The
HIKER'S
hip
pocket
GUIDE
to
Sonoma
County

by
Bob Lorentzen

D0366351

BORED FEET PRESS
MENDOCINO, CALIFORNIA
Third Edition, 2006

© 1990, 1995, 2006 by Robert S. Lorentzen
Third edition, October 2006
Printed in the United States of America on
30% post-consumer recycled paper

Illustrations by Joshua Edelman
Symbols by Jann Patterson-Watters & Taylor Cranney
Maps by Bob Lorentzen, Marsha Mello, California State
   Parks and USGS
Design by Judy Detrick and Bob Lorentzen
Layout and production by
Wendy Blakeway, DesignXperts and Janet Ashford
Edited by Anne Fox
Cover photograph © Bob Lorentzen, "Ridge Trail in
   Spring, Sonoma Valley Regional Park"

Published by
Bored Feet Press
Post Office Box 1832
Mendocino, California 95460
(707) 964-6629, (888)-336-6199
Visit our website: www.boredfeet.com

Library of Congress Cataloging-in Publication Data
Lorentzen, Bob
   The hiker's hip pocket guide to Sonoma county, third edition.
      /by Bob Lorentzen.
   256 pp.
   Includes bibliographical references and index.
   ISBN 0-939431-31-9. $16.00
   1. Hiking—California—Sonoma County—Guide-books. 2. Sonoma
   County (Calif.)—Description and travel—Guide-books. I. Title.
GV199.42.C22S655 1990   90-44136
796.5'1'0979418—dc20   CIP

ISBN-13: 978-0-939431-31-2
ISBN-10: 0-939431-31-9
10 9 8 7

Dedicated to my Dad, Karl Lorentzen, for encouraging me to explore the world, introducing me to camping and backpacking, and more recently for urging on my writing and publishing endeavors for more than twenty years.

This book is also dedicated to California Ocean Sanctuary, the movement to prevent the degradation and destruction that would result if oil exploration and development were allowed on the Northern California Coast. Save the coast for future generations, whether of people, fish, birds, whales or other life.

NO OFFSHORE OIL!
OCEAN SANCTUARY NOW!

For more information, write:
OCEAN PROTECTION COALITION
an affiliate of the
Redwood Coast Watersheds Alliance
P.O. Box 87
Elk, CA 95432

LET'S WIN THIS ONE! ACT TODAY!

In memoriam,
Gary Matson
Marcia Howe
Sam Harman
Carolyn Lorentzen
Edward Abbey

ACKNOWLEDGMENTS

For help with this third edition, I particularly want to thank Regional Parks Planner Steve Ehret for helping to make the seeming impossible a reality, Regional Parks volunteer Rick Beebe for being my guide for two days of hikes, Richard Nichols for frequently being a sounding board and consultant on changes in Sonoma County's trails, Ben Pease of Pease Press Maps for help with mapping of new trails, and Amy Racina for her friendship, enthusiasm, encouragement and suggestions, not to mention being a great role model for perseverance. For help with specific trails and parks, I thank Bill Walton of Fort Ross State Historic Park, Brendan O' Neil and Gary Shannon for help with Sonoma Coast State Beach, Dave Horvitz of Armstrong Woods/Austin Creek, Joel Miller of Lake Sonoma, and Tyler Phillips and Brian Osborn of the Red Hill trail crew. For help getting it into book form, my thanks to Wendy Blakeway of DesignXperts and Janet Ashford. And thanks to all the Sonoma County booksellers for their encouragement and feedback.

My thanks to all who helped create this book. In particular I wish to thank Anne Fox and Margaret S. Fox, the dynamic duo, Anne for her judicious red pen, Margaret for her magic with pots and promulgation; Jann Patterson-Watters for symbols and camaraderie; Judy Detrick for her formative design; Liz Petersen, production artist; David Springer for his discerning geology; Coastwalkers Richard and Brenda Nichols and Tom and Vivian McFarling for sharing their invaluable knowledge of Sonoma County trails.

For guidance and feedback on specific trails I thank Dan Winkelman and Ashford Wood of Salt Point State Park, Steve Edinger of Sonoma Coast State Beach, Fred Lew of Sugarloaf Ridge State Park, Bill Krumbein of Annadel State Park, Douglas Kauffman and Bill Grummer of Bothe-Napa Valley State Park, Kasey Cook of Lake Sonoma, Bill Barnhart and Kenneth Tam of Sonoma County Regional Parks, Ben Crabb of San Pablo Bay National Wildlife Refuge, John DeWitt of Save-the-Redwoods League, Bill Walton and Caerleon Safford of Ft. Ross State Historic Park and Matt Atkinson of Jack London State Historic Park.

With special thanks to COASTWALK and all the other groups that have worked to save the natural beauty of Sonoma County's coastal areas, when hope, reason and conservation were all that kept the coast from being built up and paved over during years of growth.

CONTENTS

WHAT KIND OF TRAIL ARE YOU LOOKING FOR?

TRAILS WHERE DOGS ARE ALLOWED
1. Headlands to Beach Loop
2. River Trail South
3. Blufftop Trail
4. Salal Trail
5. Other Sea Ranch Trails
13. Stockhoff Creek
26. Pinnacle Gulch to Shorttail Gulch
27. Woodland Ridge Loop
28. Half-a-Canoe Loop
29. South Shore to Old Sawmill Camp
32. Riverfront Regional Park
33. Ragle Ranch Regional Park
34. Helen Putnam Regional Park
35. Cloverdale River Park
36. Foothill Regional Park
40. Spring Lake/Lake Ralphine
45. Santa Rosa Creek Headwaters
47. Ponds Loop
52. Crane Creek Regional Park
53. Jack London's Wolf House Ruins
55. Canyon/Ridge Loop
56. Maxwell Farms Regional Park
58. Bartholomew Park Winery
59. Shollenberger Park

TRAILS WITH HANDICAPPED ACCESS
1. Headlands to Beach Loop
11. Salt Point to Stump Beach (first ⅛ mile with assistance)
13. Stockhoff Creek (see Other Suggestion)
16. Fort Ross Creek (to fort)
18. Vista Trail
22. Shell Beach to Wrights Beach (see Other Suggestion)
23. Bodega Dunes Loop (at start)
27. Woodland Ridge Loop (see Other Suggestion)
30. Armstrong Woods Loop
33. Ragle Ranch Regional Park (paved paths)
34. Helen Putnam Regional Park
35. Cloverdale River Park
36. Foothill Regional Park
37. Shiloh Ranch Regional Park
40. Spring Lake Loop
52. Crane Creek Regional Park
55. Canyon/Ridge Loop
56. Maxwell Farms Regional Park
59. Shollenberger Park

TRAILS FOR BIKES OR MOUNTAIN BIKES
1. Headlands to Beach Loop
10. Pygmy Forest Loop
15. Kolmer Gulch
25. Bodega Head Loop (see Other Suggestion)
28. Half-a-Canoe Loop
29. South Shore to Old Sawmill Camp

31. Austin Creek (no bikes on Gilliam Creek Trail)
32. Riverfront Regional Park
33. Ragle Ranch Regional Park (see Other Suggestion)
34. Helen Putnam Regional Park
35. Cloverdale River Park
36. Foothill Regional Park
37. Shiloh Ranch Regional Park
38. Mt. St. Helena—start from fire road ½ mile north of trailhead.
39. Ritchey Canyon—OK on Ritchey Canyon & Spring trails. No bikes on upper Redwood Trail.
40. Spring Lake/Lake Ralphine
41. Rough Go/Canyon/Spring Creek Loop
42. N. Burma/Louis/Canyon/Marsh/S. Burma Loop
43. Steve's S/South Burma/Two Quarry Loop
44. Lawndale/Marsh/Ridge Loop
45. Santa Rosa Creek Headwaters: bikes OK on fire roads
46. McCormick Ranch/More Santa Rosa Creek Headwaters
47. Ponds Loop
50. Bald Mountain Loop
51. OK on Hillside & Gray Pine Trails. No bikes on Brushy Peaks Trail.
52. Crane Creek Regional Park
54. Sonoma Mountain
55. Canyon/Ridge Loop
56. Maxwell Farms Regional Park
59. Shollenberger Park
60. Sonoma's Other Shore

TRAILS FOR EQUESTRIANS
10. Pygmy Forest Loop
15. Kolmer Gulch
23. Bodega Dunes Loop
28. Half-a-Canoe Loop
29. South Shore to Old Sawmill Camp
30. Armstrong Woods Loop (see Other Suggestion)
31. Austin Creek
32. Riverfront Regional Park
33. Ragle Ranch Regional Park
34. Helen Putnam Regional park
36. Foothill Regional Park
37. Shiloh Ranch Regional Park
38. Mount Saint Helena
39. Ritchey Canyon
40. Spring Lake Loop
41. Rough Go/Canyon/Spring Creek Loop
42. N. Burma/Louis/Canyon/Marsh/S. Burma Loop
43. Steve's S/South Burma/Two Quarry Loop
44. Lawndale/Marsh/Ridge Loop
45. Santa Rosa Creek Headwaters
46. McCormick Ranch/More Santa Rosa Creek Headwaters
47. Ponds Loop
50. Bald Mountain Loop
51. Brushy Peaks Loop
52. Crane Creek Regional Park
54. Sonoma Mountain
55. Canyon/Ridge Loop

Continued on page 248

INTRODUCTION
THIS BOOK IS FOR RECREATIONAL PURPOSES ONLY

Sonoma rolls across the green and golden hills north of San Francisco Bay. These hills shelter a promised land of rich botanical diversity, where a thousand miles of meandering back roads deliver you to new, unexpected views with each turn, and dozens of parks entice exploration on foot.

Once the untamed home of grizzly bears and mountain lions, Sonoma County's million acres now stand as a transition between the sophistication of the Bay Area and the rugged forests and mountains to the north. Premium vineyards and upscale subdivisions vie for its sheltered valleys, while a wilderness of deep woods, graceful grasslands and tangled chaparral climbs its high ridges and hunkers in its deep canyons. These wild lands provide shelter for an array of wildlife.

This book tells how to find and walk, hike, jog or ride over 300 miles of scenic trails through beautiful country. The trails range from easy walks to difficult backpacks, with choices to fit the taste of every nature lover. The trails lead to a variety of habitats: beaches, tidepools, lagoons, dunes, headlands, marshes, grasslands, forests, stream canyons, ridges and mountain tops. You may also hike to waterfalls, a wildlife refuge and ghost town sites and along old railways. Five trails explore the broken country around the San Andreas Fault, and others investigate the literary heritage of Jack London and Robert Louis Stevenson. In short, there is something for everyone. So get out of your car and use your feet, bicycle, horse or wheelchair to explore Sonoma County.

HOW TO USE THIS BOOK

This book has three sections, each organized from the north to the south. Highway 1 is the starting point for the directions to all trailheads in the first section, the Sonoma Coast. The next section covers trails inland from the coast but west of Highway 101. The third section details trails east of Highway 101, including two trails in Napa County. No trail is more than two hours from Santa Rosa. From San Francisco it will take you 40 minutes to three hours to drive to the trailheads.

In the directions to most trails, you will find milepost numbers listed like this: M.33.00. These numbers refer to white highway mileposts placed frequently (but at irregular intervals) along state highways by CalTrans, the State Department of Transportation. You can quickly determine the location of a trail by referring to its milepost number and its position in the book.

You do not have to start at the beginning of the book. Simply turn to the trail nearest your location and you will be on your way. Neighboring trails are on adjacent pages.

For each trail in the book, you will find a map, specific directions to the trailhead, the best time to go, appropriate warnings, and a detailed description with some history and/or natural history.

You will find a group of symbols below the access information for each trail. They tell you at a glance the level of difficulty, type of trail, available facilities, whether there is a fee, and whether dogs are allowed. The list of symbols follows.

After the contents you'll find a table listing the trails most suitable for a particular type of recreation: mountain bikes, equestrians, dog walking, backpacking and handicap access. You can then locate these trails in the text by referring to the trail number.

THE DANGERS
HIKER'S TEN COMMANDMENTS

When on the trail, *always* keep your senses wide open so that you can best appreciate nature's pleasures as well as her

THE SYMBOLS

WALK:
Less than 2 miles
Easy terrain

EASY HIKE:
2 to 10 miles
Easy terrain

MODERATE HIKE:
2 to 10 miles
Rougher terrain

DIFFICULT HIKE:
Strenuous terrain
Backpacking possible

**MOUNTAIN BIKE
TRAIL**

BIKE TRAIL

HANDICAP ACCESS

**DOGS ALLOWED
ON LEASH**

CAR CAMPING

**WALK-IN OR
BIKE-IN CAMPING:**
Environmental camps

13

TIDEPOOL ACCESS

PICNIC SPOT:
May be tables or just
a good blanket spot

**RECOMMENDED
FOR FAMILIES**

**INTERPRETIVE
NATURE TRAIL**

**TRAIL FOR
EQUESTRIANS**

**RESTROOMS
AVAILABLE**

WATER AVAILABLE

FEE AREA

FISHING ACCESS

**NO OIL EXPLORATION
OR DRILLING**

14

dangers. Don't let nature lull you into complacency. Here are ten rules to keep you out of danger, so that you may safely enjoy the beauty of Sonoma County.

1. DON'T LITTER. Most of these places are unspoiled. Do your part to keep them that way. Always hike with a trash bag and use it, even for matches, cigarette butts and bottle caps. I always pick up any trash I see in a pristine spot, my way of saying thanks to Mother Nature.

2. NO TRESPASSING. Property owners have a right to privacy. Stay off private property. There are enough public places without walking through someone's front or back yard.

3. NEVER TURN YOUR BACK ON THE OCEAN. Oversized rogue waves can strike the coast at any time. Watch for them. They are especially common in winter. They have killed people. More subtle are the changes of the tides: don't let rising tides strand you against steep cliffs or on a submerged tidal island. The ocean is icy and unforgiving, generally unsafe for swimming without a wetsuit.

4. STAY BACK FROM CLIFFS. Coastal soils are often unstable. You wouldn't want to fall 40 feet into the icy sea, would you? Don't get close to the cliff's edge, and never climb on cliffs unless there is a safe trail.

5. WILD THINGS: ANIMAL. Most animal pests of Sonoma County are small. Watch out for ticks (some carry Lyme Disease), wasps, mosquitoes, biting spiders, scorpions and rattlesnakes. The only large wild animal you might encounter is a mountain lion. While this is extremely unlikely, lions are sometimes seen in Sonoma's wilds. If you see one, don't run—stand tall, then move away slowly. Human animals are easily the most dangerous, particularly during hunting seasons. Always listen for gunfire, especially outside state parks. **UNDERWATER ANIMALS:** When tidepooling or at the beach, always watch for sea urchins and jellyfish. Both have painful stinging spines. Remember, too, that mussels are quarantined each year from May through October or later; at that time they contain deadly poison.

6. WILD THINGS: PLANT. These mean business too, especially poison oak and stinging nettles, which can get you with the slightest touch. Many other plants are poisonous. It is best to not touch any plants unless you know by positive identification that they are safe; this is most important with mushrooms.

7. TRAIL COURTESY. Equestrians always have the right of way on trails, because you can move aside for a horse much more easily than its rider can yield to you. Mountain bikers must yield to hikers and horses and slow to walking speed on blind corners. As wonderful as bikes are, metal machines

15

(especially when moving fast) can cause serious injury when other trail users do not know you are coming. Mountain bikes are the leading cause of trail accidents and injuries.

8. TRAFFIC. Country roads are difficult and often over-crowded. Drive carefully and courteously. Please turn out for faster traffic. You will enjoy the journey more if you do. If you stop, pull safely off the road.

9. CRIME. Be sure to lock you car when you park it at the trailhead. Leave valuables out of sight, or better yet, back at your lodging.

10. ALWAYS TAKE RESPONSIBILITY FOR YOURSELF AND YOUR PARTY. This is a trail guide, not a nursery school. The author cannot and will not be responsible for you in the wilds. Information contained in this book is correct to the best of the author's knowledge. Author and publisher assume no liability for damages arising from errors or omissions. You must take the responsibility for your safety and health while on these trails. The coast is still a wild place. Safety conditions of trails, beaches and tidepools vary with seasons and tides. Be cautious, heed the above warnings, and always check on local conditions. It is always better to hike with a friend. Know where you can get help in case of emergency.

THE HISTORY

Native Americans lived in relative peace and abundance in the wilderness that was to become Sonoma County. Evidence of habitation can be traced back at least 8000, perhaps 10,000, years. If you ask the Kashaya Pomo, though, they would tell you the people have been here since the beginning of time. Four tribes, the Kashaya Pomo, Southern Pomo, Coast Miwok and Wappo, shared the bounty of this hill country for millennia, developing sophisticated, diverse cultures that engaged in commerce and cultural exchange.

The indigenous people had contact with Sir Francis Drake when he explored the coast in 1579, with the Spaniards as early as 1775, and with the Russians in the early 1800s. The Russians became the first non-natives to settle in Sonoma County when they established Fort Ross in 1812. They treated the Kashaya Pomo fairly by nineteenth-century mores, paying to rent their land, hiring them as hunters and guides, and studying and recording their culture. (A Moscow museum holds the world's largest collection of Kashaya ceremonial artifacts.)

The Spanish had laid claim to all of California in 1521

with the conquest of Mexico, although they had never settled and seldom explored the land north of San Francisco Bay. But they considered the Russian intrusion a challenge to their sovereignty. After the Mexican war for independence from Spain ended, the Mexicans wasted no time responding to the Russian threat, establishing the last and northernmost mission at Sonoma in 1823. The local Indians were baptized and forced to labor, making adobe bricks and planting vineyards. Meanwhile, the United States also warned against Russian imperialism, proclaiming the Monroe Doctrine in 1823.

In 1833 Lieutenant Mariano Vallejo was sent to Sonoma to establish a military presence. In 1834 the outpost changed from church to civil authority. The Mexican government ordered Vallejo to divide the arable land of present-day Sonoma County into land grants. Vallejo gave them to people trusted not to join with the Russians. In 1836, when Vallejo's nephew became governor of Alta California, he promoted Mariano to General and encouraged further settlement north of the Golden Gate.

Meanwhile, the Russians had depleted the otter population and were losing money on Fort Ross. After their offer to buy land on San Francisco Bay was refused, the Russians sold out and abandoned the fort in 1841.

Americans had begun arriving in Sonoma in 1827, as word of the abundant land and mild climate spread east. Moses Carson, Kit's half-brother, settled in Sonoma before Mariano Vallejo. The first wagon train arrived in 1841. By 1846 ten percent of California's population was American.

On June 14, 1846, 33 American settlers seized the pueblo of Sonoma at daybreak, arresting General Vallejo, raising the Bear Flag and declaring independence. Less than a month later, the American war with Mexico began, as the American flag was raised over Monterey. The *Californios*, long isolated from Mexico, offered token resistance. Six months later the hostilities were over, although the formal treaty was not signed until 1848.

So the United States conquered California just in time for the Gold Rush. For the preceding twenty years, the town of Sonoma had rivaled San Francisco as the leading settlement in the north. But the Gold Rush changed that in a hurry. As a deep-water port, San Francisco was the debarkation point and the gateway to the gold fields. Sonoma, not located on the golden road, became a provincial town.

Sonoma County boomed, however, as it took on the business of supplying food and lumber to prospering San Francisco and the miners in the Sierra foothills. Bodega and Sonoma grew. Petaluma began as a hunting camp to supply

San Francisco with meat. Valley Ford, Pine Grove (later Sebastopol), Bloomfield, Guerneville, Healdsburg and other towns were born and prospered. Settlers laid out Santa Rosa in 1853 and stole the county seat from Sonoma in 1854. By 1870 Sonoma was the sixth most populous county in the state, well ahead of Los Angeles.

In the 1870s and 1880s, railroads spread throughout Sonoma County, bringing a reliable way to transport goods to market, causing new waves of growth and more boom towns. The dairy and cattle industries grew. The invention of the artificial chicken incubator established Petaluma's poultry industry. Wines were produced in greater volume and quality increased. By 1900 the county population was nearly 40,000, and the growth had just begun. Today the population exceeds 480,000.

If Sonoma County still had the extensive rail network that covered the county in 1900, trains could transport the increasing crowds of commuters who threaten gridlock on the existing roads.

As you read about and explore the trails, many more details of Sonoma County's complex history will fall into place.

THE CLIMATE

The climate of Sonoma County differs considerably from one part of the county to another. The coast is cool and often foggy, mild enough for year-round hiking if you are prepared for varying conditions. Inland areas tend to be somewhat cooler in winter, much hotter in summer, with the hottest extremes in the north and east. In planning your excursions, keep in mind the following about the seasons in Sonoma County:

November to March are the rainy months, time to bring rain gear and waterproof boots. Still, there are often fine sunny days between storms.

April and May offer mild sunny days, often windy, with occasional rain storms. The wind may be gentle, or fierce and unrelenting. The landscape is at its most lush and beautiful. Bring layered clothing and hats.

June, July and August bring hot, sunny summer days inland, often too hot for comfortable hiking except perhaps in the early morning. Occasionally the fog will move inland to cool things off. On the coast it may be sunny, but thick, chilly fog can move in suddenly. You may be comfortable in shorts, but always bring layered clothing in case the fog comes in. Sometimes you can beat the fog by heading a few miles inland. (This is the most crowded season, especially August.)

September and October are a beautiful time. Fog is less common. Though there may be rainstorms, most of the days are calm and warm. The land is dry, the hills golden, and the sunsets often spectacular.

GET READY, GET SET, HIKE!

You should be chomping at the bit to get out on the trail by now. Here are a few suggestions of what you might need to take on your hike: layered clothing—sweater, sweatshirt, hat, windbreaker or rain coat; insect repellent; sunscreen; sunglasses; and small first aid kit (at least bring moleskin for blisters). Not essential, but highly recommended for all but the shortest walks: water container, extra food, pocket knife, flashlight and extra batteries, matches and fire starter, map, compass (helps if you know how to use it), and of course you would not want to be caught without your *Hiker's hip pocket Guide*!

Additional suggestions: camera; dry socks; binoculars; and field guide to birds, wildflowers and/or trees. If you are backpacking, you should consult an equipment list for that purpose.

When you are out on the trails, remember to slow down, open your senses and enjoy. Most people hike at a rate of 2 to 3 miles per hour. But beach sand or steep terrain may slow all but the most hardy to as little as one mile per hour. Leave ample time to do the hike you plan at a pleasant pace. Hike not to count the miles, but for the enjoyment and appreciation of nature. Happy trails to you!

THE SONOMA COAST

Sonoma County's pristine 62 mile coastline has remained sparsely populated and mostly untamed despite having been first settled more than 190 years ago. The survival of its wild character owes much to its rugged, fractured and varied topography, but even more to the fact that the County's highest concentration of public lands is here.

Three tribes of Native Americans originally inhabited this coast and the adjacent ridges. The Coast Miwok lived from Wrights Beach south. The Kashaya Pomo, still present in the area, lived from Shell Beach north to Stewarts Point. The Southern Pomo controlled the short segment of coast in the area where Sea Ranch is today. These tribes lived an abundant, generally peaceful life thanks to the bounty of the sea, rivers, forests and grasslands.

White explorers came early and relatively often to visit this land. Sir Francis Drake landed somewhere (a point of much historical controversy) along this coast in 1579 to make repairs to his ship, meeting some of the coast dwellers.

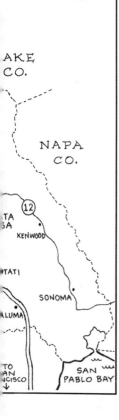

Spaniard Sebastian Vizcaino named many coastal landmarks during his voyage in 1602. Other Spanish galleons sailed the coast before and after, during a period of intense trade with the Philippines. It was not until 1775 that Juan Francisco de la Bodega y Quadra put ashore at the bay that was to take his name, surveying the surrounding area. But the Spaniards never made a permanent settlement on the coast north of San Francisco.

The Russians established a colony at Fort Ross in 1812, having camped at Bodega for eight months in 1809. They quickly decimated the abundant population of sea otters and seals, selling the valuable pelts primarily to the Chinese. The Russians left in 1841.

In belated response to the threat of Russian colonization, the Mexicans finally made a stab at settling the coast. They made two land grants in the 1840s, the 35,000-acre Rancho Bodega to Captain Stephen Smith of Boston, who established the first sawmill on the coast, and the 20,000-acre Rancho German to Captain Ernest Rufus, a German.

But the Americanization of California and the onslaught of the California Gold Rush quickly changed the character of settlement along the coast. Lumber boom towns sprang up to supply the huge demands of San Francisco. Stewarts Point and Timber Cove began in the 1850s, followed by Gualala, Black Point, Fisk Mill, Duncans Landing, Louisville and several more. A stage was in operation around 1860, and a railroad reached Duncans Mills on the Russian River in 1877. Soon the Russian River was a popular vacation spot for San Franciscans.

Today the ports, mills, railroads and most of the towns are long gone, but the vacationers still come every summer. They come with good reason, for this coast offers some of the most spectacular, untamed beauty in all of California. South of the Russian River the coastal terrain is fairly gentle, backed by grasslands. North of the river mouth a rugged, precipitous coast with few signs of human habitation meets the wild Pacific, offering solitude and breathtaking beauty.

21

GUALALA POINT REGIONAL PARK

The park sits in a spectacular setting on the south shore of the normally placid Gualala River, extending upstream from its mouth for about 1½ miles. The land, once the northernmost portion of the Rancho German land grant, was donated to Sonoma County when Oceanic Properties created the extensive subdivision called Sea Ranch. The 325-acre park covers the diverse habitats of beach, rugged sea cliffs, grassy headlands, tidal river and redwood and bay laurel forest. It is in the extreme northwest corner of Sonoma County.

1.

HEADLANDS to BEACH LOOP
WINDBREAKS AND WILDFLOWERS

The western portion of the park is covered by a fine network of trails offering several choices. Though the following trail report details the unpaved headlands-to-beach loop, a paved bicycle and wheelchair path can easily be followed out to the same beach and headlands area.

The modern visitor center fits nicely into the beautiful headlands landscape. When it's open, the center has informative displays and provides a welcome refuge from the strong winds often blowing here. Hiking here is nice anytime of year. However, whale and bird watching is best December through March, and spring is especially nice for wildflowers.

From the visitor center, follow the paved path northwest for 250 feet. There beside a rest bench you meet a grassy trail that continues northwest where the paved path swings west. Take the grassy path leading gently downhill through lush headlands. In 300 feet a trail on your right heads down to a pleasant shady picnic area near the river.

Continuing northwest, in 500 feet you meet a trail on your left, which leads southwest on the leeward side of an old cypress windbreak to another picnic area. The main trail continues west-northwest around the windbreak, passing over headlands filled with wildflowers. On your right the Gualala River is a prime habitat for aquatic birds. Many species of grasslands birds live near the trail.

Around ⅜ mile your footpath joins the paved trail, continuing to the beach near the river mouth. In late summer or early

HEADLANDS to BEACH LOOP:

DISTANCE: 1¼-mile loop.

TIME: One hour.

TERRAIN: Grassy headlands between river and sea
cliffs leading to broad beach at river mouth, then to
rocky point.

BEST TIME: Spring for wildflowers. Whale watching
is best December through March. Anytime is good.

WARNINGS: Watch for killer waves on beach: six
people were swept into the sea here in February 1986;
one of them drowned. Watch for poison oak tangled
with other plants.

HOW TO GET THERE: Turn west off Highway 1 at
M.58.2, about one mile south of the town of Gualala.
Drive .5 mile to the visitor center parking lot.

FEES: Day Use: $5/vehicle. Car and walk-in camping:
$18/night. Hike/bike camping: $5/person/night.

FURTHER INFO: Gualala Point Regional Park
(707) 785-2377.

fall, you can ford the river near its mouth, continuing north
to the end of the beach. At medium to high water, however,
the river is not safe to ford.

Our described trail turns southwest on a fork of the paved
path, quickly coming to picnic tables and a restroom. Leave
the paved path here to follow the grassy path past the picnic
ground, passing another spur to the beach on your right.
Climb past two view benches and along a cypress windbreak.
Your trail eventually passes through the dense windbreak and
meets a junction at ⅝ mile.

Turn right to follow the trail west onto a narrow rocky
promontory known as Whale Watch Point. It soon comes
to sandy bluffs on the leeward side of a cypress windbreak
overlooking ocean cliffs to the south. You may continue
250 feet farther west to the windswept point beyond the
windbreak. Look north from the point for a fine view of
the beach and the town of Gualala. The wooded ridge
beyond extends west to the point of Haven's Neck and

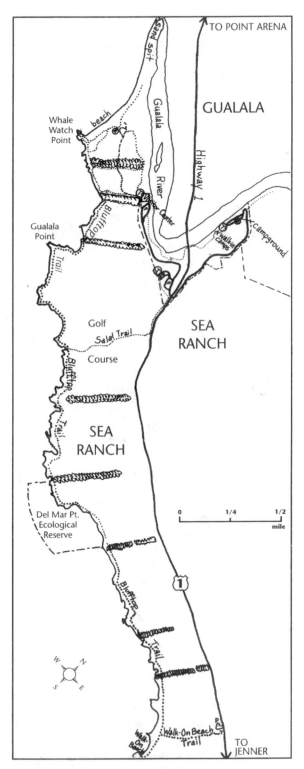

TO POINT ARENA

GUALALA

Sand Spit

Gualala River

beach

Whale Watch Point

Highway 1

Walk On Campsites

Campground

Gualala Point

Bluff top Trail

SEA RANCH

Golf

Salal Trail

Course

Bluff top Trail

SEA RANCH

Del Mar Pt. Ecological Reserve

Bluff top Trail

0   1/4   1/2
mile

N

1

Bluff top Trail

Walk On Beach Trail

Walk On

TO JENNER

the big sea stack called Fish Rock. This is truly one of the grand views of this stretch of coast.

Returning to the junction, take the right fork southwest along the bluff's edge. You quickly pass a flat, rocky tidal shelf. Continuing along the bluff, at ⅞ mile you plunge into a broad cypress windbreak, a home for many small birds. As you clear the cypress thicket, you meet the windbreak trail forking to the left. (You may return by that trail if you prefer.)

The trail continues southeast near the edge of the bluff. Two benches provide fine views of the coast. Just 300 feet after the second bench, you come to a fence and a sign indicating the park boundary. The start of Blufftop Trail leads through the fence here (see Trail #3). You turn northeast here, following the fence and windbreak along the Sea Ranch boundary. In another 300 feet you enter a "tunnel" through pines. Leaving the tunnel, you meet the paved path in 20 feet. Follow the bike path for 500 feet back to the visitor center and your car.

2.

RIVER TRAIL SOUTH
ALONG A QUIET STEELHEAD STREAM

The campground along the Gualala River lies at the western edge of a dense redwood forest on a quiet tidal stretch of the river. You can often hear the surf crashing just a mile to the west. The roar intrudes upon, but does not overcome, the quiet of the campground.

Though there are many large redwoods here, the many old stumps show evidence of pioneer logging. Most of these have springboard cuts still showing on their eroded surfaces, indicating that the trees were cut before the introduction of chainsaws. The sawyers would stand on these springboards five or ten feet above the ground to avoid cutting through the thicker, often scarred wood at the tree's base. Many of these old stumps have new plants growing healthily from their tops. If you walk through the campground, you will see the following plants atop stumps: elderberry, huckleberry, sword fern and bay laurel.

Where the redwood trees stop near the southwest end of the campground, bay laurels grow very large, with gnarled trunks up to four feet in diameter.

River Trail leads south through this dense bay laurel forest from the south end of the campground. Seven great walk- or bike-in campsites are located in this forest along the first 400

feet of trail. Just beyond the last campsite, the trail comes to a clearing in the forest; a dense tangle of brush competes for the lush riverine environment.

At ⅛ mile the trail swings right and follows the river bank, then winds through tall brush to cross a sturdy bridge over a side stream. Your path ascends into grasslands with much coyote brush.

About ¼ mile from the trailhead, you pass under the highway bridge. Cliff swallows nest under the bridge, especially on its west side. From March through September, the swallows will be chattering and feeding over the river. Your trail then leads through a stand of alders before climbing away from the river and following a fence. Then you leave the grassy river flat and climb the face of the bluff. The tangle of brush along the trail includes many species: tanoak, bay laurel, ceanothus, hazel, Oregon grape, blackberry, wild rose, wild strawberry, paintbrush, silktassel, lupine, honeysuckle and poison oak. The trail switchbacks twice, coming to a bench at ⅜ mile where you may rest and enjoy the view.

As you climb to the top of the bluff, the flora changes to bluff grassland scattered with Douglas fir and low cypress. Three more benches feature views north. Another ⅛ mile along the bluff's edge brings you to a pleasant picnic area. It is less than ¼ mile to the visitor center, where you can connect with the network of headlands and beach trails (see Trails #1 and 3).

RIVER TRAIL SOUTH:

DISTANCE: One mile round trip to blufftop bench, 1⅛ miles round trip to visitor center.

TIME: One half hour to one hour.

TERRAIN: Down the river canyon, under the highway bridge, then climbing the bluff to headlands.

BEST TIME: Spring for wildflowers, but nice anytime.

WARNINGS: Watch for poison oak and stinging nettles.

HOW TO GET THERE: Turn east off Highway 1 at M.58.2, about one mile south of the town of Gualala. Go .7 mile to the campground. Trailhead is .1 mile farther. If not camping here, you must park on road shoulder outside campground and walk in ⅛ mile to trailhead.

FEES: Day use: $5/vehicle. Car and walk-in camping: $18/night. Hike/bike camping: $5/person/night.

FURTHER INFO: Gualala Point Regional Park (707) 785-2377.

ENVIRONMENTAL CAMPS: 7 walk- or bike-in camps are located from 75 feet to 400 feet along the trail in a dense bay laurel forest by the river.

3.

BLUFFTOP TRAIL
ALONG THE SEA RANCH COAST

State law mandated this trail in 1980, after years of litigation that went all the way to the state appeals court. The trail was finally opened in 1987. Today it serves as part of the California Coastal Trail. Though the trail passes many houses in the Sea Ranch subdivision, including one stretch so heavily built it is known as the Malibu Wall, it provides the only public access to a marvelously convoluted coast with headlands rich in wildflowers. On one spring visit, I counted more than two dozen varieties of wildflowers in bloom.

This description starts at the north end of the trail, where

*it meets the trails of Gualala Point Regional Park. You can
also reach the Blufftop Trail via the Salal Trail (see Trail #4)
and the Walk-On Beach Trail (see Trail #5).*

From the visitor center at Gualala Point Regional Park,
follow the paved path northwest for 200 feet. Then walk
the pavement southwest along the park boundary fence for
another 250 feet. Where the pavement turns right, take the
dirt path that continues southwest through the trees and
along the fence.

At ¼ mile a break in the fence marks the start of Blufftop
Trail, signed as "PUBLIC ACCESS TRAIL." Turn left,
heading through the fence and the cypress windbreak. The
Blufftop Trail soon turns south, following the edge of the
bluff. For the next ⅛ mile, the nearby shore is mostly hidden behind dense cypress. From ⅜ mile you gain vistas of
Gualala Point ahead. Before ½ mile you reach a point with
unobstructed views south to Gualala Point and northwest to
Whale Watch Point.

Then your trail plunges through another windbreak. At ⅝
mile your trail jogs right, passing above a small, inaccessible
pocket beach. You head southwest to Gualala Point, shrouded
in bushy cypress. Take a short spur on the right before ¾
mile for a great view of Gualala Point Island just offshore, a
nesting ground for Brandt's cormorants and other sea birds.
Other vistas look north to Whale Watch Point in the park
and Fish Rock beyond the town of Gualala.

Beyond ¾ mile you leave a dense cypress thicket for open
headlands. Your trail continues southeast, hugging the edge
of the bluff. Grand views of a convoluted rocky shoreline
command the eye's attention. The wooded ridgeline forms
a backdrop, with many Sea Ranch homes in between. Near
one mile you cross a bridge over a small gully jammed with
salal, wild rose and coffeeberry to follow the rugged shore.
Large yellow bush lupine are scattered along the grassy
headlands. You soon descend into a canyon where forest and
soft chaparral plants mix. After crossing a creek at 1¼ miles,
you meet Salal Trail (Trail #4).

Climb the steps heading southeast up onto a headland with
tall grasses, coyote brush, bush lupine, berry vines and Douglas iris. You wind along the bluff near the shore. Beyond 1½
miles your trail winds onto a point, passing the wind-sculpted
end of a cypress windrow, gaining another view of the rocky
coast ahead, which is eroded into many shapes.

At 1⅝ miles you come to a creek with still pools overlooking the shore. Cross the bridge over the creek and climb to
a view back to the waterfall where the creek drops to the

BLUFFTOP TRAIL:

DISTANCE: 6½ miles round trip.

TIME: Three to four hours.

TERRAIN: Along headlands near the bluff's edge, crossing several creeks and passing through numerous cypress windbreaks.

BEST TIME: Spring and early summer for wildflowers.

WARNINGS: Trail closed by a washout beyond junction with Walk-On Trail; no access to Walk-On Beach. Do not trespass on adjacent private property. Watch for poison oak. Be careful along the bluff's crumbly edge. Stay on the trail and away from the edge.

HOW TO GET THERE: Turn west from Highway 1 at M.58.2 into the day-use area for Gualala Point Regional Park. Go .5 mile to parking area at end of road.

FEES: $5/vehicle, day use.

FURTHER INFO: Gualala Point Regional Park (707) 785-2377.

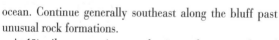

ocean. Continue generally southeast along the bluff past unusual rock formations.

At 1⅞ miles you cut in around a tiny rocky cove and wind through more bush lupine, then head south. At 2 miles you approach another windbreak, this one marking the boundary of the Del Mar Landing Ecological Reserve. The Reserve was created to protect the rocky intertidal zone, habitat to an abundance of marine invertebrates. No fishing or collecting is allowed here.

The trail soon forks. Follow the right fork along the edge of the bluff. At 2⅛ miles a wooden beam and an old rusty stake mark Del Mar Landing, where lumber schooners were loaded at the end of the nineteenth century.

You soon come to the end of Del Mar Point. Your trail turns north briefly, then east. Around 2¼ miles you pass a rock outcrop nearly buried in angelica and other lush vegetation. Delicate star tulips, or cat's ears, grow among the grasses nearby. Blufftop Trail continues along the bluff's edge. Near 2½ miles you head into a broad windrow. An

afternoon-sunny bench overlooks the shore. Cross a bridge over another small creek.

Continue southeast through the wildflower-dappled headlands. Beyond 2⅝ miles you are alongside a rocky cliff with fantastically eroded rocks. The rocks here are similar to the extensive tafoni rock formations at Salt Point (see Trail #11), visible along the coast to the south. Your path bends to the right and heads out to a small rocky point, then turns east to cross a bridge. The small creek below is hidden in a dense tangle of vegetation. Beyond the creek grows a thicket of salal and cow parsnip.

Soon your trail veers right, heading out to a small point, then meanders east along the bluff edge. By 3 miles you pass another old windrow. After two more houses, Blufftop Trail traces the bluff edge with a large open grassland on your left. You pass a keyhole cove on your right.

In ¼ mile you come to the junction with Walk-On Beach Trail, 3¼ miles from your starting point. At press time Blufftop Trail south is closed due to an eroding bluff. Until a new route is opened you must return the way you came. Or you can head northeast to Walk-On Beach Trailhead, which would be perfect if you arranged a shuttle vehicle ahead of time. Otherwise, return along Blufftop Trail to Gualala Point Regional Park. You may also turn right when you reach Salal Trail, follow that back to the park, then walk another ½ mile along the road to the visitor center.

SALAL TRAIL
COASTAL CREEK HABITAT

This short trail is one of my favorites because it offers such variety in a short invigorating hike, not to mention some very unusual habitats. The hike is even better if you loop back on Blufftop Trail instead of the way you came.

Salal Trail leads southeast from the restroom and picnic area. The grassy path parallels the park road to the park entrance on Highway 1. Your trail turns right, then parallels Highway 1 south for ⅛ mile.

About 500 feet after crossing the golf course access road, Salal Trail descends ten wooden steps, leaving the highway for a wooded creek canyon. This little creek canyon forms a habitat distinct from the coastal grasslands surrounding it. Many species thrive in the cool, damp, wind-protected environment, including fragrant wild azalea, madrone, salal, bay laurel, coffeeberry, silktassel, alder, berries and oaks.

Your trail heads down the canyon, coming quickly to stands of redwoods, Bishop pines and droopy Douglas firs around ⅜ mile. California hazel and toyon grow in the understory. You soon cross a concrete golf cart path, then come to a small wooden bridge and a paved road.

Cross the road and continue southwest, passing a pumphouse before the trail comes back alongside the creek on your left in an area lush with willows, alders, sword ferns, skunk cabbage, salmonberry, wax myrtle, Bishop pines and cypresses.

Beyond ½ mile you cross a wooden bridge beside wild azaleas. Now with the creek on your right, plunge into a dense tunnel of growth dominated by silktassel, alder, flowering currant, huckleberry and thimbleberry, with fairy bells and corn lily in summer. Around ⅝ mile you come to a rocky, more open portion of the trail where paintbrush thrives. Then you drop into another tunnel of brush, mostly bay laurel.

You come to a dense stand of redwoods on the creek. The trees are snapped off just above the level of the surrounding grasslands, attesting to the protection this little canyon provides from prevailing strong winds. This pretty spot has a small waterfall, plus redwood sorrel and five-finger ferns. Continue along the left side of the creek. In 300 feet, you find a dense salmonberry thicket beside the trail. Salmonberries ripen in May and June. At ¾ mile you come to another paved path, this one with miners lettuce growing beside it.

DISTANCE: 1½ miles round trip (or 2⅜-mile loop with
the north portion of Blufftop Trail).

TIME: One hour.

TERRAIN: Grassy headlands spotted with cypress, then down
narrow, wooded coastal creek canyon to rocky beach.

BEST TIME: Spring for azaleas and other wildflowers,
but anytime is nice.

WARNINGS: Do not trespass on adjacent private property. Watch for poison oak and nettles.

HOW TO GET THERE: Turn west from Highway 1 at
M.58.2 into the day-use area for Gualala Point Regional Park. Take the first left inside the park, parking
near the restrooms.

FEES: Day use: $5/vehicle.

FURTHER INFO: Gualala Point Regional Park
(707) 785-2377.

The trail bends left and passes through a brushy area where
you should watch for nettles.

In 150 feet a small rocky beach comes into view at the
mouth of the creek. The wooded habitat gives way to soft
chaparral plants: skunk cabbage, cow parsnip, horsetail
ferns, grasses and assorted wildflowers.

You come to a junction with Blufftop Trail (see Trail #3),
which goes north for one mile to meet the trails of Gualala
Point Regional Park, and south for 2 miles to meet Walk-On
Beach Trail. You can prolong your hike by going either left
or right. Or you can simply descend the stairway to the tiny
beach, enjoy the shore, and return the way you came.

OTHER SEA RANCH TRAILS

SHORT AND SCENIC

WALK-ON BEACH TRAIL (¾ mile round trip) descends from the parking lot into dense coastal scrub forest of cypress, Bishop pine, grand fir, tanoak, willow and madrone. As you head south, watch for poison oak in the understory. You cross a paved road in 400 feet, then head southwest through grasslands west of a large cypress windbreak. Beyond ¼ mile you come to a junction with Blufftop Trail (see Trail #3). NOTE: A slide has closed access to Walk-On Beach at press time. It may reopen by late 2007. If it has, go left here for ¼ mile to reach the stairway and ramp at the far end of Walk-On Beach.

SHELL BEACH TRAIL (1.2 miles round trip) descends south, then southwest through pine forest with abundant coffeeberry. At ⅛ mile you cross a paved road, then continue over grasslands scattered with trees. Beyond ¼ mile you walk between houses and a dense riparian corridor on your left, then cross a second paved road. At ½ mile Shell Beach Trail jogs right for 250 feet, then crosses a bridge over a creek. Turn left here and descend to the pleasant sandy beach, consisting

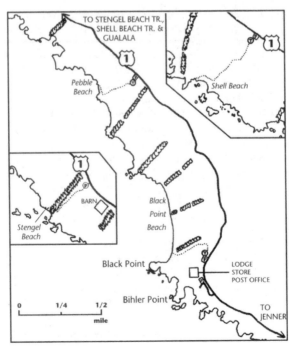

DISTANCE: ½ mile to 1¼ miles round trip.

TIME: One half to one hour (each trail).

TERRAIN: Coastal grasslands leading to small pocket beaches.

BEST TIME: Spring for wildflowers, low tide for best enjoyment of beaches and tidepools. Nice anytime.

WARNINGS: Respect adjacent private property—do not trespass. Watch for rogue waves when on the beach. Trails are open 6 a.m. to sunset.

HOW TO GET THERE: All on west side of Highway 1 at the following mileposts (just south of Gualala):

Walk-On Beach Trail: M.56.50

Shell Beach Trail: M.55.20

Stengel Beach Trail: M.53.96

Pebble Beach Trail: M.52.30

Black Point Beach Trail: M.50.83

FEES: Day use: $5/vehicle.

FURTHER INFO: Gualala Point Regional Park (707) 785-2377.

of two barely attached crescent coves sheltered by offshore rocks and protected somewhat by the point to the north.

STENGEL BEACH TRAIL (.4 mile round trip) descends west then heads southwest, soon following a beautiful old cypress windbreak and a fence. In 500 feet you meet a private trail and a break in the fence. Your trail bends right and heads through the break to the steep beach stairway. Descend 40 steps, then carefully find your way down the last 20 feet of slanting rock to narrow, secluded Stengel Beach.

PEBBLE BEACH TRAIL (.6 mile round trip) heads south between shore pines on a gentle descent. At 300 feet you cross a private path at a right angle. Your trail turns west through Bishop pine forest. A lush creek runs on your right, home to corn lily, ferns and other water-loving plants. At ⅛ mile you leave the creek and forest for grassy headlands. Near ¼ mile the trail approaches a cypress windbreak. You meet another private path on the left. Go right, crossing a small wooden bridge. In 150 feet you meet the stairway to Pebble Beach. The beach is gray, pebbly sand with good tidepools at low tide.

BLACK POINT BEACH TRAIL (.5 mile round trip to beach, up to 1.5 miles total round trip), arguably Sea Ranch's wildest hike, descends gently north, then northwest across lush, grassy headlands. After 300 feet you cross a private dirt road. The trail soon turns west, heading directly toward the sea cliff. Cross a private Sea Ranch trail, then come to a sturdy set of stairs descending 84 steps to the south end of the beach. To the south is Black Point, a rock outcrop with windblown cypress, once site of a Southern Pomo settlement and long a landmark to navigators on both land and sea. To the north the black sand and pebble beach extends about ½ mile at medium to low tide.

OTHER SUGGESTION: If you rent a house in the Sea Ranch subdivision, you will have access to all the private trails there as well as trails described in this book.

SALT POINT STATE PARK
INCLUDES THE NEXT SEVEN TRAILS

Salt Point State Park is Sonoma's slice of coastal heaven. The park's 7000 acres sprawl along five miles of convoluted shore, extending inland more than two miles to 1000-foot-high wooded ridges. The adjoining Kruse Rhododendron State Reserve adds 317 acres of second-growth forest. Ten creeks dissect the uplifted marine terraces of the park.

In November 1993 a wind-whipped wildfire, apparently started by someone camped illegally, raged through the park, scorching 450 acres. The fire damage has already begun to heal.

The changing seasons bring a diversity of moods to the land here. In winter the surf roars and crashes and the creeks sing. In spring wildflowers sparkle in lush green grasslands. In summer grasslands fade to gold and brown, while the ocean takes on a glassy calm. Immense beds of giant bull kelp grow offshore. Great blue herons stand on the heads of the kelp, seeming to walk on the still waters as they pick their meals from the sea.

The Kashaya Pomo were the original human inhabitants of the land. They had villages on the ridges and descended to the shore to harvest sea food. The Pomos camped in the forest to stay out of the wind. They cooked their catch on the

leeward side of rocks, where middens are found today. They salted the surplus, trading it and salt with inland tribes, mostly for obsidian to make tools and weapons.

When the Russians established Fort Ross in the early 1800s, their Aleut hunters camped at Gerstle Cove to hunt otters. The Russians left in the 1840s, soon replaced by Americans, who came to cut redwoods and low-grade sandstone blocks. They loaded the lumber and stone on ships, hauling the materials to San Francisco to build the booming city.

Overland transportation improved when Wells Fargo established a stage line from the Russian River to Fisk Mill and Plantation about 1860 (later extended to Gualala), but the infamous gentleman bandit Black Bart often robbed the stage. The stage road was improved around 1870 with the help of the Sonoma County Board of Supervisors, but even then it took driver Lew Miller 12 hours to negotiate the wild ride from Jenner to Gualala. Today Highway 1 follows much of the original stage route.

Salt Point State Park offers an enchanting maze of trails that interconnect the ten biotic zones within the park. In one day of hiking you can start on windswept headlands overlooking the ocean, climb through tall forest to reach the stunted growth of the Pygmy Forest or the sag ponds and valleys along the San Andreas Fault, then return to your campground. Whatever season you visit Salt Point, the pristine land provides new and diverse treasures of wildflowers and moods.

6

CHINESE GULCH/
PHILLIPS GULCH LOOP
KRUSE RHODODENDRON STATE RESERVE

The Kruse family started a sheep ranch in these coastal hills in 1880. The marginally productive land could not raise enough sheep to support the family, so they diversified into logging and tanbark harvesting. In 1933 the family donated these 317 acres to the state as a Rhododendron Reserve, preceding the establishment of adjacent Salt Point State Park by almost 40 years. In the 1970s another 1350 acres of the original Kruse Ranch were added to Salt Point State Park. They make up the extreme northern portion of the park.

This easy hike has three chances for early return, should you decide to shorten your hike. From April to June, the brilliant pink blossoms of native rhododendrons brighten the forest along your trail.

From the parking area, your trail climbs 50 feet east to a trail map and the posted start of the Rhododendron Loop. Continuing east between redwood split rail fences, you climb through mixed forest of redwood, Douglas fir, grand fir and Bishop pine, with scattered tanoak and madrone. In spring evergreen violets, clintonia and lillies brighten the trail. The muffled roar of the surf filters through the forest, the ocean less than ½ mile away.

In 300 feet dense clusters of rhododendrons line the trail. Soon the short Rhododendron Loop goes left for a quick return to the parking area. Take Chinese Gulch Trail, climbing gradually northeast into dense forest. The murmur of a stream rises from the east. You leave the split rail fences behind as your trail bends left, coming to a one-person seat on a twisted wax myrtle to your left. Other plants in the crowded understory include evergreen and red huckleberry, manzanita, salal, sword fern and evergreen violet.

Climb into tall forest with a dense understory. You soon pass a circle of redwoods encompassing a large fragment of a charred stump. The notches in the stump, called springboard cuts, indicate that it was cut long ago, before the advent of chainsaws, as were most of the redwood stumps along this trail.

Climb east at ⅛ mile, passing second-growth redwoods to four feet in diameter. You meet and climb along the rim of the steep canyon of Chinese Gulch. Passing a rest bench, descend into the gulch at ¼ mile. A spur on the right de-

CHINESE GULCH/PHILLIPS GULCH LOOP:

DISTANCE: 2⅜-mile loop, with several shorter options.
TIME: One hour.
TERRAIN: Rolling, wooded hills cut by several canyons.
ELEVATION GAIN/LOSS: 360 feet+/360 feet–.
BEST TIME: May.
WARNINGS: Watch for poison oak.
HOW TO GET THERE: Turn east off Highway 1 at
 M.42.75 onto Kruse Ranch Road. Go .4 mile to trail-
 head parking area.
FURTHER INFO: (707) 847-3221.

scends quickly to the gravel road, your second chance for
an early return.

Stay left to cross a bridge over the creek. Along the creek
redwood sorrel blooms most anytime of year. Hedge nettle,
violets, deer and sword ferns and a dense carpet of moss
also thrive here.

Climb steeply out of the canyon, passing clintonia, slink
pod and trillium, then crossing a small bridge over a tributary.
You switchback left above two large stumps with springboard
cuts, then switchback to the right. Cross a short boardwalk at
the top of a steep slide, then contour through the forest.

Beyond ⅜ mile your trail swings left, climbing past a
rest bench. Walking through an open understory, you soon
switchback left. The trail levels at ½ mile as you pass through
a redwood circle. You switchback steeply to the right, climbing to cross a gully at ⅝ mile. Your trail levels, then starts a
gentle descent. Tanoaks dominate the forest here, providing
a different, more luminous quality of light.

At ¾ mile your descending trail approaches a gulch where
a bend of the road comes into view. You drop steeply to the
gulch and a junction. You can go right, coming to the road
in just a few feet for a shortcut to the trailhead.

The described hike goes left to climb southeast, then steeply
east to ⅞ mile, where your trail levels. You dip through a small
gully. Then the understory becomes dense again, jammed
with rhododendron and huckleberry. Soon tall golden chinquapin and dense Labrador tea, with pungent white flowers
in summer, crowd the trail.

At one mile you climb northeast as the forest thins. You

promptly return to dense forest with a crowded understory. Start a gradual descent, crossing the road at 1⅛ mile, then descending south on the Phillips Gulch Trail.

You soon draw near Phillips Gulch Creek, below on your left. Follow the sound of rushing water to 1¼ miles. Then your trail bends gradually right, crosses a side gully and levels. Most of the next mile is descending or level. At 1⅜ miles you cross another bridge over a tributary, then continue a gradual descent through mixed forest.

After another small bridge the trail levels, following an old wagon road. Descending gradually at 1½ miles, you pass through a dense stand of young redwoods. Soon your path bends right, leaving the old road to cross a gully at 1⅝ miles. Climb gently through forest with an open understory. You pass a circle of redwoods on your left, descend briefly, then level.

At 1¾ miles you meet one more junction. The trail on the right climbs quickly to meet the road. Taking the right fork saves little time, although it eliminates considerable climbing. Take the left fork for some of the prettiest scenery on this hike.

The left fork descends west, then southwest. You descend six switchbacks into a canyon that feeds Chinese Gulch Creek. The sixth switchback, at 2 miles, overlooks the creek in the side canyon. Follow the creek downstream, crossing it on a bridge at 2⅛ miles, just above its confluence with Chinese Gulch. In another 75 feet you cross Chinese Gulch at a beautiful spot where a bench provides a resting spot. The murmur of the creek mingles with the distant roar of surf. Lush vegetation, including salal, corn lily, elk clover and huckleberry, thrives in the moist environment.

From here you have nowhere to go but up. The trail climbs switchbacks through a dense stand of redwoods. At 2¼ miles you overlook Chinese Gulch. You climb steeply by two more switchbacks, pass the toilets and come to the parking lot.

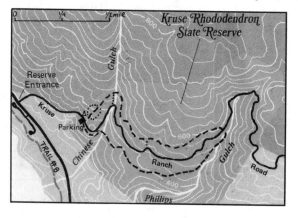

7.

FISK MILL COVE to HORSESHOE COVE
FOLLOWING THE PARK'S NORTHERN SHORE

From the parking area, your trail descends northwest through mature Bishop pine forest for 150 feet to a junction. Stay right, continuing northwest through the forest with a carpet of pine needles underfoot. Your path forks again in 150 feet.

The short, 250-foot spur on the left climbs to an observation platform atop Sentinel Rock, offering a spectacular view. Broadleaf ceanothus, evergreen violet and poison oak grow in the understory along the trail. From the wooden deck at the end of the spur you look northwest to the high headland of Horseshoe Point, west to open ocean and south toward Salt Point. Tiny Fisk Mill Cove lies 120 feet below. Coast silktassel, toyon, leather fern, iris, coastal onion and sticky monkeyflower grow beside the deck.

Returning to the main trail, you descend northwest to a rough gully crossing overlooking the cove. Your trail climbs gradually north through the forest, then levels to wander back to the edge of the bluff. You make a winding descent into Cannon Gulch. At ⅜ mile you switchback left, descending to meet a vague spur on the left that descends steeply to the spectacular pocket beach of Fisk Mill Cove. The cove was called *Tabatewi* by the Kashaya Pomo, meaning "place of much gravel." You may see Pacific loons, great blue herons, grebes, murres and pelicans.

Going right on the main trail, you descend to a creek crossing with lush coastal scrub including red elderberry, star Solomon's seal, salmonberry and western coltsfoot beneath Bishop pines and stunted redwoods.

Climb steeply out of the gulch and through a broken fence to meet a trail that branches right, heading north-east to Highway 1. You turn left to continue along the headlands. As you turn away from Fisk Mill Cove, a spur trail branches left. Go 75 feet to a beautiful spot above the shore, a cemetery for the pioneer Fisk family, who moved to this coast in 1860.

Return to the main trail, a rutted double track heading northwest through tall grasslands toward a fence. As you join a broader trail from the highway, veer left toward bluff's edge to pass through the fence. You descend to cross a small creek at ⅝ mile, where a spur on the left descends to a rocky beach.

Your trail leaves the gulch and forest to head west along the shore. You dip through another small gully where wax myrtle, cypress and Bishop pine grow, then continue west over open headlands, with golden brodiaea in spring.

At ¾ mile you meet a broad trail. The right fork heads east to Highway 1 at M.43.22. Take the left fork to head southwest toward the south-facing point. You veer inland to cross a gully, then continue southwest to a fork. Take the faint left fork toward a rock outcrop.

At ⅞ mile the rock is right before you. Veer to the left of the rock, heading south to the bluff's edge, site of the loading chute for the Fisk lumber mill, where schooners were loaded in the boom days of the timber trade. You pass several posts and rings that were used to anchor and feed the cables to ships waiting offshore. The many offshore rocks made navigation difficult for the nineteenth-century sea captains. Ice plant grows along the bluffs.

Pick your way west along the shore, passing bush lupine, paintbrush, goldfields, hairy cat's ear, checker mallow and but-tercups. At one mile you approach the point. Turn northwest, then north along the park's westernmost shore, heading toward the high headland of Horseshoe Point.

Around 1⅛ miles your trail veers right, rounding a small cove. Continue north along the convoluted coast. At 1¼ miles you have three trails to choose from. All of them merge not far ahead as you cut inland to wind around a mushroom-shaped cove, then head along the shore.

FISK MILL COVE to HORSESHOE COVE:

DISTANCE: 4¼ miles round trip to point, 6¼ miles
round trip to north end of trail.

TIME: Two to four hours.

TERRAIN: Along the shore on gentle bluffs cut by
stream canyons, then climbing to dramatic promontory of Horseshoe Point, with optional descent along
the shore of Horseshoe Cove.

ELEVATION GAIN/LOSS: 360 feet+/360 feet– round trip
to point, 560 feet+/560 feet– round trip to end of trail.

BEST TIME: Spring, summer for wildflowers.

WARNINGS: Watch for poison oak. Stay back from
edge of crumbly bluffs. Ford of Cannon Gulch may be
impassable after storms.

HOW TO GET THERE: Turn west off Highway 1 at
M.42.63 into Fisk Mill Cove parking area. Turn right
and drive .1 mile to Bluff Trailhead (.1 mile before
end of road).

FURTHER INFO: Salt Point State Park (707) 847-3221.

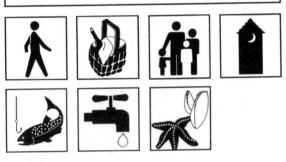

At 1⅜ miles you cross the small creek of scrub-filled Dead-
man Gulch, where mimulus, coltsfoot, yellow water iris, alder
and willow tangle with other seaside plants. You stay near the
sea's edge, passing to the left of a scrub-draped rock outcrop
sheltered by a stand of pines at 1½ miles.

Continue along the shore, winding through fields of bush lupine where native blackberry intertwines with the introduced
Himalaya species. Soon a spur on the left winds southwest to a
small point with a fine view of the coast. Continuing northwest
beside the shore, you pass several more small coves and points.
Harbor seals and California sea lions haul out on offshore
rocks. Red-shafted flickers live in the grasslands.

Around 1⅝ miles multiple paths provide a choice of routes
along the shore. Continue northwest, hugging the edge of the
bluff, heading toward the tree-shrouded rise of Horseshoe Point.
Sea palms grow on the offshore rocks. You soon join a trail with
better tread, heading northwest over gently sloping grasslands.
A rocky, sparsely wooded ridge runs to the right of the trail.

42

From 1¾ miles you climb gradually along the shore. Around 1⅞ miles a prominent sandstone outcrop covered with a garden of succulents stands between you and the ocean. The outermost rocks shelter many shorebirds. You continue northwest, climbing gradually toward the rocky point, through grasslands with scattered cow parsnip, sea thrift, purple seaside daisy and coast buckwheat.

When you meet a sandstone shelf, turn right and climb steeply up a grassy chute into the pines. The pines shelter iris, buttercup, sticky monkeyflower and coast silktassel. The trail becomes vague here, but you promptly meet a better path. Turn left and climb northwest, paralleling the ridge on your right. At 2 miles you climb steeply but briefly. Dense, low-growing ceanothus and salal shelter delicate star tulips in spring.

You top the ridge at 2⅛ miles. Follow it briefly northwest to the 186-foot-high summit of Horseshoe Point. Hen and chicks and other succulents thrive on the moisture-catching rock outcrop, along with poison oak. The large boulder just west of the summit makes a fine viewpoint and picnic spot if it is not too windy. You have a grand view up and down the rugged, winding coast. Gualala Point sprawls seaward 13 miles northwest. To the northeast of Horseshoe Point, the protected waters of Horseshoe Cove jog east to only 300 feet from Highway 1.

You can retrace your steps to the trailhead for a 4¼-mile round trip. If you wish to continue east, then north around the shore of Horseshoe Cove, the trail gets rougher and less traveled. To continue, double back along the ridge for a few hundred feet to a low saddle where a rough, winding footpath descends steeply east, then passes through an old fence in a sea of beach grass. The rough trail continues east along the bluff. Lush vegetation grows along the path, including blue Mendocino gentian, poppy, paintbrush, hedge nettle, beach morning glory, purple seaside daisy, Douglas iris, coffeeberry, yarrow, bush lupine and beach strawberry. You turn north to descend to a low spot on the headlands at 2⅜ miles, then climb to another high point at 2½ miles. From this vantage you look north to the main arm of Horseshoe Cove and south to another arm. Descend along the bluffs to 2⅝ miles, where you cross a gulch.

Continue another 300 feet to a fork. Take the left fork to a high, short promontory at the bluff's edge. You overlook a steep cliff face where cormorants and pigeon guillemots can be seen nesting on the cliff and fishing in the churning surf below.

You can continue north to 3⅛ miles, where your trail winds east to meet Highway 1 at M.44.54 at the northern

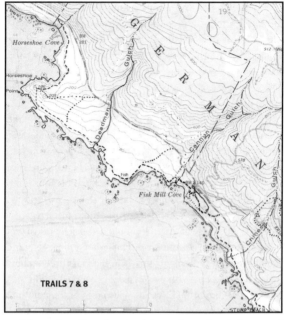

TRAILS 7 & 8

park boundary. From here, unless you have shuttled a second
vehicle, you must return to Horseshoe Point, then return the
way you came, winding along the shore. Or you can take the
broad path that winds east from the southern summit. It
returns to Highway 1 at M.43.9, but you can veer right on
a path ⅛ mile before the highway and return to the shore to
retrace your steps southeast along the headlands to the Fisk
Mill parking area.

OTHER SUGGESTION: You can also walk to Horseshoe
  Point and Cove from parking areas at M.43.68, M.43.9,
  M.44.26 and M.44.54 (no day-use fee).

8.

FISK MILL to STUMP BEACH
OUTCROPS, COVES, GULCHES AND SURGE CHANNELS

Your trail south along the coast from the Fisk Mill Cove
parking area starts at the same trailhead as the trail north,
Trail #7. At the junction 150 feet down the trail, take the
left fork. The sign says South Cove .3 mile. Descend south
through pine forest with views of the nearby coast. Around
⅛ mile you pass a picnic table and come to a vague junction
beside a large Bishop pine.

Go left at a fork, making a winding ascent southeast through the forest rather than heading out to the bluff's edge. At a signed junction, continue southeast through pine forest where coffeeberry grows densely in the understory. Beyond ¼ mile descend to cross a bridge over a gully, then meet the shore at the top of eroded cliffs.

Your trail winds north then east, passing along the seaward base of a wooded rock outcrop at ⅜ mile. You soon descend to cross a bridge over a gully with lush salal, ferns and berry vines. Climb steps, veer right at a fork to head southwest and pass through a grassy clearing, then veer left to meander south through forest.

At ½ mile you walk along the base of another rock outcrop at the top of steep bluffs. Coast silktassel, coffeeberry, paintbrush, seaside daisy and poison oak grow beside your trail. You descend to a spot with a magnificent view south along the coast. A trail descends from the left (from the Fisk Mill South parking area).

Follow the wooded bluff southeast, passing a rock with an egg-shaped hollow where succulents dangle overhead. You cross a bridge arond ⅝ mile, then leave the forest for open, grassy headlands. A rough trail on your right descends steeply to tiny South Cove.

Continue south along the shore to a point overlooking offshore rocks, a popular haul-out for harbor seals. Your trail turns south-southeast, following the bluffs over open headlands. You cross grassy Chinese Gulch just above where its stream plunges to the surf line in a waterfall.

Your vague trail climbs southeast, passing to the left of a patch of Douglas iris and coming to a fork around ¾ mile. Veer right, heading south along the coast. Two spurs on the left lead to Highway 1 at M.42.14 in about 300 feet.

Follow the bluff's edge along the shore, passing bush lupine, seaside daisies, irises and buttercups. At one mile a flat rock shelf lies along the tideline. Notice the magnificently eroded shore, with surge channels where the surf pulses through shoreline rocks on the right.

At 1⅛ miles you ford the creek of Phillips Gulch, where mimulus and beach silverweed grow. On your right the creek plunges 30 feet to the surf. You climb a steep incline along the bluff's edge. After 200 feet your trail veers left, climbing to the east side of the rocky top ahead. You reach the top at 1¼ miles, where another spur leads to the nearby highway. Continue south, then southeast, soon coming to an overlook of the huge cove of Stump Beach.

To reach Stump Beach, head east along the high bluff, passing Bishop pines. Continue through grasslands to a power

FISK MILL to STUMP BEACH:

DISTANCE: (all round trip) 2¼ miles to Stump Beach
    overlook, 3⅛ miles to blanket picnic spot, 3½ miles to
    Stump Beach.
TIME: One or two hours.
TERRAIN: Along rolling headlands cut by several creeks
    above the shore, then descending to pocket beach.
ELEVATION GAIN/LOSS: 280 feet+/280 feet-, round
    trip to overlook. Add 160 feet+/160 feet- to beach.
BEST TIME: Spring, early summer for wildflowers.
WARNINGS: Stay back from edge of bluffs. Watch for
    poison oak in coastal scrub. Ford of Chinese Gulch
    may be impassable after storms.
HOW TO GET THERE: Turn west off Highway 1 at
    M.42.63 into Fisk Mill Cove parking area. Turn right
    and drive .2 mile to trailhead at the end of the road.
FURTHER INFO: Salt Point State Park (707) 847-3221.

line, then stay left at a fork, paralleling the highway, to cross
a gully. Then head southeast through the forest to another
clearing by 1½ miles, where seaside daisies and asters grow.
Sheltered by the trees, this small clearing is a pleasant spot for
a blanket picnic, with a fine view of Stump Beach Cove.

To descend to Stump Beach, follow the trail as it descends
south, then climbs east before contouring south through pine
forest. At 1⅝ miles your trail begins its descent to the beach,
soon switchbacking right to descend west to the beach at the
mouth of the creek before 1¾ miles. You can extend your
hike by linking with the Salt Point Trail (Trail #11) at the
southwest corner of the beach.

When ready to return, retrace your steps along the bluff's
edge or follow the upper headlands back to South Cove, then
follow the trail back to your starting point.

9

STUMP BEACH/PLANTATION/ PRAIRIE/NORTH LOOP

CLIMB TO AN OLD STAGECOACH STOP

From the trailhead opposite the entrance to the Stump Beach parking lot, follow the Stump Beach Trail that heads south (not east as the hiker sign placement might indicate). The broad path soon climbs east, leaving an area scorched by the 1993 wildfire. Ascend through forest of Bishop pine, Douglas fir, grand fir and tanoak with an understory of huckleberry, wax myrtle, sword fern and bunch grasses.

By ⅛ mile you ascend along the edge of the deep canyon of Miller Creek. Lady ferns and salal soon join the understory. Before ¼ mile redwoods join the forest mix. Continue east, then northeast on a moderate ascent.

Wind around the top of a gully at ⅜ mile and continue your ascent as rhododendrons join the understory. At ½ mile you approach a larger gulch, then cross it on a bridge.

At ⅝ mile your trail turns north and the ascent eases. Large redwood stumps with springboard cuts indicate that this forest was first logged long ago. Some of the second growth redwoods and firs approach four feet in diameter. Continue on a zigzagging climb, crossing the head of another gulch at ⅞ mile.

Beyond one mile you cross the top of yet another gulch. Tanoaks begin to dominate the forest, with scattered conifers and madrones. Ascend gradually as your trail heads north, with the largest gulch yet on your right. Ascend moderately again beyond 1¼ miles, passing pockets of large redwoods.

Your trail levels around 1½ miles, then descends before an easy climb to Stump Beach Trail's end at Kruse Ranch Road. You can return the way you came for a hike of 3¼ miles round trip. Another choice would be to turn left and walk Kruse Ranch Road for about ¾ mile into Kruse Rhododendron State Reserve and hike the Chinese Gulch/Phillips Gulch Loop (see Trail #6) from its top end, then return via Stump Beach Trail for a 7⅛-mile hike.

Our described loop turns right to ascend north, then east on Kruse Ranch Road to the historic settlement of Plantation (no services; note that portions of the road leave state park property, but it is a public road). Along the way you pass the largest redwoods on this loop as well as houses and small farms.

Climb gradually along the road (some portions gravel, some paved) to 2 miles, then descend gradually to 2⅛ miles. At

47

DISTANCE: 8-mile loop, or shorter hikes of 3¼ miles
round trip or 7⅛-mile semi-loop.

TIME: Three or four hours.

TERRAIN: Climbs through forest, follows country road
through historic settlement, descends along San Andreas
Fault, then climbs to prairie, then pygmy forest, before
descending through coastal forest and grasslands to
Stump Beach before returning to trailhead.

ELEVATION GAIN/LOSS: 1200 feet+/1200 feet-.

BEST TIME: Spring, early summer for wildflowers.

WARNINGS: Use caution crossing Highway 1. Stay off
adjacent private property.

HOW TO GET THERE: On Highway 1 in Salt Point State
Park at M.41.2, trailhead is on east side of highway opposite the entrance to Stump Beach parking.

FURTHER INFO: Salt Point State Park (707) 847-3221.

2¼ miles the hard-packed dirt road turns north on a gentle
ascent through mixed forest.

At 2⅜ miles your road turns east, picks up some pavement,
and dips through Plantation, a former stagecoach stop on
the original coast road—passing the old school, an old barn
and other historic buildings, an antique gas pump and a
modern sculpture.

From 2½ miles your road ascends steeply. You climb past
the gate for Plantation Ranch, then follow their old split
rail fence on the right, passing very large redwoods. When
the fence on your right ends, look closely on the right for
Plantation Trail. It leaves the road just 125 feet beyond the
end of the fence. It does NOT head southeast as shown on
the state Park map. Rather, it descends west from beside
a large chunk of old redwood root. When I hiked this trail
in November 2004, the small sign marking the trail was
knocked over.

In only 200 feet Plantation Trail bends left to contour
southeast through dense forest, generally following the
San Andreas Rift Zone for most of its length. At first the
fault runs along to your left. Your trail descends steeply
beyond 2⅞ miles, then resumes its contour southeast
beyond 3 miles. Beyond 3⅛ miles you are directly over
the rift zone and following it, revealed here by a broad,

relatively flat shelf in otherwise steep country. You pass a seasonal sag pond on your left.

Beyond 3¼ miles the rift zone runs along on your right. Ascend moderately from around 3⅜ miles. At 3½ miles a huge redwood stump is on your right and a seasonal seep flows down from the left. Ascend gradually, making a big bend left and reaching Plantation Trail's end beyond 3⅝ miles. Raspberries grow beneath redwoods at the junction.

Turn right and descend southwest and south on the unmarked Prairie Trail. (A left turn ascends to Seaview Road.) Descend moderately to 3⅞ miles. As the trail levels, you once again cross the rift zone. Pass a large sag pond on your left before 4 miles near the headwaters of Miller Creek. The murky pool, where a few water lilies struggle for survival, is surrounded by tall forest.

Your trail climbs gradually south, then moderately southeast. Climb gradually from 4⅛ miles, passing woodwardia ferns and toyon.

Beyond 4⅜ miles you suddenly leave the forest for the open and gently rolling, grassy prairie, where abundant wildflowers grow in spring. Just beyond 4½ miles Prairie Trail ends. Wood rose grows eight feet tall near the junction. A left turn would descend South Trail, which leads 1.3 miles to Highway 1 at the park's south boundary. Turn right and climb slightly on Central Trail, following the edge of the prairie with a forest peppered with large madrones on your left.

Around 4⅝ miles a "hedge" of native blackberry grows on our right, then abundant huckleberry grows on your left. Your broad trail soon turns southeast to climb away from the prairie.

At 5 miles you meet a junction on your right. Turn right and ascend north on North Trail. It climbs to 900 feet elevation beyond 5⅛ miles, the high point of this loop. Abundant golden chinquapins grow beside the trail. You might see their spiny seed pods on the ground.

Begin a gentle descent around 5¼ miles. You climb over a small rise at 5⅜ miles. As you descend from it a sign announces that you are entering the pygmy forest. Most of the plants are the same, just smaller—Bishop pine, tanoak, chinquapin, huckleberry—but near the sign you'll also see Mendocino cypress and Fort Bragg manzanita, which has the smallest leaves. You descend quickly to a nearly level basin with poor soils and drainage. Plants are smaller here, except for the few Bishop pines whose roots have broken through the hardpan soil.

At 5½ miles a wide spot in the trail marks the heart of this pygmy forest, where mature trees are shorter than most people. Continue through the dwarf forest. You soon encounter an ancient dune, long ago uplifted from the shoreline. The forest here is transitional (part pygmy, part normal) but you pass one pygmy redwood only 20 feet tall and abundant, fragrant Labrador tea. Climb briefly at 5⅝ miles, then descend moderately through tall forest of primarily tanoak and madrone with scattered redwoods. A steep descent around 5⅞ miles soon eases as Bishop pines join the forest.

At 6 miles the broad Water Tank Trail forks left. Descend southwest on the sandy North Trail as Douglas fir, salal and rhododendron join the forest mix. Make a winding moderate descent on the broad track through the forest.

Beyond 6¼ miles your trail descends along the edge of

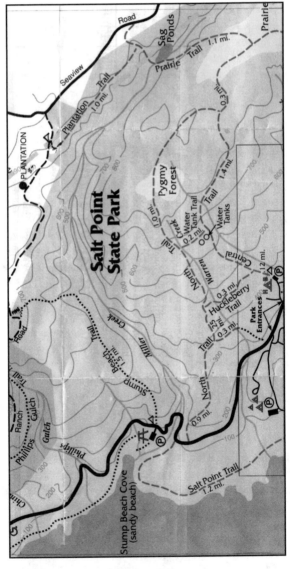

Warren Creek's canyon on your left. You'll soon hear the surf pounding, at least on big surf days.

Descend to a confusing junction beyond 6⅜ miles. Bear right, then right again to continue on North Trail. (The trail sign doesn't mention Huckleberry Trail, the .3-mile connector to Central Trail to the south.) North Trail descends fitfully through forest of redwoods and firs with scattered Bishop pines. Before 6⅝ miles you pass a massive stump of a climax redwood easily twelve feet in diameter.

You soon encounter another junction. The unmarked left fork heads south .3 mile to Highway 1. Go right on North Trail as redwoods become uncommon in a coastal forest with a grassy understory. Beyond 6⅞ miles your trail skirts the burn zone of the '93 fire on the left. The trail was used as the fire line here, healthy forest on the right contrasting with snags on the left along with a dense growth of young, fire-sprouted Bishop pines.

Beyond the top of a hill at 7 miles, you descend toward the nearby coast. The fire line broke here, allowing the fire to burn north nearly to Sea Ranch. The descent steepens as you pass tent-sized sandstone boulders with coastal views beyond. The trail soon swings right to descend northwest. Around 7¼ miles your trail winds left and descends to Highway 1.

To return to the trailhead, cautiously cross the highway and walk the shoulder for about ⅛ mile to a fire-road trail that heads west from the first big bend. Follow that trail as it climbs northwest briefly, then descends north toward Stump Beach Cove. After you pass the last tree, a scrubby pine, beyond 7⅝ miles, bear right to leave the trail, heading north toward the north end of Stump Beach. As you top a small rise, you'll spot the grassy trail that descends east to the beach at 7¾ miles. Cross Miller Creek, turn left and walk 200 feet to find the trail and stairs climbing to Stump Beach parking lot. Walk up to the highway and carefully cross it to return to your starting point at 8 miles.

10.

PYGMY FOREST LOOP
CLIMB TO THE FOREST OF DWARVES

Your trail leaves from the parking area for the Hike/Bike Campground, where you may want to use the toilets, water faucet or phone. Climb north on the fire road, ascending through mixed forest with an understory of huckleberries, salal, ferns and redwood violets.

At ⅛ mile you reach a junction. North Trail goes left, eventually leading to Stump Beach. You go straight, climbing along Pygmy Forest Trail. The steady climb encourages you to breathe deeply the fresh coastal air. Rhododendrons, clintonias and trilliums flower abundantly in spring.

By ¼ mile Labrador tea joins the understory plants. This pungent and poisonous relative of the rhododendron often occurs in pygmy forest, but covers a much broader range as well. Soon tall woodwardia ferns grow on the left of your steadily climbing trail. Also known as giant chain ferns, they often occur with redwoods, as they do here.

At ⅜ mile, you climb to a junction beside two water tanks. Go left for the shortest route to the pygmy forest. Your fire road climbs gradually to reach the third terrace, where it levels briefly. Madrone, tanoak, wax myrtle and manzanita mix with grand and Douglas firs, redwoods and Bishop pines. Watch for cottontailed pygmy brush rabbits. You climb intermittently, then descend briefly to cross the headwaters of Warren Creek. You meet the upper end of North Trail at ⅝ mile, turning right to continue a gradual climb. You climb steeply again beyond ¾ mile, ascending to the fourth terrace.

At ⅞ mile your trail levels. In 200 feet you suddenly enter pygmy forest, growing on level, nutrient-leached soil. Not far beneath the surface lies a dense hardpan that prevents most plants from breaking through to any nutrients in the soil below it. Along with stunted Bishop pines and redwoods grow two uncommon species that occur primarily on pygmy soils: Mendocino cypress and Fort Bragg manzanita. While Mendocino cypress occasionally grows more than 100 feet tall on nutrient-rich soils, the species is most prevalent on pygmy soils. A 100-year-old tree here may be only three feet tall. Fort Bragg manzanita has the smallest leaves of all the manzanitas.

On the Mendocino Coast, the fourth-terrace pygmy forest occurs around an elevation of 400 feet, with isolated pockets of fifth-terrace pygmy at about 600 feet elevation. Since the fourth-terrace pygmy forest at Salt Point occurs around 900 feet above sea level, one can surmise that this portion of the coast has been (and may still continue to be) uplifted at a faster rate than the coast sixty miles north.

The trail passes through true pygmy forest for about ¼ mile. At 1⅛ miles the road resumes a gradual climb. You quickly leave the most dwarfed area of the pygmy forest for an area of transitional vegetation. In the transitional zone, you have many of the pygmy associated species, but they tend to grow larger and be mixed with other species. Bear grass also grows here.

PYGMY FOREST LOOP:

DISTANCE: 2⅝-mile loop, 5-mile loop or longer.
TIME: One or two hours.
TERRAIN: Climb through redwood forest to pygmy forest at 900 feet elevation and return.
ELEVATION GAIN/LOSS: 650 feet+/650 feet–.
BEST TIME: Spring for wildflowers, anytime nice.
WARNINGS: No water along trail.
HOW TO GET THERE: Turn east off Highway 1 at M.39.78. Go straight to day-use parking, near Hike & Bike Campground.
FEES: Day use: $6/vehicle. Car camping: $25/night.
FURTHER INFO: Salt Point State Park (707) 847-3221.

Your path curves right to climb gradually southeast through transitional pygmy. Soon a large hairy manzanita grows twenty feet tall on the right of the trail. Your path bends right and descends gradually.

At 1⅜ miles North Trail ends as it comes to another fire road. You can go left here for a longer loop of 5 miles, heading east to a large prairie with abundant wildflowers in spring. (In the prairie a spur forks left to descend ⅝ mile to a sag pond along the San Andreas Fault at Miller Creek, then climbs to Seaview Road at one mile.) From the prairie you can descend South Trail to meet a power-line footpath that branches right (200 feet before the highway) to Woodside Campground and your trailhead.

Our described route goes right at the junction, descending west through mixed forest. At 1½ miles your trail steepens and bends left. Then your descent eases.

Beyond 1⅝ miles your path levels on the third terrace for nearly ¼ mile. You pass a spot where the road turns suddenly to loose sand. This is the top of an ancient dune that formed along the shore about 300,000 years ago, then was uplifted along with this entire coast.

Your descent steepens again as it bends left to cross Squaw Creek around 1⅞ miles. You may spot coffeeberry on the right, soon followed by corn lilies on the left. Descend alternately steeply and gradually through forest.

At 2¼ miles you return to the junction where the two water tanks stand. Retrace your steps downhill, returning to the parking lot at 2⅝ miles.

> **OTHER SUGGESTION**: You can also reach the PYGMY FOREST by ascending NORTH TRAIL (M.40.74) or SOUTH TRAIL (M.38.73), or by descending PLANTA-TION TRAIL from Kruse Ranch Road or Seaview Trail from Seaview Road, east of the park.

11.

SALT POINT to STUMP BEACH

ALONG TWISTING, HISTORY-RICH ROCKY SHORE

One of the earliest towns on the northern Sonoma Coast was Louisville, situated on Salt Point overlooking Gerstle Cove, where the parking area for this trail is today. Louis Funcke and Louis Gerstle established Louisville in 1870, naming it after their Kentucky hometown. The founders planned to capitalize on San Francisco's booming growth by shipping timber and stone to the city to feed the building boom. Their town plan showed streets all over the Salt Point headlands.

By 1872 California's largest hotel stood on the bluff above Gerstle Cove. A big lumber operation was in full swing, with a horse-drawn railway up the coast to Stump Beach, where the canyon of Miller Creek was extensively logged. The sandstone rocks of Salt Point were quarried into building blocks, used mostly to build streets and retaining walls. Two ship-loading operations ran down to the cove, a wooden loading chute and a high-line cable operation. The quarried rock was loaded by the latter.

By the late 1870s, Louisville was declining. The most accessible trees had been cut, and only the quarry was productive. Neither the town nor the hotel had fulfilled the grandiose dreams of its founders. Today nature has reclaimed this wild coast.

From the parking area, a paved trail descends southwest, winding over headlands covered with yellow bush lupine. Quarried blocks of sandstone lie beside the trailhead. The paved trail winds, descending gradually past two interpretive signs, coming to the tip of Salt Point at ⅛ mile, where the pavement ends. Harbor seals haul out on the offshore

rocks. If the sky is clear, you may see Bodega Head southeast along the coast near the Sonoma-Marin county line. You may even see the headlands of Point Reyes jutting seaward beyond the Head.

From the point, a dirt path heads northwest along the shore. Dense lupine grows beside the trail. Sea palms cling to the tidal rocks on your left. At a fork, you can take either trail past a rock outcrop where poppies and sea thrift grow. Where the trails merge ahead, your path improves. Tidal rocks to the left of the trail have been eroded into intriguing shapes by the action of the waves. A rest bench overlooks the shore around ¼ mile. Where the double track turns east, take the narrow bluff trail along the shore.

Continue northwest paralleling the shore. At ⅜ mile you pass quarried rocks. Your trail soon veers right to wind around a cove. You ford seasonal Warren Creek at the top of the cove, where calla and corn lilies grow upstream. The big rock to the east was one of the main quarry sites.

Wind west along the bluff's edge on a narrow path, paralleling the broad old road just inland. A dense tangle of coastal scrub covers the headlands. The plants include coyote brush, cow parsnip, angelica, broadleaf ceanothus, blackberry, salal, sword fern, coffeeberry, yarrow, beach morning glory and beach strawberry.

The footpath fords a small stream where woodwardia fern, twinberry and wax myrtle grow with other soft scrub plants. Continue along the shore, passing many discarded quarry stones. Irises, hairy star tulips, coast goldfields and buttercups add color in spring and summer.

55

SALT POINT TO STUMP BEACH:

DISTANCE: 3⅜ miles round trip to Stump Beach, 3 miles for headlands loop, 6½ miles for Stump Beach-North Trail-Pygmy Forest loop.

TIME: One to three hours.

TERRAIN: Along open, convoluted shore with unusual rock formations, then descending to a large cove.

ELEVATION GAIN/LOSS: 120 feet+/120 feet–, round trip. 180 feet+/180 feet– for headlands loop. 1040 feet+/1040 feet– for combined loop.

BEST TIME: Spring and summer for wildflowers. Moderately low tide for exploration of shoreline rock formations.

WARNINGS: Watch for oversize killer waves at shoreline, especially in winter.

HOW TO GET THERE: Turn west off Highway 1 at M.39.90 (signed Gerstle Cove Campground). Go straight past campground for .5 mile, then take right fork to Salt Point parking area.

FEES: Day use: $6/vehicle. Car camping: $25/night.

FURTHER INFO: Salt Point State Park (707) 847-3221.

Merge with a broad path before ⅝ mile and head west toward a point, then turn northwest to parallel the convoluted shore. Your trail crosses a grassy headland that extends west to a rocky point. Rejoin the broad path and continue north along the shore, then veer right to round another cove.

You merge with a rutted broad path at ⅞ mile. Climb gradually on the broad path over headlands covered with bush lupine. At one mile the climb steepens briefly, then levels in another 250 feet. Soon a side trail on your left heads west.

The side trail leads over grassy headlands for 400 feet to overlook tidal rocks sculpted into fantastic shapes, tafoni. Do not go near the sea's edge here unless it is summer or the sea is calm and the tide is out. In winter, waves smash over these tidal rocks, sometimes sending spray 100 feet in the air. If conditions are right, you can go down to explore the tafoni, rocks carved into lace and honeycomb formations and other wondrous shapes by wave action. Notice the natural depressions in the rock that catch sea water during winter and storm tides. When the water had evaporated from these basins, the local Indians came to gather the pure sea salt that remained. They used it to preserve fish and game. The Kashaya Pomos had such a surplus of salt that they traded with tribes as far away as Clear Lake. The salt was a foundation of the Pomos' prosperous culture, traded for obsidian and other goods from the inland tribes. The Pomos name for Salt Point was *Kabesilawina*, meaning flattop rock.

Return to the main trail, and descend north. Beyond 1¼ miles you pass a rock outcrop to the right of the trail. Around 1⅜ miles your trail swings to the right and heads east along the rim of Stump Beach Cove. In another ⅛ mile, when the two-wheel track bends right to climb southeast, you should veer left, continuing along the edge of the cove.

At 1⅝ miles you meet a steep old road that descends to Miller Creek and Stump Beach. The fine blond sand of the beach is well protected by the high walls of the deeply set cove, providing a fine rest or picnic spot with a superb view. Another trail climbs steps southeast to reach the parking area at M.41.2, where there are picnic tables and a toilet.

When you leave the beach, climb back up the steep road to the headlands. From there you can retrace your steps along the bluff trail for a round trip of about 3⅜ miles.

Or you can turn left and climb southeast on the two-wheel track for ⅛ mile. As the trail descends slightly, you come to

TRAILS 11 & 12

a fork. Take the right fork, heading south across the grassy headlands. You parallel the highway on a faint trail with grand views of the rolling headlands of Salt Point. About ¼ mile from the junction, you will see two trail signs on your left. If you want to prolong your hike, turn east past the signs to cautiously cross Highway 1. You can climb east into the forest on North Trail (at M.40.7). As the sign says, it is 1.8 miles to the pygmy forest, where you join Trail #10, which you follow back to Woodside Campground.

If you would rather take the shortest route back, continue south across the rolling headlands to the Salt Point parking lot at the southern tip of the point for a loop of 3 miles.

OTHER SUGGESTION: STUMP BEACH can also be reached from parking lot at M.41.2 for a shorter, but less dramatic approach to the cove. NORTH TRAIL can also be reached from M.40.74.

12.
SALT POINT'S SOUTHERN COAST
SPARKLING COVES SHROUDED IN PINE FORESTS

The effects of the nasty November 1993 wildfire that scorched 450 acres of beautiful Salt Point State Park show most conspicuously on this short, easy hike along the park's southern shore. Still, it is heartening to see how quickly the land regenerates. Mushrooms, wildflowers and young trees have begun to restore the area's beauty. Though the older trees are scorched the coastal views remain spectacular.

While this trail is described from the southernmost picnic area near Gerstle Cove, you can instead start your hike from the park's campgrounds. It is ⅜ mile from Gerstle Cove Campground, ⅞ mile from Woodside Campground to the trailhead. You can also link this hike with Trail #11 for a grand tour of the coast from the southern boundary to Stump Beach.

The park map does not show the trail running south from the South Gerstle Picnic Area. But when you reach the end of the road, a well trod path starts at a gate and descends to cross Squaw Creek, where Bishop pine, California buckeye and silktassel still grow right to shoreline. South Gerstle Cove lies at the outlet of the small creek.

After you pass the cove, a sloping grassy bluff lies on your right, where grass nut, or Ithuriel's spear, sends clusters of violet flowers skyward in spring. Look for iris, angelica and

DISTANCE: (all round trip)1⅛ miles to South boundary, 2¼
    miles to Gerstle Cove, 2⅜ miles to Salt Point parking.
TIME: One half hour to south boundary, one hour to
    Gerstle Cove.
TERRAIN: Along a convoluted shore with alternating
    grasslands and pine forests.
BEST TIME: Spring, early summer for wildflowers.
WARNINGS: Watch for poison oak. Stay back from crum-
    bly bluff edge.
HOW TO GET THERE: Turn west off Highway 1 at
    M.39.90. Go straight for .5 mile, then turn left and drive
    .5 mile to parking lot for picnic area.
FEES: Day use: $6/vehicle. Car camping: $25/night.
FURTHER INFO: Salt Point State Park (707) 847-3221
NOTE: Salt Point's 20 ENVIRONMENTAL CAMPS are now
    located east of Woodside Campground. A HIKE/BIKE
    CAMP ($3/person/night) is also east of the highway.

yellow mat in the grasslands too. If you have a closer look,
return to the main trail to avoid a washout ahead. Before ⅛
mile you come to a point that looks north to the cove. Veer
left and climb inland to cross a small creek at a rough, eroded
spot, then bear right in 50 feet at a vague fork to walk the
gently sloping, rock-rimmed grasslands of the open bluff
above small coves. Pink shades of owl's clover and the purple
of aster and seaside daisy sparkle in the grass.

Your trail heads south paralleling the shore. At ¼ mile you
approach a rocky point, revealing views to the southeast.
Ocean Cove and Timber Point are in the foreground. The
high ridge behind Sonoma Coast State Beach lies beyond.
On a clear day you can see Bodega Head and the headlands
of Point Reyes jutting seaward. Nearby offshore rocks are a
favorite haul-out for harbor seals. Continue along the shore
past lupine, passing the convoluted, rocky point between you
and the blue Pacific.

Veer east to the very end of the grassland and find a narrow
path through the Bishop pines along the shore that survived

the fire, returning you to the broad main track. It continues until you reach the end of the grassy headlands around ⅜ mile. The violet flowers of elegant brodiaea grow in the forest nearby. Just inland, huckleberry is among the first perennials to regenerate beneath charred forest. Your trail crosses rough ground, fording two eroded seasonal creeks and leaving the forest to climb over the top of a picturesquely eroded rock at ½ mile. You must wind inland to walk around a small cove and steep eroded gully, passing Indian potato.

Your trail improves, following the shore for another 300 feet to overlook a deep cove just short of the wooded ridge marking the southern park boundary, also the southern extent of the fire. Bishop pine forest still grows at the sea's edge in this spectacular, protected spot. Offshore from the ridge, a sea stack has a triangular window. The park boundary also marks the southern boundary of the original Rancho German, granted by the Spaniards to Captain Ernest Rufus in 1841. Rancho German extended north along the shore all the way to the Gualala River.

Retrace your steps, more or less, returning to the trailhead at 1⅛ miles. If you feel lazy today, you can end your hike here. But you have barely begun to tap the treasures of this shore. You can extend the hike by going northwest along the blufftop below the road.

From the gate just south of the restroom, head northwest then west toward North Gerstle Cove (hidden), beyond which Salt Point juts west. At 1¼ miles you pass scorched pines, nearly hidden now by young pines. Soon you dip into a small gully, passing through a stand of Bishop pines to a rough creek crossing. Returning to the grassy blufftop, continue west along the shore. At 1⅜ miles a spur on the right climbs to Gerstle Cove Campground. Continuing along the bluff, you soon overlook Gerstle Cove Reserve. Your trail winds to the right around the cove, crossing the top of a small eroded gully at 1½ miles. Then wind out to the road following its shoulder west.

At 1⅝ miles you come to an A-frame overlooking North Gerstle Cove, the Salt Point Visitor Center (open weekends in summer). It has exhibits of the park's ten biotic zones and a fine view of the cove from the deck.

To visit the cove or continue to Salt Point, you can go west from the visitor center to parallel a paved road. Then turn left and descend south on a dirt road to meet the paved Gerstle Cove access path (a short ⅛ mile side trip to the cove's shore).

You can continue south toward Salt Point. At 1¾ miles a restroom, fish cleaning station and cold-water diver's shower lie on the right. Just 100 feet ahead is the start of Trail #11. You can continue along the shore or return to the trailhead from here to complete a 2⅜-mile hike.

13.

STOCKHOFF CREEK
REDWOOD CANYON AT STILLWATER COVE

Your trail begins at the lower end of the day-use parking lot. Descend northeast into a dense forest of grand fir, Douglas fir, Bishop pine and redwood. Huckleberry, tanoak, wax myrtle, redwood sorrel, salal, slink pod, forget-me-not, and sword and bracken ferns grace the lush understory. As you approach Stockhoff Creek, large red huckleberry bushes and a red elderberry grow on the left.

At ⅛ mile you come to a junction. Cove Trail goes left, descending .2 mile to Stillwater Cove. Our described hike turns right on Canyon Loop Trail. Trillium, evergreen violet and five-finger fern join the understory plants. Stay on the right, passing a bridge over the creek. Continue up the creek, climbing along the sidewall of the canyon, then descend to cross a small bridge over a tributary.

Climb again, then descend to a rest bench at ¼ mile. You soon return to the mostly level flood plain of the creek, where corn lilies grow beside the trail. They bloom in late summer, although the blossoms may linger well into winter. Some redwood stumps along the trail have springboard cuts still showing. Early-day loggers wedged a platform into these cuts, providing a place to stand to make the saw cuts above the tree's swollen base.

You reach the park's eastern boundary before ⅜ mile. Since there's no longer a bridge here, ford the creek to head down-stream briefly. Your trail switchbacks to the right, climbing up and away from Stockhoff Creek. Clintonia grows beside the trail (red flowers in spring, blue berries in summer and fall). You climb gradually above the west side of the creek.

Before ½ mile you switchback steeply left and climb north-

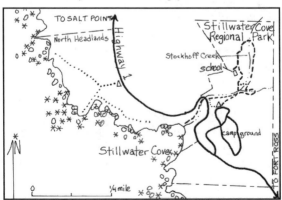

STOCKHOFF CREEK:

DISTANCE: ⅞-mile loop, 1⅛ miles including trip to cove.
TIME: One hour.
TERRAIN: Up a wooded creek canyon to an old one-room schoolhouse.
ELEVATION GAIN/LOSS: 140 feet+/140 feet–.
BEST TIME: Spring for wildflowers.
WARNINGS: Watch for poison oak and stinging nettles.
HOW TO GET THERE: Turn east off Highway 1 at M.37.02 and follow signs to day-use parking.
FEES: Day use: $5/vehicle. Car camping: $18/night (hot showers for campers!).
FURTHER INFO: Stillwater Cove County Park (707) 847-3245.

east. Two water-loving plants, both with small white flowers, grow here. Bedstraw is a spreading or climbing vine, while redwood inside-out flower grows close to the ground. Climb 150 feet to drier habitat where the uncommon rattlesnake plantain is found. This member of the orchid family has green leaves with a white center stripe, spikes of tiny white flowers in summer.

Your trail climbs through the forest, then comes to a junction at ⅝ mile. Turn right and climb into North Meadow where you approach a white schoolhouse with red trim in a clearing surrounded by redwoods. The Fort Ross District School has led a charmed, well traveled life. Established at Fort Ross in 1885, it was moved board by board to Seaview Ridge in 1924. The school was moved again in 1938, then to its present site in 1974. Peering in the windows, one might guess the students had just left for vacation.

Your return loop heads back into the forest from the front of the school. Return to the junction and bear right, descending an old road through an enchanting forest. You soon return to creekside, crossing the stream on a sturdy bridge. Along the creek grow fat Solomon's seal, western coltsfoot, thimbleberry, hedge nettle, elk clover, stream violet, and other riparian plants mentioned earlier.

Just 20 feet from the bridge, you return to the first junction of this hike. You can choose to take the left fork for a quick return to the starting point at ⅞ mile. Or take the right fork down the creek to Stillwater Cove beyond one mile. From there you must return via the trail since the grand old stairway is closed, and seemingly beyond repair. At the junction, turn right and climb the trail to your car around 1⅜ miles.

OTHER SUGGESTIONS: The stairway to STILLWATER COVE is closed, but you can get there via COVE TRAIL. At M.37.28 a WHEELCHAIR-ACCESSIBLE PATH descends to the beach at the cove. At M.37.57 a trail explores the park's NORTH HEADLANDS.

FORT ROSS
STATE HISTORIC PARK
INCLUDES THE NEXT FOUR TRAILS

Although the Fort Ross park brochure shows no trails, more than 15 miles of paths and fire roads explore the park's diverse terrain. You just need to know where they are, and, it should not need saying, use them at your own risk.

Fort Ross State Park comprises 3157 acres of steep, wild country in one of the most rugged areas of the California coast. The next four trails explore different facets of this isolated land: gentle headlands atop surf-pounded cliffs, rolling forests and grasslands cut by deep stream canyons, protected coves and beaches, and the remote tidal beaches and rocks of Sonoma's Lost Coast, hidden at the base of towering cliffs. Three of the trails explore the San Andreas Fault, which has had a big role in shaping these awesome slopes.

In your rush to explore these natural wonders, do not forget to explore Fort Ross (open 10–4:30 daily) itself, the imperial nineteenth-century outpost of czarist Russia. It provides the only physical link with one of California's strangest and most amazing historical epics.

In March 1812, 25 Russians and 80 native Alaskans led by the peg-legged adventurer Ivan Kuskov landed here with the intention of establishing a permanent colony for the czar and his Russian American Fur Company. They paid the Kashaya Pomo blankets, pants, tools and horses to use the Pomo village of May-tee-nee. The Russians quickly built a sturdy fort of redwood and several houses, naming it Rossiya to honor their homeland.

The Russians and Alaskans were no strangers to the California coast even then. In fact the presence of Russian

fur hunters on the coast had provoked the Spanish to settle San Francisco 40 years before Fort Ross began. A Russian trading party had visited the Presidio of San Francisco in 1806. In 1808 Kuskov had led a hunting expedition that camped at Bodega for eight months, sneaking their baidarkas (fur-covered kayaks) into San Francisco Bay to hunt otters under the noses of the Spaniards. That expedition returned to Russia with over 2000 pelts. At around $100 a pelt, the Russians could not afford to stay home.

Aside from the valuable furs, the Russians hoped to establish trade with Spanish California and produce enough food to supply their struggling colonies in Alaska. If they were able to gain any territory through the escapade, so much the better. By the time the Spaniards learned of the fort, it was already built and well armed. Kuskov had chosen the high bluffs for Fort Ross because he knew they could be defended from attack.

The Russians hurried to solidify their anchor on the coast, establishing farms at Bodega, Freestone and Willow Creek and paying the Pomos to build, hunt and farm for the colony. The native Alaskan Aleut hunters traveled hard in their quest for otter pelts, ranging as far as Baja California. One report states that they gathered 200,000 pelts in their years of residence in California. Fort Ross soon had nine buildings inside the stockade and 40 or 50 outside, defended by 41 cannons.

The outpost reached a maximum population of 300 or 400. It served as a meeting place for European explorers, scientists and scholars visiting the West Coast. They explored most of present-day Sonoma County, becoming the first to accurately map the area and investigate its biology and ethnology. The most famous visitor may have been David Douglas, the Scottish botanist who lent his name to fir trees, irises and other plants of the area.

The systematic hunting of the Alaskans quickly depleted

the sea otter population. Meanwhile, poor soil, gophers, insects and fog combined to cause crop failures, and grizzlies marauded the large herds of horses and cattle. Within 20 years of its founding, the colony was losing money and in serious decline. In 1839 it was put up for sale.

As the last commandant, Alexander Rotchev brought a brief renaissance. A renowned writer and scholar, he was married to Princess Elena Gagarina, who had given up high society for love. They both agreed that their years at Ross were the happiest of their lives. When French diplomat de Mofras visited in 1841, he was charmed by the Rotchev's choice library, French wines and the piano on which Elena played Mozart. Even the Mexicans dared to visit in these last years. A group of 30 rode all day from Sonoma, then danced all night.

The Mexicans declined to buy the colony and in December 1841 John Sutter offered 30,000 pesos for it. Sutter did not want the land, only the supplies, equipment and livestock for his Sacramento Valley ranch. Within a few months the Russians were gone.

The Kashaya took over the fort, reclaiming their land for three decades. In 1873 the Call family acquired the fort and 15,000 acres. They ranched and logged the area into the twentieth century; some still live nearby today.

The state of California bought the fort and three acres in 1906 and began to preserve and restore it. The 1906 earthquake collapsed the chapel, which has now been rebuilt three times. The commandant's house to the right of the fort's main entrance is the only building that survives in original form, making it one of the oldest wooden buildings west of the Mississippi River. But the other buildings have been meticulously restored, providing a marvelous feeling of the Russian settlement that nearly changed the history of California.

14.
FORT ROSS NORTH HEADLANDS
TO NORTHWEST CAPE AND BEYOND

The trail to Northwest Cape leaves from the southwest corner of the main parking area. Head southwest on a gravel road. After the road bends left, you meet a grassy path on your right, near a handicap parking spot. Follow the path southwest to pass through a narrow stile through a fence at ⅛ mile.

Descend a long-used path toward the tip of Northwest

DISTANCE: 2¾-mile loop or 3¼ miles round trip, or
   short 1¼-mile loop.
TIME: One or two hours.
TERRAIN: Gentle headlands descending to Northwest
   Cape, then northwest on headlands to overlook of
   Kolmer Gulch Cove and Beach.
ELEVATION GAIN/LOSS: 120 feet+/120 feet−.
BEST TIME: Spring, early summer for wildflowers.
WARNINGS: Stay back from steep, crumbly bluffs.
   Watch for poison oak.
HOW TO GET THERE: Turn west off Highway 1 at
   M.33.00 into main parking area for Fort Ross State
   Historic Park.
FEES: Day use: $6/vehicle.
FURTHER INFO: Fort Ross State Historic Park
   (707) 847-3286.

Cape, passing between rock outcrops where iris grow, then
crossing an animal path. As you leave most of the rocks behind, your trail becomes vague and forks. Take the left fork,
descending south to approach the steep bluff edge where yellow bush lupine, sticky monkeyflower and coast buckwheat
grow. Follow a vague trail southwest along the bluff, coming
to Northwest Cape at ⅜ mile. The invasive bush lupine has
grown so thick recently that the path is hidden in spots.

On your left the very tip of the point juts south. Be careful
and stay back from the edge of the cliff. You have a grand
view east to the fort and southeast to Fort Ross Cove, with
Sonoma's Lost Coast to its right. On a clear day you can see
Point Reyes nearly 40 miles down the coast.

Head northwest, following the bluff's edge. The eroding shelf
on your left has exposed layers of topsoil, sand and sandstone.
You may see killdeer darting over the grass. Again the lupine
obscures the path. Head generally northwest and north. The
grasslands offer goldfields and tidy-tips in spring.

Beyond ⅝ mile you reach the western tip of the cape, where
angelica and iris grow. Follow the shore northeast, passing

rocks covered with bright orange lichen on their north sides. Sword ferns cling to the base of the rocks. Pass a steep, dangerous path to a beach; a better one lies ahead.

Beyond ¾ mile you pass a gully where the rough side trail on the left descends to the rocky shore and tidepools. Continue north along the bluff's edge, climbing gradually to pass to the left of a low rocky hill. You can turn east here, heading toward the tall trees that shelter the fort for a short hike of 1¼ miles.

The described route goes left to cross a seasonal creek at ⅞ mile. Head northwest through grasslands. The headlands are more lush here, providing shelter for great blue herons, northern harriers, black-shouldered kites and other birds. Pass another small gully as your trail parallels the edge of the bluff.

By one mile you return to bluff's edge, where a rough path descends to the rocky tidal zone. Continue along the bluff to cross a small creek where it tumbles off the edge. The stream shelters windblown Bishop pine and wax myrtle, mimulus, coast buckwheat, lupine, beach morning glory and iris. Calla lilies grow nearby. Pick up an animal trail to continue northwest over open grasslands, nearing the bluff's edge again at 1⅛ miles.

Beyond 1¼ miles you cross a creek at its mouth, where yarrow grows beneath wind-sheared pines and wax myrtle. Remnants of a dilapidated wooden bridge are strewn about. It served as a crossing for the logging railway that ran along these bluffs during the heyday of the Call Ranch.

Continue northwest along the headlands, where many Douglas iris bloom in spring. An alternate track forks left to meander along the bluff's edge to a point, but the described trail goes straight. Around 1⅜ miles the paths merge and cross a seasonal creek. Continue northwest along the heavily grazed headlands. Around 1½ miles you veer right to circumvent a pocket cove where the surf crashes 80 feet below. Pelagic cormorants nest on the cliffs below you and Brandt's cormorants are often seen here. Double-crested cormorants nest to the south on offshore rocks near the mouth of the Russian River.

Continue northwest across the grassy bluffs. Soon the blufftop narrows and steepens. Highway 1 draws nearer your path. You pass coyote mint, purple seaside daisy, poppy and aster as you return to the bluff's edge.

You meet a faint trail around 1⅝ miles. It climbs for 250 feet to meet Highway 1 at M.34.08. You can walk northwest only 100 feet, coming to an overlook of Kolmer Gulch Beach and its cove 80 feet below. The beach is a mixture of light sand from west of the San Andreas Fault (where you are) and dark, gravelly sand that has washed down the creek from east of the fault, about a mile upstream. (To explore the fault east of here, see Trail #15.) Do not descend to the beach from the overlook. You can walk to the beach on a rough ¼-mile trail from the other side of the gulch. It leaves Highway 1 at M.34.53, descending southwest.

Retrace your steps southeast across the headlands toward Fort Ross. After the creek with the old railroad bridge, you can shorten the return trip by veering left and heading southeast toward a rock outcrop. After you cross another creek, turn east, then southeast to meet an abandoned stretch of Highway 1. Then walk the old highway southeast back to the trailhead.

15.

KOLMER GULCH

FOLLOWING THE SAN ANDREAS RIFT ZONE

In 1990 Fort Ross State Park tripled in size, adding a magnificent area of steep, open hillsides and wooded canyons extending east to 1600-foot elevation Seaview/Meyers Ridge, where tremendous vistas encompass the precipitous coastline and the fort. The Save-the-Redwoods League purchased 2157 wild acres surrounding the old park on three sides, then sold the land to the state for half the price.

The expanded park includes some shaky ground. About two miles of the San Andreas Rift Zone bisect the new acreage from northwest to southeast. Several old logging roads provide access to the fascinating rift zone. On this hike, you will see fault trenches and sag ponds amidst rolling country torn by the fault. Try not to visit on the day of the big one!

Your trail, beginning at the Stanley Spyra Memorial Grove, is an old logging road behind a locked gate, where the rift zone crosses Fort Ross Road. In 1906 the road and fence here were offset 7½ feet by the big quake. To the left of the trailhead stands an immense bay laurel, its many-branched trunk nearly 40 feet in circumference. Descend gradually northwest past a pioneer rose bush and a huge, fallen Douglas fir snag.

In 250 feet a depression on your left shelters redwoods to ten feet in diameter. Many old redwoods here were snapped off during the 1906 temblor. This gully is a fault trench, a surface manifestation of the tear in the earth's crust that lies below. The rift zone crosses the road ahead. Then a fault trench follows the road on the right, where several sag ponds lay hidden in young redwood forest. Sag ponds are

KOLMER GULCH:

DISTANCE: 1¾ miles round trip to Kolmer Gulch Camp, 5¼ miles round trip for full hike.

TIME: One to three hours.

TERRAIN: Through forests and meadows along San Andreas Rift Zone, passing slough trenches and sag ponds, then descending into heavily wooded Kolmer Gulch.

ELEVATION GAIN/LOSS: 340 feet+/340 feet– to camp, 780 feet+/780 feet– for full hike.

BEST TIME: Spring for wildflowers and sag ponds, summer to see old orchard in its glory.

WARNINGS: Watch for poison oak.

HOW TO GET THERE: Turn east off Highway 1 at M.33.00 onto Fort Ross Road, opposite main entrance to Fort Ross. After .5 mile, the fort's old fenced orchard is on the right. Your trailhead is a fire road, just beyond on left. Do not block the gate.

FURTHER INFO: Fort Ross State Historic Park (707) 847-3286.

seasonal or year-round pools where water does not drain from the fault trench.

As you leave the forest for open meadows, notice the gently rolling terrain around you. This gradual country, so unlike the steep, convoluted hills that dominate this stretch of coast, contains several parallel fault trenches with many sag ponds.

At ⅛ mile your road forks. Take the right fork, signed Upper Kolmer Gulch. You immediately cross a tributary of Kolmer Gulch where it flows northwest following the rift zone. Your road bends left, climbing along the fault.

At ¼ mile the path levels. On your left you overlook a deeply eroded gulch along the rift zone. As you descend gradually northwest, Steer Field Road forks right to climb steeply.

You cross a tiny stream where giant horsetail ferns grow, then resume the climb northwest, passing redwoods, huckleberries and woodwardia ferns. Soon your trail levels again, as Tan Oak Trail forks right to climb steeply north. Between the forks Oregon grape and Douglas iris grow beneath redwoods.

Take the left fork, descending gradually. At ½ mile coast silktassel grows on the right. Continue a gradual descent, passing many stumps beside much healthy regeneration. On your left the terrain still drops steeply into the gulch. Bush lupine and coyote brush grow on the right.

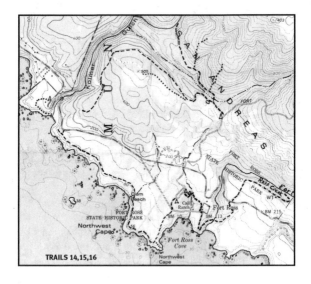

TRAILS 14,15,16

At ⅝ mile another fault trench lies on the left. You descend along the lip of the trench to overlook a year-round sag pond. Red and green duckweed covers the surface of the pond. You come to a large logging landing. The main road bends right to descend northeast, then north. At ¾ mile the road bends right to descend steeply toward the sound of rushing water.

Before ⅞ mile you come to Kolmer Gulch Camp, along the creek in an area much disturbed by logging. The camp has picnic tables, barbecue pits and water piped from a spring, a great picnic spot (no camping allowed). From here you can explore up or down the creek. Descending along the creek, it is less than ⅛ mile to the junction of creek and fault line where the terrain gets rough. Downstream the creek turns northwest to follow the fault line for about ¼ mile before resuming its southwest-flowing course.

Retrace your steps up the road, returning to the first fork at 1⅝ miles. You can return from here to reach the trailhead at 1¾ miles. Our described hike goes right to explore more of this fractured country. Follow the west fork climbing northwest, soon passing a large sag pond on the left. The ocean forms the horizon to the southwest. Your road levels, with the deep gulch now on your right.

Your route bends sharply left at 1¾ miles, starting a long, backward-S curve that descends gradually through heavily grazed meadows. As your route turns northwest to approach a forest of young Douglas fir, a spur on the left heads west, offering a side trip to a grand view. It passes through a fence in 300 feet, climbing gently through grasslands to wonderful views of Bodega Head, Tomales Bay and Point Reyes Penin-

70

sula. Continuing on the main fork, follow the rim of the gulch northwest through the forest. You pass through a mixed forest of Bishop pine, redwood, Douglas fir, bay laurel and wax myrtle. Spearmint grows in moist spots along the road.

Crest a small rise at 2 miles, level briefly, then climb gradually to 2⅛ miles, where you level before ascending again. The deepening canyon that drops away on the right marks the rift zone. Beyond it the terrain rises steeply to the headwaters of Kolmer Gulch.

You crest another rise at 2¼ miles, where you can look northeast to the steep glades at the precipitous head of the gulch. Tiny evergreen violets grow on the road shoulder along with abundant iris and yerba de selva. The road winds northwest, beginning a gradual descent at 2⅜ miles.

At 2½ miles you reach a landing to the right of the road, now grown in with young firs and pines. The road turns west, then southwest, paralleling deep and wooded Kolmer Gulch on your right. I spotted a wild sow in early spring, trailing her litter of multicolored piglets on this little traveled path. (Stay away from wild pigs; they can be vicious!)

Around 2⅝ miles your descent gradually increases. You may hear the rumble of traffic rising from Highway 1 about ¾ mile away. As you turn south, the vegetation turns lush with redwood sorrel, salmonberry, foxglove and Siberian miners lettuce in the understory. Make a winding descent to 2¾ miles, where an osprey nest perches atop a broken-top redwood down toward the gulch. Many tree stumps line the road, but the forest along the bottom of the gulch is undisturbed.

Descend southwest, then south. Climb briefly around 3 miles, where three trees lay across the track in spring 2005. Resume a gradual descent where the dark green foliage of grand firs begins to mix with the redwoods, pines and Douglas firs. The road drops steeply on the right, descending west.

By 3⅛ miles, where the road becomes vague, turning to a narrow path, you can see the ocean through the trees. The vague narrow track turns south through forest, heading away from Kolmer Gulch.

Before 3¼ miles the old logging road becomes clear again, although covered with grass. Iris grow in large patches. Follow it southwest then west, descending with expanding coastal vistas. You leave the forest, passing the last of the trees at 3⅜ miles, where you can see Highway 1 about 200 feet below. Beyond it is the rugged coast north of Fort Ross (see Trail #14). (You could easily descend to the highway from here and walk the headlands southeast to the fort, but you had better have arranged a car shuttle beforehand.) The barking of sea lions may rise on the wind.

Retrace your steps up the road, returning via the same route you descended, reaching the junction nearest the trailhead around 5⅛ miles. Stay right and ascend to the trailhead at 5¼ miles.

OTHER SUGGESTION: THE OLD FORT ROSS ORCHARD is across the road from the trailhead. It contains some of the oldest cultivated trees in the west, including original Gravenstein apple stock. A short trail explores the orchard, which straddles the fault line.

16.

FORT ROSS CREEK
CLIMB TO SAN ANDREAS FAULT

The rugged, wooded canyon of Fort Ross Creek cuts deeply through steep, rolling grasslands east of the fort. About ½ mile upstream from its mouth, the creek meets the San Andreas Fault. Over many millennia, lateral ground movement along the fault has caused the creek to turn northwest following the fault for ½ mile, running perpendicular to its general northeast to southwest course. This wondrous manifestation of plate tectonics is most easily seen on a map. This intriguing hike explores the creek along the fault line, beautiful country with grand views of the fort and its surroundings.

From the parking area, take the trail to the right of the visitor center. You head south into cypress forest, then turn southeast, passing a spur on the right to the picnic area. Then your trail

FORT ROSS CREEK:

DISTANCE: 3¼ miles round trip.

TIME: Two hours.

TERRAIN: Easy descent to Fort Ross Cove and mouth of creek, then climb to old Russian cemetery. Cross Highway 1 and climb dirt road to ridge overlooking wooded creek canyon. Optional descent to creek along San Andreas Fault.

ELEVATION GAIN/LOSS: 440 feet+/440 feet– round trip to ridge, 520 feet+/520 feet– round trip to creek.

BEST TIME: Spring, early summer for wildflowers.

WARNINGS: Watch for poison oak. Steep uneven terrain beyond end of road descending to creek.

HOW TO GET THERE: Turn west off Highway 1 at M.33.00.

FEES: Day use: $6/vehicle. Car camping: $15/night.

FURTHER INFO: Fort Ross State Historic Park (707) 847-3286.

swings left, following a split redwood fence to the visitor center's back door, where a deck offers a fine view of Fort Ross through the trees. Descend to cross a seasonal creek on a sturdy bridge, then veer right to follow the creek downstream.

Beyond ⅛ mile your paved path veers left toward the fort. On clear days you can see Bodega Head and Inverness Ridge on Point Reyes beyond the fort. On your right are buildings of the Call Ranch, established in 1873. Soon your path bends right to follow the rough-hewn redwood walls of the fort, coming to the entrance at ¼ mile. If the fort is open, you can explore the exceptional historic buildings of the compound (be sure you do before leaving the area). The trail to Fort Ross Cove and Creek continues south to a paved road in 250 feet.

Go left on the road briefly, coming to the fort's south door. You turn right on the gravel road that descends south for ⅛ mile to the bluff's edge, then makes a big bend left to descend northeast to Fort Ross Cove.

The cove was the site of California's first shipyard. The

Russians constructed at least four seagoing (but not very seaworthy) ships here during the heyday of the fort between 1818 and 1824. Although the Russians had considerable shipbuilding skills, they knew virtually nothing about working native California woods. Only the last of the ships demonstrated much seaworthiness. Archaeologists have excavated the shipbuilding site recently to learn more about the Russians' stay here. The fort's bathhouse, cooperage, tannery and blacksmith shop were also at the cove.

Beyond ½ mile from the trailhead, you come to picnic tables and a trash can along Fort Ross Creek at the head of the cove. From here a trail, signed "Cemetery", heads east, crossing the creek, then climbing along a gulch. The dense vegetation includes willows, hazel, coyote brush, elderberry, elk clover, sticky monkeyflower, coffeeberry, thimbleberry, flowering currant, coastal manroot and poison oak. In spring you may also see paintbrush, blue dicks, bee plant, mugwort and columbine.

Beyond ¾ mile your trail switchbacks left and climbs through grasslands where hairy honeysuckle, baby blue eyes, soap plant, blue-eyed grass, and narrow-leaved mule ears grow. At ⅞ mile you come to the old Russian cemetery. On this grassy knoll lie the Russian adventurers who were not lucky enough to return to their fatherland. The original wooden Russian Orthodox crosses, long ago returned to the soil, have now been replaced with replicas.

Go northeast, then east through a break in the fence to cautiously cross busy Highway 1. Then climb northeast on the dirt fire road, signed "Authorized Vehicles Only," behind another gate. As you climb look southwest for a view of the fort. Notice the deep, wooded canyon of Fort Ross Creek as it climbs north on your left, then bends sharply right to cut through the headlands in front of you.

At 1⅛ miles your road bends right and climbs east, following the rim of the forested canyon of Fort Ross Creek on your left. You can hear the murmur of the creek rising through the forest. Your road bends southeast and climbs steeply past irises, blue-eyed grass and hairy cat's ears, then levels atop a 320-foot hill, where you have a bird's eye view of the fort and the rugged coast. Start a gradual descent, passing a pump house and three water tanks. At 1⅜ miles you enter forest with abundant hazel in the understory. The road soon bends left and comes to a semicircle of old tourist cabins, now housing for archaeologists doing research in the park.

At 1½ miles the road ends. Go north between the last two cabins to find a hole in the fence; you are overlooking Fort Ross Creek where it intersects with the San Andreas Fault.

There is no real trail beyond this point, so you might want to retrace your steps from here. But if you are game to explore, it is not far down to the cool, gurgling creek. Just upstream a sturdy fence marks the park boundary. When the 1906 earthquake occurred, the fence that was here at the time was torn and offset 12 feet. It is this same displacement, occurring in smaller and perhaps larger increments over eons, that has caused the half mile jog in the direction of the creek.

Pick your way downstream, following the flat-bottomed, steep-walled canyon. Large redwoods grow with bay laurels along the flat; Douglas firs and tanoaks favor the slopes. Calypso orchids, trilliums, redwood sorrel, slink pod, twisted stalk and other plants of the deep forest grow in the understory. You can go about ⅛ mile downstream before a couple of massive log jams make further passage difficult. Find your way back to the fire road and retrace your steps to the trailhead.

17.

SONOMA'S LOST COAST
WALKING THE SAN ANDREAS FAULT AT ABALONE HOTEL

The primarily gentle terrain of the rest of the Sonoma Coast does not prepare one for the rugged and wild grandeur of the Lost Coast between Fort Ross and Russian Gulch. The area is relatively small, only six miles of coast, but inch for inch it matches the craggy beauty of Big Sur or the King Range, the more famous Lost Coast. If you are fit and check your tide tables scrupulously, you can walk the secluded beach at the base of dizzying cliffs, a place that belongs to the wild Pacific Ocean more than to Sonoma County. You will see magnificent tidepools, walk through the San Andreas Fault and visit a land that is usually seen only from sea. For this hike I recommend sturdy boots for the uneven, sometimes loose footing, and hiking with a friend. You must not attempt the hike in winter, when a high tide is rising, or during storms.

From the end of the dirt road, head southeast to dip through a gully that shelters willows, phacelia, horsetail ferns, mimulus and sun cups. Pass through the fence and follow it southwest onto a narrow promontory. You then carefully descend a steep, winding path southeast over loose soil to the shoreline before ¼ mile. (If this descent feels unsafe, the Lost Coast is NOT for you.)

Head southeast along a beach of large rocks. Fort Ross Reef lies offshore just below the water's surface. It teems with

SONOMA'S LOST COAST:

DISTANCE: 5⅜ miles one way to Russian Gulch, 9¾
    miles round trip to cove before climb out.

TIME: All day to do full hike.

TERRAIN: Rugged beach walking punctuated by
    scrambles over rock outcrops.

ELEVATION GAIN/LOSS: 370 feet+/370 feet–, one
    way; 340 feet+/340 feet–, round trip.

BEST TIME: Moderate to low tide.

WARNINGS: Watch for killer waves along beach. Stay
    off this beach during storms and in winter. You need
    a tide lower than 3.0 feet during your hike. Inquire
    about conditions before you go. Use extreme caution
    on slippery tidal rocks. Hike with a friend and wear
    sturdy boots.

HOW TO GET THERE: Turn west off Highway 1 at
    M.31.36 to entrance for Fort Ross Reef Campground.
    Go left immediately, pass through a gate, leaving the
    gate as you found it. Then drive .3 mile to end of road
    and the trailhead.

FEES: Day use: $6/vehicle. Car camping: $15/night.

FURTHER INFO: Fort Ross State Historic Park
    (707) 847-3286.

sea life, including abundant abalone that gives this area the nickname "Abalone Hotel."

At ⅜ mile offshore rocks provide nesting grounds for cormorants and other sea birds. Continue down the coast on a beach of pebbles and small rocks interspersed with clusters of large rocks. In some places, massive piles of driftwood lie along the beach. You round a shelf of sandstone at ⅝ mile, then reach the mouth of Mill Gulch.

Just before ¾ mile you pass old cast iron wheels still mounted on their axle at the base of the cliff, then meet the narrowest point on the beach so far on the hike. At +5 feet tide, you must climb the rocks above the surf to proceed. **Do not pass this point in winter or during storm seas, or if the tide is rising**. If tide and seas are low enough you can continue south.

You soon have a view of rugged cliffs rising on your left, with Highway 1 rounding a big curve 400 feet above. Harbor seals frequent the offshore rocks. You round another point where you need to watch for waves at high tide. Then the beach turns east to meet the San Andreas Fault.

At one mile you come to the base of a slide with a base of gray clay. As you look at the slide and the cliffs above, you are looking into the San Andreas Fault. The rocks here are fractured down to their molecular structure. The gray clay is actually mylonite, pulverized rock with a structure like ground glass. The fault is about ¼ mile wide here. In other places it gets as wide as one mile. This slide slid massively in winter 1995, closing Highway 1 for nearly two years and drastically altering the landscape as seen from the beach. In 2005 the gray clay was barely visible beneath darker soil.

Much seaweed and driftwood lie along the beach, now composed of small stones that provide easier walking. At 1⅛ miles the beach narrows at the base of another slide. The small creek of Timber Gulch empties onto dark sand at 1¼ miles. The dark sand indicates that you are now on the North American Plate rather than the Pacific Plate, where you began the hike.

Enjoy walking the fine, dark sand, the Riviera of the Lost Coast. You pass more seeps at the base of slides. Pass a narrow spot beyond 1½ miles that is safe to pass at a tide lower than +4.5 feet. By 1⅝ miles the lower beach is composed of small rocks, but the upper beach is fine, dark sand. This leads into a beach of all sand, more relief for your rock-weary soles.

At 1¾ miles you pass another small creek, where the cliffs on your left rise abruptly. You are now east of the fault line. The rocks here are not fractured. The cliffs stand tall without continuous crumbling, rising 1600 feet in less than a mile. Another small seep at 2 miles, where a waterfall drops to the beach, is jammed with lupine, monkeyflowers and other moisture-loving plants. Continue along the broad, sandy beach, passing more seeps on the cliff-face above the beach.

Before 2⅛ miles the broad beach ends at a rock outcrop. Walk southeast over uneven large rocks, where a large seep has formed algae-covered mineral terraces. The narrow beach becomes broader at 2¼ miles. Continue past a creek with a large rock pile at its mouth to briefly walk a patch of fine dark sand. As you pass a pyramid-shaped rock in the surf zone at 2⅜ miles, the sand gives way to large boulders. Another offshore rock is a popular perch for pelicans and cormorants. Between the two rocks, an emergency exit trail climbs steeply to Highway 1.

Continue along the beach of mixed rock and sand. You

might pass the remains of cars along the base of the steep cliff. After another small creek, the beach provides moderately easy walking for ⅜ mile. Around 2⅞ miles, sea fig and seaside daisy grow on the cliff above the rocky beach.

At 3 miles the beach becomes broader, with dark, fine sand and small pebbles. Pass several more seeps on the cliff-face. Beyond 3⅛ miles a steep gulch cuts through the cliff. Sheep graze on the steep bluffs above.

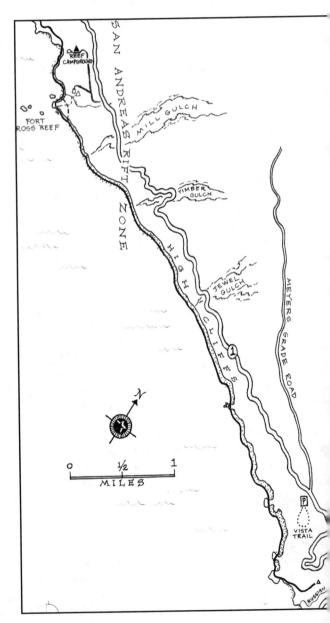

The beach broadens to its widest and sandiest so far on the hike, offering easy walking at the base of steep cliffs. At 3¼ miles you approach a rocky point over which you must scramble. It is far easier than it looks as you approach. Pick your way over the rocks for good views up and down the Lost Coast. Then hop down the south side and continue over large rocks on the beach. The easiest path is at the base of the cliff.

Around 3½ miles walking on fine sand provides a respite. Pampas grass grows on the steep bluffs. Harbor seals often fish offshore here. You pass rich tidepools where many sea vegetables grow. Anemones, sea stars, bat stars, turban snails and hermit crabs also abound. You pass a small cove, then meet a narrow passage at 3¾ miles where the best route climbs over a rock shelf.

Then you walk a gravelly beach. Before 3⅞ miles a 50-foot-tall sea stack stands at tideline, with more sea stacks ahead. Pick your way over uneven terrain. You soon pass the base of a taller sea stack, a pointed landmark that can be seen for miles up and down the coast. It stands above the tideline. Scramble between massive rocks. Sea rocket grows in the shelter at their base. You pass more rocky tidepools where mussels, gooseneck barnacles and sea palms thrive.

At 4 miles you walk a rocky beach with gradual bluffs on the left. Soon the beach turns to gravel as you approach a huge, domed rock outcrop that juts seaward. You reach the base of the huge rock at 4¼ miles.

If you are hiking back the same way you came in, this is a good place to turn back. Russian Gulch lies 1⅛ miles southeast over rugged terrain. The immense rock presents cliffs to the ocean, precluding any chance of walking around the west face.

To continue, you must scramble up the steep chute between the outcrop and the steep, grassy headland to which it is attached. Use extreme caution as you climb the loose, crumbly rock along the chute. In just 200 feet, you top the notch, about 75 feet above sea level. Be careful as your path plunges steeply down to a small, rocky beach on the other side of the big rock. In 250 feet the beach ends. You must scramble over a jumble of rocks for 250 feet.

At 4⅜ miles you return to beach sand briefly, then hop a few more boulders to a large sandy beach. The dark sand provides easy walking to 4⅝ miles, where you pass a seep along the cliff. The beach narrows at a point where you might have to scramble over rocks at high tide.

Beyond the narrow spot, you return to sandy beach, passing a big sea stack at 4¾ miles. You approach one last cove, nestled between two giant rock outcrops and the bluffs. The beautiful emerald pool looks as if it might be a haven for mermaids. In fact it provides fine tidepooling at a minus tide.

At 4⅞ miles you can go no farther along the beach. To return to the trailhead, retrace your steps from here for a 9¾-mile round trip.

If you are hiking through to Russian Gulch, you have nowhere to go but up. A narrow, steep and rocky path climbs southeast to the low point on the ridge to the left of the rock outcrop. Use caution on the steep climb. At the top you have a magnificent view of the coast southeast. Russian Gulch, your destination, is the larger of the two sandy coves. Bodega Head juts seaward 12 miles away.

A well trod trail heads east over rolling grasslands for ⅛ mile. Then the trail turns southeast, following the bluff's edge for 400 feet. At 5⅛ miles your trail turns left and descends northeast toward the parking lot at Russian Gulch, passing through grasslands and coastal scrub. Watch carefully for poison oak in the scrub. You climb over a fence and come to the parking area at 5⅜ miles. Welcome back to civilization!

OTHER SUGGESTION: You can also start this hike from FORT ROSS, adding 1½ miles in each direction, but this is considerably more difficult to do in a day. Most difficult route is to start from RUSSIAN GULCH at the south end (see Trail #18).

SONOMA COAST STATE BEACH
INCLUDES THE NEXT EIGHT TRAILS

Actually a string of many beaches separated by rocky bluffs, plus extensive ridges and canyons inland, this state park unit offers 9300 beautiful acres along a diverse, mostly gentle 18 miles of coastline from the Vista Trail in the north to Bodega Head in the south. The beaches become crowded during summer and holiday weekends, but you can always find some solitude if you look in the most remote corners. A marvelous array of wildflowers brighten the creeks and headlands in spring and early summer.

In winter you will often have this expansive coast nearly to yourself. Ferocious surf and wild seas indicate the rugged, untamed nature of these gentle lands. You must always use caution along North Coast beaches and headlands, watching for oversized waves and keeping in mind your route of escape. But especially in winter keep the wild ocean at safe distance. In 35 years, these beaches had 73 known drownings and 80 reported rescues. Winter also brings the greatest abundance of bird species. More than 200 species have been counted in the Audubon Society's Christmas count, of a total of more than 300 species found during the year.

In addition to the developed trails described in the next eight hikes, many beaches and headlands offer short, easy access where you can just sit or picnic, contemplating the majestic meeting of shore and sea. Some offer fishing, tidepooling and diving as well. Here are the mileposts of places otherwise not covered in the text.

M.15.94: Rock Point

M.15.22: Gleason Beach

M.14.68: Portuguese Beach

M.14.40: Schoolhouse Beach

M.14.20: Carmet Beach

M.14.05: Marshall Gulch

M.13.60: Arched Rock Beach

M.13.4: Coleman Beach

M.13.20: Miwok Beach

M.13.05: North Salmon Creek Beach

M.12.6: Park headquarters, in case of emergency.

M.12.41: South Salmon Creek Beach

18.

NORTH OF JENNER
SHORT TRAILS EXPLORE STEEP, WILD COAST

Between Jenner, at the mouth of the Russian River, and Fort Ross, 13 miles up the coast, Highway 1 tortuously twists and climbs over one of the most spectacular sections of its entire length, along the faces and folds of rugged cliffs that rise up 1300 feet from the sea. The San Andreas Fault dissects the shore here. The collision of the North American and Pacific tectonic Plates causes these towering cliffs. It is worthwhile to take your time on this tangle of highway, pulling out for the hurried local traffic, stopping to admire the sweeping views, taking a walk or two to admire the details of wildflowers and the cliffs plunging to the sea.

Several short, easy trails investigate these awesome headlands, each one exploring a different aspect of the varied, rugged terrain. The northernmost of these trails begins 600 feet above the Pacific, where Highway 1 reaches its dizzy summit at the junction with Meyers Grade. The 275 acres of the Black Ranch were acquired for public access through the efforts of COASTWALK and the Coastal Conservancy. The Vista Trail offers wheelchair access to this plunging, view-rich headland and views of the Lost Coast below (see Trail #17). The second trail is a level beach walk at Russian Gulch. The third hike surveys rolling headlands where a lumber loading chute once was and where peregrine falcons sometimes nest in summer. The fourth trail descends from the rolling, wildflower-rich headlands to the secluded north end of the beach where the Russian River meets the Pacific.

VISTA TRAIL (¾ mile paved, handicap-accessible loop, see previous map) heads southeast from the parking lot, offering grand views. Turn south past soap plant, with abundant

NORTH OF JENNER:

DISTANCE: ½ mile to 3½ miles round trip.

TIME: One half hour to two hours (each trail).

TERRAIN: Vista Trail: High bluffs overlooking steep headlands.

    Russian Gulch: Easy walk to beach.

    North Jenner Headlands: Descend rolling, grassy headlands to convoluted bluff's edge.

    Descent to Russian River mouth: Steep descent from bluff to beach.

ELEVATION GAIN/LOSS: Vista Trail: Minimal on paved loop. Russian Gulch: negligible. North Jenner Headlands: 160 feet+/160 feet– round trip. Descent to Russian River mouth: 180 feet+/180 feet– round trip.

BEST TIME: Spring, early summer for wildflowers.

WARNINGS: Stay back from steep, unstable cliffs. Watch for poison oak.

HOW TO GET THERE: All on west side of Highway 1 north of Jenner at the following mileposts:

    Vista Trail: M.26.3

    Russian Gulch: M.24.55

    North Jenner Headlands: M.23.83

    Descent to river mouth: M.23.21

FURTHER INFO: Sonoma Coast State Beach (707) 875-3483.

blue-eyed grass, buttercups and sun cups in spring. Stay left at a fork for views over the steep canyons of Russian Gulch Creek. Beyond ⅛ mile your path bends right, coming to a picnic table beside a rock outcrop. It offers grand views south to Bodega Head, with Point Reyes visible beyond it on the clearest days.

The paved track descends gradually as the coastal views expand to include immense offshore rocks near Russian Gulch, the sandy beach at the Russian River mouth, Goat Rock and Duncans Landing. Beyond ¼ mile your trail begins a gentle climb as it winds west to another picnic spot.

The path continues its ascent, winding north now. The

pavement forks at ⅜ mile. Take the spur on the left 250 feet for a glimpse of the Lost Coast below (see Trail #17), Fort Ross Reef offshore and Northwest Cape at Fort Ross beyond the steep headlands to the northwest.

The main trail makes a gentle ascent to ½ mile where it levels, then meanders west to another picnic table. This spot offers a fine view of the coast sprawling northwest to Fort Ross.

The path quickly brings you back to the first fork. Go left 450 feet to return to the parking lot.

RUSSIAN GULCH TRAIL (¾ mile round trip) parallels the creek from the parking lot, winding through willows and red alders to reach the surf in ⅜ mile. The ⅛-mile-wide beach is sheltered by 120-foot cliffs.

NORTH JENNER HEADLANDS TRAIL (1½ miles round trip) descends southwest across rolling grassy headlands where coyote brush, bush lupine and purple aster grow. You reach the bluff's edge before ⅛ mile, then turn left to follow it southeast. Douglas iris, yarrow, pennyroyal, paintbrush, seaside daisy and pearly everlasting grow in the grass, while coast buckwheat, California fuchsia, angelica and hen and chicks hug the cliffs above the ocean. Beyond ¼ mile your path bends right to follow the bluff's edge out to a point, where you have views up and down the rugged coast. The promontory ¼ mile west is sometimes home to peregrine falcons in summer.

Your trail climbs north, then turns east, climbing gradually to meet a steep spur on the right at ⅜ mile that descends steeply south to a cove. You continue along the bluff's edge, veering right on a spur as the well trod path forks left to return to the road. You follow the vague trail along the top of the cliff through low coastal scrub with paintbrush and

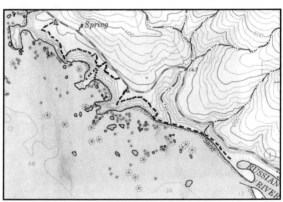

sticky monkeyflower. At ½ mile, climb east to wind around several eroded gullies, then descend south to bluff's edge. At ⅝ mile you reach a point overlooking a cove where harbor seals haul out on the rocks. Side trails descend steeply to the small beach.

The main trail winds east to Highway 1 to get around a big gully. You can return northwest to the trailhead from here or descend southwest to return to the bluff's edge at ¾ mile, then follow it southeast for another 250 feet before another big gully forces a return to the road at M.23.34. Retrace your steps, more or less, to the trailhead.

TRAIL TO NORTH SIDE OF RUSSIAN RIVER MOUTH (1¾ miles round trip): Descend southwest across the grassy headlands. The trail descends ⅛ mile to a point where you have a view of the river mouth and surrounding coast. A spur heads to the tip of the point, but follow the trail that turns east along the blufftop, nearly returning to the road at ¼ mile. Black sage, paintbrush, coast buckwheat and other plants grow on the bluff face. Walk a wood plank across a tiny creek, then head southeast toward the river mouth, passing bush lupine and poppies. At ⅜ mile your trail starts a gradual descent as the trail becomes vague. You soon veer right amidst shoulder-high lupine and begin a steep, winding descent south down the cliff face. You reach the beach by ½ mile, just 300 feet from its north end. Walk southeast along the beach. Walk ⅜ mile down the beach to the river mouth.

19.

POMO CANYON to SHELL BEACH
FROM REDWOOD FOREST TO COASTAL VIEWS

Willow Creek has carved a broad, deep canyon similar to that of the nearby Russian River. The creek's grasslands, rimmed by dense forest, are a favorite hunting ground for red-tailed hawks and black-shouldered kites. If the road is closed to Pomo Campground, you must walk the level ½ mile to the trailhead, adding one mile to total hike.

From the parking lot at the end of the road, a trail heads southwest toward the Environmental Camps and into the redwood forest. Just before the restrooms in 50 feet, turn right on the signed Dr. David Joseph Pomo Canyon Trail, passing beneath a bay laurel. The trail climbs gradually, heading north through redwood forest. You quickly pass two trails

branching left, but stay on the main trail, passing campsites
overlooking the meadow along Willow Creek.

Soon your trail veers left, starting a steady climb up a
ridge forested with young redwoods, tanoaks and gracefully
arched bay laurels. Shift into low gear for the steady climb
ahead. At ⅛ mile a trail sign confirms that you are on the
right path. Soon your climb eases briefly in a clearing where
huckleberries thrive. You quickly return to the forest, continuing to climb the ridge.

Your ascent slackens around ¼ mile. You soon leave the
broad skid road you have been following for a footpath
that veers right. Pass a Douglas fir eight feet in diameter.
Coffeeberry and California hazel grow nearby. This native
relative of the filbert has velvety oval leaves. Its nuts are a
favorite of squirrels.

Your trail narrows at ⅜ mile, passing ancient Douglas firs, bent
and forked by the powerful coastal winds they have endured over

Trails 19, 20, 21, 22

their several-hundred-year lives. A break in the forest offers views north to the grassy ridges near the Russian River. You leave the forest for a brushy clearing where gooseberry bushes tangle with hazels, thimbleberries and ferns.

Before ½ mile you are again under a forest canopy of arching bays and wind-topped firs. The trail ducks under a horizontal bay trunk and resumes a steady climb.

At ⅝ mile you leave the forest, breaking into grasslands. The new Red Hill Trail forks left (see Trail #21). Your trail turns left and climbs south along the grassy ridge. In spring and summer these meadows are filled with poppies, lupines, iris, blue-eyed grass, blue dicks and other wildflowers. Even in fall the pink to purple blooms of godetias and the yellow flowers of tarweed grace the trail. Look northwest for a vista of the mouth of the Russian River.

Your trail climbs west, then levels at the top of a small gully. Beyond ¾ mile you approach a saddle between two rock outcrops. Your path soon veers right and wraps around the rock outcrop on your right. You might detour for an easy scramble to its rocky top, where the fine view extends up the coast beyond the river mouth all the way to Northwest Cape at Fort Ross. You will find coast buckwheat, hen and chicks, poppy, sticky monkeyflower and leather ferns growing on the rock's north and west faces.

87

Returning to the trail, head west to duck under a bushy bay tree and begin a gradual descent. Around ⅞ mile, look northeast to see 4722-foot Cobb Mountain rising beyond the canyons of Willow Creek and the Russian River. Join an old road and descend through grasslands scattered with coyote brush. A spring on the left is a favorite animal watering spot.

Cream cups and baby blue eyes grow in grasslands as you pass a brush shrouded rock outcrop at one mile. Descend gradually, heading west with forest on your left and vintage Sonoma coast and hills everywhere else. Coffeeberry mingles with the coyote brush. Swing left and climb a short hill into redwood forest where trillium and twisted stalk grow, crossing a murmuring stream. Another short climb tops out at 1⅛ miles. Then you descend, redwood/fir forest on your left, dense scrub of coffeeberry, red-flowering currant and California blackberry on your right. Then descend through a thicket of thimbleberry with hazel and oceanspray.

You cross another brook at the edge of a beautiful redwood grove. A spur trail on your left climbs into the grove, where red clintonia grows in spring. The main trail descends north, then west around a big bend. Climb a small hill and pass under an old, single-wire phone line. At 1¼ miles the town of Jenner appears to the northwest. Cross two more creeks in the next ⅛ mile as you head west through soft chaparral interspersed with grasslands. Then descend along a fence line where poison oak grows.

At 1½ miles the view west opens up to the ocean and horizon as your descent turns moderate. Soon you can see Highway 1 winding far below. Continue along the hidden fence on a gradual descent nearly to 1¾ miles, gaining the best view yet of Jenner and the Russian River mouth. You finally turn left to pass over a ridge where the fence is no longer in place. Now you wind south, descending to cross a small creek at the top of its canyon, then joining another road to climb the ridge to your west. Just before you gain the ridgetop, you pass a side trail on the right that leads to a picnic table with a grand view.

Now you tend southwest on a series of short ups and downs through wildflower-studded meadows with views north to Jenner and the Russian River. From 2⅛ miles you ascend the last hill between you and Shell Beach. An old road on the left at 2¼ miles now leads to the new Red Hill property of state parks (see Trail #21). The main trail climbs quickly to the summit. From this ridge you overlook the entire southern Sonoma Coast. On a clear day you see Bodega Head to the south, with Point Reyes jutting seaward beyond it.

If you want a shorter, easier round trip hike than the full

excursion described here, this is your ideal turnaround point. By turning back now, you will save one mile and nearly 1000 feet in elevation gain and loss. (Or you may have a shuttle car waiting at the west end.) If you have most of the day left, you can make it to Shell Beach, rest, then trudge back over the ridge to Pomo Canyon.

Near the summit you pick up an old paved road and follow it on a steepening descent. As the road swings gradually left, you have views of large on- and offshore sea stacks below. At 2½ miles a large boulder stands on your left. You pass under a power line.

At 2⅝ miles you switchback left as your descent eases. You quickly come to a gate and the western trailhead at 2¾ miles. Just across Highway 1 (at M.18.2), the road to the Shell Beach parking area descends west. Use caution crossing the highway. It is ⅛ mile from the trailhead to the parking area, another ⅛ mile to the beach (The Coastal Trail heads north from the northwest corner of Shell Beach parking lot. It heads south from the southwest corner.)

If you plan to return to the Pomo Canyon Trailhead today, be sure to leave at least two hours of daylight and carry a flashlight.

20.

BLIND BEACH to SHELL BEACH
THE KORTUM TRAIL

About 100,000 years ago, all but the start of this hike was below sea level, being carved by waves into the gently sloping terrace you see today. This portion of the California coast has been uplifting since then, pushed upward from sea level by the collision of the offshore Pacific tectonic Plate and the onshore North American Plate. Despite the major earthquakes that this region is subject to, most of the uplifting has been extremely gradual. On the average this shore rises one inch every 100 years.

In recent history, since white settlers arrived in the 1800s, ranchers grazed their cattle and sheep here. Cattle continued to graze the headlands from Blind Beach to Shell Beach until about 1992. The headlands south of Shell Beach were closed to grazing in the 1980s.

The difference in policy between the two areas has produced striking results that will be evident if you hike all 4 miles of trail. The recently grazed land has fewer native species and abundant invasive species. The southern segment of

BLIND BEACH to SHELL BEACH:

DISTANCE: 3¾ miles round trip to Shell Beach; 8 miles round trip to Wrights Beach (including Trail #22).

TIME: Two hours round trip to Shell Beach, four hours round trip to Wrights Beach.

TERRAIN: Over the ridge of Peaked Hill, then down to gently sloping, grass-covered marine terrace overlooking the shore.

ELEVATION GAIN/LOSS: 380 feet+/300 feet– round trip to Shell Beach Trailhead; 140 feet+/220 feet– one way.

BEST TIME: Spring, early summer for wildflowers.

WARNINGS: Stay off Goat Rock: every year people fall or are swept into the sea from this spectacular but dangerous sea stack. Stay back from the very edge of the crumbly, unstable bluffs. Watch for poison oak, especially on the last part of the trail.

HOW TO GET THERE: Less than one mile south of the Russian River, turn west off Highway 1 at M.19.15 onto Goat Rock Road. Go .75 mile to the Blind Beach parking area.

FURTHER INFO: Sonoma Coast State Beach (707) 875-3483.

trail has recovered many of its native species. The northern 2 miles are recommended for the views and the marine terrace geology; the southern 2 miles merit attention more for the native plants.

The disruption of the environment here could have been much worse. In 1972 a subdivision was planned for these coastal terraces. Some streets were installed and a few houses built before coastal preservationists managed to halt construction. After that battle was won, former county Supervisor Bill Kortum and the group COAAST fought to acquire the land for a state park. They went on to build the trail you will hike today. In 1990 it was designated as the Kortum Trail.

If you have two cars in your party, you can park one at each end of the trail and not have to retrace your steps.

From the Blind Beach parking lot, follow the road south for 300 feet to find the trailhead. From there the trail angles south to pass through a fence. Head southeast across

grasslands with scattered Douglas iris, phacelia and coast buckwheat. Cylindrical posts mark the trail.

After ⅛ mile the trail climbs toward Peaked Hill. Remaining native vegetation includes coyote brush, cow parsnip, yarrow and buttercup. At ¼ mile you approach rock outcrops along the ridge. Hedge nettle and miners lettuce grow in protected pockets beside the rocks.

If the day is clear as you top the ridge, take a faint trail on the right that climbs quickly to the windswept 377-foot summit of Peaked Hill. At the rocky top an inspiring view of this rugged coast stretches to the horizon, with Bodega Head pointing seaward 10 miles south.

Beyond the ridge your trail turns east and descends. At ⅜ mile you parallel the road, then pass through another fence. Descend south along the fence with sweeping coastal views. Descend to a small rock outcrop at ½ mile. At the rocks your path crosses a small gully and bends left to descend southeast. Your descent eases as you approach a large onshore sea stack. You come to the imposing sea stack. It shelters leather ferns, hen and chicks and other coastal scrub plants. The trail goes to the right of the rock outcrop and descends to bluff's edge at ⅝ mile.

Head south-southeast along the bluff, where many Douglas irises and buttercups grow. A tall sea stack offshore called Gull Rock provides nesting for Brandt's cormorants, western gulls and pigeon guillemots. Around ¾ mile you cross a creek with still pools. Your trail traverses level headlands just inland from steep cliffs. Pass another immense onshore sea stack, now believed to have been a scratching post for the immense wooly mammoths that lived here during the Ice Age. A closer look reveals several large polished spots on the big rock. Six large sea stacks stand offshore. At one mile descend into a scrub-choked gulch to cross a small bridge. As you climb out of the gulch, notice the canyon's eroded wall. You can see layers of rounded, ocean-polished pebbles laid down when this was the ocean floor.

Your trail continues across level headlands. Before 1⅛ miles a rough trail provides access to a small, rocky, low-tide beach (be careful!). The main trail continues across the headlands, soon following a new boardwalk over seasonal wetlands. Pass through an old fence at the head of a small gully and come to the end of the boardwalk at 1¼ miles. Beyond 1⅜ miles you follow another boardwalk, crossing a small creek as your trail turns south. Your trail jogs east around a big ravine that cuts the headlands ahead.

At 1½ miles you come to the end of the boardwalk. Kortum Trail angles southwest, once again drawing near the bluff edge. Pass through a fence beyond 1⅝ miles and meet a gravel path. For a close-up view of the convoluted shore, turn right and follow the gravel west. At bluff's edge a small waterfall drops on your right when the creek is flowing.

The main trail follows the gravel east. The headlands south of the fence have not been grazed. They are covered with a thick layer of natural vegetation including coyote brush, cow parsnip, paintbrush, yarrow, purple miniature and bush lupine, flowering currant, twinberry, slim Solomon's seal and poison oak. Red hot poker, an introduced species with showy orange and yellow flower spikes, also grows here.

You reach the Shell Beach parking lot at 1⅞ miles from the trailhead. You can 1) retrace your steps, 2) descend a trail on the right to Shell Beach ⅛ mile, great tidepools at low tide), 3) climb east over the ridge on Trails #19 or 21, or 4) continue south on the Kortum Trail to Wrights Beach (see Trail #22).

OTHER SUGGESTIONS: GOAT ROCK BEACH lies at the end of the road, providings a mile of broad sand to wander. A SHORT TRAIL descends from Blind Beach parking lot to the beach in ⅝ mile. TRAIL #22 can be combined with #20 for a long ramble on coastal bluffs. TRAIL #19 can also be linked with this trail for a spectacularly varied, but arduous 10½-mile hike.

21

SHELL BEACH to RED HILL
CLIMB TO SWEEPING VISTAS ABOVE POMO CANYON

Red Hill Trail was completed in 2005, expanding the options for hiking in the upper reaches of Sonoma Coast State Beach. The trail traverses portions of the old Sequeira Ranch, a 910-acre property that was acquired in 2001 and converted to state park land with the help of four public and two private organizations: State Parks, the county's Agricultural and Open Space District, the Coastal Conservancy, Stewards of Slavianka, LandPaths and the Sonoma Land Trust. Sonoma Coast State Beach now includes 9300 acres, making it the largest state park in Sonoma County.

From the Shell Beach parking lot, walk up the paved road and cautiously cross Highway 1 to find the western trailhead for the Pomo Canyon Trail at ⅛ mile. Walk around the gate and follow the old dirt road as it climbs northwest through grasslands. Your two-rutted track rounds a sharp bend to the right at ¼ mile as the climb increases to moderate.

Ascend with expanding vistas of the rugged coast, passing under power lines and past a large boulder on your right at ⅜ mile. As the road bends to the right, the ascent eases, coming to a summit around ½ mile. From this ridge you can see the entire southern Sonoma coast, with Bodega Head to the south and Point Reyes jutting seaward beyond it on the clearest days.

From the ridge, the track descends slightly, coming to a junction around ⅝ mile. Pomo Canyon Trail continues climbing on the left. Turn right on another old ranch road, start of the new Red Hill Trail. It heads southwest, descending slightly before bending left to climb gradually northwest through the grasslands, passing between two large rock outcrops. The ascent turns moderate, then eases beyond ⅞ mile.

Soon the old road swings right to climb south. Watch for a green post on the left marked "Red Hill." Leave the old road here for the new footpath that ascends gradually east, then south through lush grasslands with abundant coyote brush.

Beyond one mile your trail climbs southeast, coming to a fence before 1⅛ miles. Pass through a stile and follow the round green posts with an angled top, climbing southeast, then east through pasture lands still actively grazed by cattle. At 1¼ miles you cross a cow path at a diagonal. Continue following the round-post marked path east-southeast through grasslands with abundant Douglas iris.

SHELL BEACH TO RED HILL:

DISTANCE: 4¼ miles round trip, or 5⅜-mile loop with western portion of Pomo Canyon Trail.

TIME: Two or three hours.

TERRAIN: Climbs through grasslands to a high hill with commanding views. with optional loop through forests, chaparral and grasslands.

ELEVATION GAIN/LOSS: 980 feet+/980 feet- to Red Hill. For loop: 1180 feet+/1180 feet-.

BEST TIME: Spring for wildflowers, a clear day for views.

WARNINGS: Use extreme caution crossing Highway 1. Watch for poison oak. Do not block gate at trailhead. Park closes at sunset.

HOW TO GET THERE: Turn west off Highway 1 about two miles south of the Russian River at M.18.22 into Shell Beach parking area.

FURTHER INFO: Sonoma Coast State Beach (707)875-3483.

Around 1⅜ miles your track turns northeast as the ascent steepens to moderate. You soon turn east and pass over a saddle, generally following the main cow path, with Red Hill rising on your right. You have grand views on your left of the ridges around the Willow Creek and Russian River canyons. Climb gradually through grasslands, with a steep, wooded hillside on your right and a small pond below you on the left.

Climb to another ridge around 1¾ miles where the trail forks. From the junction you can see Cobb Mountain (4722 feet) and Mount St. Helena (4339 feet) northeast. The main trail continues ahead, but turn right and follow the spur trail to Red Hill. It climbs south up the ridge, winding through grasslands and into the trees on Red Hill's north slope, a welcome refuge from the strong winds that often blow here. You wind through a compact but gnarled grove of old redwoods. Climb to the top of the grove at 2 miles where the redwoods are even more gnarled. Look two redwoods north on your left for a mossy seat cut with a back rest on a redwood stump, a pleasant resting spot on a warm day.

Your trail climbs out of the grove, winding through grasslands east of the grove, then winding south toward the summit. You soon climb along the edge between the grasslands and the leeward side of the forest, where tanoak, hazel, oceanspray, bay, native California blackberry and poison oak grow. Ascend to the summit of Red Hill, elevation 1062 feet, at 2⅛ miles, where an old rock cairn stands just west of the real top. When it's clear you have a sweeping vista of the coast, with Bodega Dunes and Bodega Bay laid out like a map before you.

When you've had your fill of the grand view, descend the spur back to the junction. For the easiest hike you can turn left and retrace your steps to the trailhead for a 4¼-mile round trip. If you choose to continue east, the green posts do not continue but the trail does. Follow it as it descends southeast to a new footbridge near the head of a creek around 2⅝ miles. Eventually there will be a junction just east of the bridge, with a future inland or high route of the California Coastal Trail heading south from here. For now, the only trail descends southeast through grasslands with scattered brush, soon gaining a ridgetop and coming to Pomo Canyon Trail at 3 miles. A right turn would descend to Pomo Canyon Campground in slightly more than ⅝ mile. Turn left to loop back to your starting point on the Pomo Canyon Trail (see Trail #19). It will bring you back to the Shell Beach parking lot at 5⅜ miles.

22.

SHELL BEACH to WRIGHTS BEACH
NATIVE PLANTS ON THE KORTUM TRAIL

Your trail starts at the southwest corner of the Shell Beach parking lot. You head east, paralleling the lot for the first 150 feet, then turn south to cross a bridge over the first of five creeks between here and Wrights Beach.

The creek canyon shelters a dense tangle of plants, including sticky monkeyflower, cow parsnip, purple bush lupine, twinberry, paintbrush, flowering currant and salmonberry. From the creek you climb to headlands covered with coastal scrub. Your trail follows the creek west. If you look at the cutbank across the creek, you can see a cross-section of the ocean sediments laid down long ago on this ancient marine terrace.

Before ⅛ mile your trail reaches the bluff's edge, where beach strawberry and narrow-leaved mule ears grow. You can see Shell Beach below. As you follow the bluff southeast past tufts of native grasses, the diversity of plants in the coastal

DISTANCE: up to 4¾ miles round trip; 2½ miles to
   north end of Wrights Beach.
TIME: Two or three hours.
TERRAIN: Over headlands with native vegetation, cross-
   ing several creeks, then descending to the dark sand of
   Wrights Beach.
ELEVATION GAIN/LOSS: 100 feet+/200 feet– to
   Wrights Beach; 300 feet+/300 feet–, round trip.
BEST TIME: Spring, early summer for wildflowers.
WARNINGS: Stay back from crumbly bluff edge. Watch
   for poison oak in coastal scrub. Watch for killer waves,
   stay back from tide line when walking on the beach.
HOW TO GET THERE: Turn west off Highway 1 at
   M.18.22 into Shell Beach parking area.
FURTHER INFO: Sonoma Coast State Beach
   (707) 875-3483.

scrub vegetation diminishes. Still, buttercups, lupine, blue-
eyed grass and paintbrush brighten the way.

You soon turn east, following the green posts away from the
ocean, climbing gradually. At ¼ mile your trail bends right and
climbs past mugwort and purple bush lupine. You soon descend
into a second gulch, where the coastal scrub includes many of the
same plants you saw at the previous creek, plus other species:
thimbleberry, sword fern, coastal manroot and nettle.

You cross a bridge and climb back onto the marine terrace.
The house that once sat on the right has been removed by
state parks. Cross the old driveway of the house around ⅜
mile, then traverse the headlands. You soon turn right and
descend to bluff's edge, following it briefly.

At ½ mile you approach Furlong Gulch, the deepest canyon
along the Kortum Trail. Your trail bends left, descending to
the bottom of the canyon. Three switchbacks descend toward
the beach and a creek crossing on a new bridge before ⅝ mile.
Purple seaside daisy and coast buckwheat grow on the canyon
floor. A dark sand beach lies at the mouth of the canyon.

Cross a small bridge and climb by steps back onto the headlands. At the top the trail now forks. The left fork climbs to the parking area at Carlevard Way. Take the right fork past a lone picnic table and follow the edge of the bluff south. Sea thrift grows profusely along the trail. Before ¾ mile you pass a small promontory on your right, a pleasant rest spot with great views up and down the beach. The trail winds inland near houses briefly, then returns to bluff's edge at ⅞ mile.

Your trail turns left and heads inland again. A spur on the right leads to an overlook of Wrights Beach. You come to the pavement of a cul-de-sac at one mile, part of a subdivision planned for these headlands before coastal advocates stopped the development and established a park instead.

From the pavement your gravelled trail descends southeast into a scrub-filled gully, crosses a bridge and climbs back to the headlands to follow the edge of the gully west.

At 1⅛ miles your trail begins descending to the beach. By 1¼ miles the trail ends, depositing you on the long, dark sand strand of Wrights Beach. Steep, varied bluffs rise above the beach, dense coastal scrub alternating with bare, jagged rock. Continue south along the beach.

At 1⅜ miles you pass a gully jammed with dense, lush vegetation. Then you walk the fine sand at the base of layered rock formations. Stay back from the water line on the steep beach; dangerous rip currents and rogue "killer" waves can occur here.

Around 1½ miles the beach is composed of wave-polished pebbles, a good spot for beachcombing. At 1⅝ miles the beach broadens. You begin to see more people on this broad playground of a beach. At 1⅞ miles the first sites of Wrights Beach Campground nestle at the base of bluffs to the east.

At 2 miles from Shell Beach Trailhead, the day-use parking and picnic area lies at the mouth of the canyon east of the beach. You can continue along the beach for almost ⅜ mile to the base of Duncans Point, where the beached sea stack called the Hogback and the small island of Death Rock lie. But if you do, stay back from these outcrops, no matter how low the tide or calm the ocean. Death Rock is closed to hikers, being one of the most dangerous, deadly spots on the entire California Coast.

If you did not plan a car shuttle to Wrights Beach, retrace your steps to the Shell Beach Trailhead.

OTHER SUGGESTIONS: You can camp at WRIGHTS BEACH CAMPGROUND ($6 day use, $25-35 to camp) at M.16.8 and do the hike in reverse. WRIGHTS BEACH also has a WHEEL-CHAIR-ACCESSIBLE PATH to the beach.

23

BODEGA DUNES LOOP

SHIFTING SANDS ON THE SAN ANDREAS

The Bodega Dunes sprawl over 900 acres of coast, from the mouth of Salmon Creek (source of much of the sand) to Bodega Harbor. The shifting sands reach inland for up to one mile, bordering the west shore of the harbor. The livestock of early settlers overgrazed the dunes, depleting the native vegetation. This caused the dunes to shift, threatening homes, farms and Bodega Harbor. In the 1930s European beach grass was planted to stabilize the dunes. Women rode wagons pulled by tractors up and down the dunes, planting grass shoots by hand.

The dunes are home to many mammals, including deer, jackrabbits, mice, voles, foxes, raccoons, weasels and badgers. Birds that inhabit the dunes include red-tailed hawks, northern harriers, short-eared owls, California quail and ring-necked pheasants. Many sea birds frequent the beach and the mud flats of the harbor. Monarch butterflies winter in eucalyptus trees in the campground.

From the parking lot, a paved trail passes picnic tables and restrooms, then heads southwest into dunes covered with European beach grass. The pavement ends as a boardwalk begins. The boardwalk bends right, passing through an area closed to foot traffic to protect and restore dune vegetation.

In 400 feet you reach an observation deck (wheelchair access to this point) overlooking long, dune-backed South Salmon Creek Beach. Descend the ramp to the fine blond sand of the beach, reaching the shore around ⅛ mile.

Always keep an eye on the surf, being aware that oversized rogue waves can strike any time, but especially in winter. It is best to hike at least 50 feet above the high-water line, unless it is a calm summer day.

Head south along the beach toward Mussel Point, which juts seaward 1½ miles south. As you walk the beach, watch for harbor seals fishing in the surf. From November through April you may see the breathing spouts of California gray whales beyond the breakers. Sanderlings and sandpipers feed along the wet sand at water line.

At ¼ mile you pass two trails leading east over the top of the foredune, the first ridge of the dunes running parallel to the shore. Continue south along the beach. At ⅜ mile the foredune is lower than it was up the beach. Continue south, passing several more trails leading east into the dunes.

BODEGA DUNES LOOP:

DISTANCE: 3½-mile loop.

TIME: Two or three hours.

TERRAIN: Along the beach, then into rolling dunes, climbing to the precipitation ridge before circling back to trailhead.

ELEVATION GAIN/LOSS: 180 feet+/180 feet−.

BEST TIME: Spring and summer for wildflowers.

WARNINGS: Blowing sand makes this hike unpleasant in high winds; light winds OK. Just as walking beach sand is more strenuous than walking a firm path, walking in loose dunes is even more strenuous; pace yourself accordingly. Watch for and yield to horses on the trail.

HOW TO GET THERE: Turn west off Highway 1 at M.11.70 into Bodega Dunes Campground. Go .4 mile to entrance kiosk, then take first right, going .8 mile to picnic area and trailhead.

FEES: Day use: $6/vehicle. Car camping: $25/night.

FURTHER INFO: Sonoma Coast State Beach (707) 875-3483.

The beach broadens at ⅝ mile, where much driftwood lies along the high-tide line. You are crossing the San Andreas Fault here, as it heads northwest into the Pacific (returning to land just south of Fort Ross). Looking inland through gaps in the fore-dune, you can see high dunes rising to 160 feet ⅜ mile inland. Bodega Dunes Campground lies east of the high ridge.

Continue south along the beach, passing several more paths into the dunes. You may pass several rough driftwood forts built by happy beachcombers. The structures wash away after occasional peak high tides. At ⅞ mile a broad path leads east over a low point in the foredune. The beach is narrower here than at the start or up ahead. Around 1⅛ miles it becomes broader once again. A tall signpost on the foredune marks a trail heading east and southeast into the dunes, "Osprey Trail to Lower Miwok Trail." Continue along the beach to the next obvious trail. The shore begins to angle west of south toward the green rise of Mussel Point.

Just beyond 1¼ miles you pass another trail into the dunes, this one unsigned. The beach ahead is very broad. Take the path southeast through a gap in the foredune, the route of the described loop. (You can continue along the beach to the granite shelf at the base of Mussel Point, but the point, a research area for the University of California Marine Laboratory, is closed to the public. Add ⅝ mile to walk to the point and back.)

As you leave the beach and approach the dunes, notice the salt-tolerant plant called sea rocket growing along the base of the foredune. Foredunes form only where vegetation grows that traps blowing sand. Follow the trail into the dunes, in just 200 feet passing a sign, "Osprey Trail to Miwok Loop Trail." Follow the trail as it bends left to a major trail junction before 1⅜ miles.

At the junction, which has two picnic tables and horse tethering posts, four trails radiate like spokes from this hub: clockwise from the one you came up, they include 1) a return to the beach, 2) the lowest and shortest route back to the parking lot and campground, 3) the main route, marked with green posts with an angled top (no horses, please), 4) the unmarked equestrian loop, which you will join soon.

Take choice #3 east (signed "Osprey Trail to Miwok Loop Trail"), following the green posts east, immediately coming to a fork, where you go right. At first the dune vegetation consists of European beach grass with scattered pockets of ice plant, both species introduced after the original vegetation (of rye grass, bromegrass and bush lupine) was overgrazed. You soon pass the first clumps of yellow bush lupine, the most hardy survivor of the original plants, which has been moving west in recent years. Your winding trail gradually climbs. Around 1½ miles, you pass several native species. Coyote brush, beach primrose, beach morning glory and sand verbena grow along the trail of soft sand.

You soon climb to a saddle between high dunes, from which you can see the ocean southeast, near the entrance to Bodega Harbor. The equestrian trail enters from the right. Descend from the saddle and tromp southeast coming to another junction beyond 1⅝ miles. The trail straight ahead, marked by the green posts, leads to Bodega Head in 1¾ miles, described in reverse direction as Trail #24.

You turn left to climb northeast on a trail open to equestrians. You quickly reach the top of a dune. Just before the top, another trail branches right, heading east to Westside Regional Park on the shore of Bodega Harbor. From the top of the dune, look east to Bodega Harbor and south to the highest of the Bodega Dunes, one of the tallest in the state at 161 feet. At the next junction at 1¾ miles, stay left on the horse trail to head north.

100

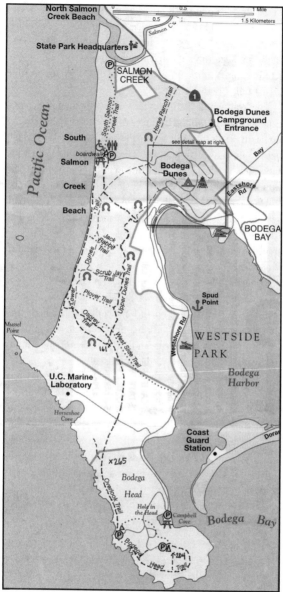

Your trail heads north just west of the crest of the dunes, passing purple seaside daisy, yarrow, coyote brush, bush lupine and beach grass. The trail levels, winding through the dunes. Before 1⅞ miles, bear right at an unmarked fork to head east. A dune on your right is shrouded in dense vegetation dominated by bush lupine. Growing in the shade of the other plants are lush miners lettuce and mosses.

Turn north again, following the ridge of the dune with views east to Bodega Bay and southeast to the ocean and coast. Your route stays level to 2 miles, then climbs to top another

101

dune. Pass ice plant and other dense vegetation mixed with the ubiquitous beach grass. Descend briefly to 2⅛ miles, coming to a junction with Plover Trail, which heads west to the beach. Continue north through dunes, soon climbing to another top. You are on the west face of a high dune with a view to the breakers.

Your trail winds along a high ridge of the dunes, heading generally north. Around 2⅜ miles you come to a marked junction with Scrub Jay Trail west to the beach. Stay on the inland path to descend between two dunes, then bend left to wind through a canyon. Soon you climb in deep, loose sand to pass through a lupine-filled gap, then climb to another dune top.

After a second lupine-choked gap at 2⅝ miles, you descend, swinging right to approach houses sheltered by trees. The trees form a precipitation ridge, a place where wind carrying sand is deflected upward by the trees, causing the wind to drop its sand, creating a ridge.

Swing parallel to a weathered fence and descend briefly to an unmarked junction. To reach Bodega Dunes Campground, continue northeast and north for ⅜ mile on the high trail that follows the eastern park boundary. But to return to the trailhead, go left (no horses allowed), descending gradually northwest along a swale in the dunes.

Young cypresses form a hedge row on your right. Beyond 2⅞ miles the cypress are short and windblown. Continue along the windrow. Beyond 3 miles your trail ends at another horse trail. The left fork leads to the beach. You go right, heading north, climbing gradually in loose sand, a cypress windrow now on your left. Cross two paths that bisect your northward route. After the second one, a shell midden lies beneath cypresses on your left at 3¼ miles.

You meet the paved road in 500 feet. Follow the road north to the parking lot and trailhead before 3½ miles.

OTHER SUGGESTION: You can also HIKE NORTH ALONG THE BEACH from the parking area. It is 1¾ miles round trip to the mouth of Salmon Creek.

24

BODEGA HEAD NORTH to DUNES
THROUGH A RESTRICTED RESERVE

*This trail starts on state park land, then enters the 326-acre
Bodega Marine Reserve, an area otherwise off-limits to the
public. Please stay on the trail to protect the Reserve. You will
pass from rocky shoreline, over the highest point on Bodega
Head, through coastal prairie and into rolling vegetated
sand dunes, with options of continuing to the beach or further exploring the extensive dunes. The Marine Laboratory,
accessible by the paved road near Gaffney Point, is open to
the public on Fridays from 2 to 4 p.m.*

From the west parking lot, your trail heads north past picnic
tables along the west shore of Bodega Head. In 200 feet cross
the top of a gully, where a spur descends west to a small
pocket beach. Your trail continues north, climbing steeply.
Once abundant fields of invasive ice plant here have mostly
been eradicated, allowing native plants to recover.

As you continue a steady climb, ignore the well trod left
forks that lead out to the eroded headlands along the shore.
A shell midden above the shore marks a native American
gathering spot. Soon a carpet of purple seaside daisies lines
your path. Buttercups, lupine, poppies, sea thrift and coast
buckwheat mix with the daisies. At ⅛ mile your climb levels
briefly, then resumes. Fine views of this rocky shoreline unfold. Beyond ¼ mile the climb eases. Large, invasive yellow
bush lupine dominate the vegetation here, and the iceplant
still thrives.

You soon come to a fork where the through trail veers right.
Go left for a short side trip to Horseshoe Cove Overlook. Near
the fork grow cream cups, goldfields, soap plant, sea thrift
and tiny lupine. The broad spur climbs steadily, passing
several granite outcrops. Your path levels, then comes to the
rock-studded overlook beyond ½ mile.

You have a bird's-eye view of U-shaped Horseshoe Cove,
the University of California Marine Laboratory on its north
shore, the green arm of Mussel Point stretching seaward and
Bodega Dunes beyond. Your height provides an excellent
vantage for whale watching. The picturesque granitic rocks
at the overlook shelter hen and chicks, leather ferns and an
assortment of colorful lichens. The area to the north is closed
for research purposes. The staff of the Marine Lab ask that
you go no farther.

BODEGA HEAD NORTH to DUNES:

DISTANCE: 4¼ miles round trip to junction with Trail #23, 5⅛ miles round trip to beach.

TIME: Two or three hours.

TERRAIN: Climb along bluff to Horseshoe Cove Overlook, then descend through coastal scrub to Bodega Dunes and return.

ELEVATION GAIN/LOSS: 440 feet+/440 feet– round trip to dunes junction; 560 feet+/560 feet– round trip to beach.

BEST TIME: Spring and summer for wildflowers. A clear day for outstanding views.

WARNINGS: Stay on trail and off adjacent property of U. C. Marine Reserve, where experiments are in progress.

HOW TO GET THERE: Turn west off Highway 1 in the town of Bodega Bay at M.11.05 onto East Shore Road. Go .3 mile to stop sign, then right on Bay Flat Road for 3 miles, then veer right for .6 mile to the west Bodega Head parking lot.

FURTHER INFO: Sonoma Coast State Beach (707) 875-3483.

As you return to the junction, a clear day will afford vistas of Tomales Bay, Bolinas Ridge beyond Tomales Point, Inverness Ridge and even Point Reyes. Turn left for the trail north through the Marine Reserve to the dunes. It heads east, then northeast through dense ice plant interspersed with bush lupine.

At ⅞ mile a dense grove of eucalyptus thrives in a protected canyon downhill on your right. You begin a gradual descent north, the sights and sounds of busy Bodega Harbor rising from the right.

At one mile your descent increases. You quickly come to the boundary sign for the U. C. Reserve. Please stay on the trail within the Reserve. Descend ⅛ mile, cross the paved road and continue generally north on a narrow, now level path marked by green posts. You pass through grasslands with scattered bush lupine.

In spring and summer, hardy coastal manroot vines climb on the bush lupine and coyote brush. Descend toward the transition zone between the coastal scrub/grasslands and the vegetated dunes ahead. The differences in vegetation form a nearly straight boundary line.

At 1¼ miles your trail turns left and meanders along the

boundary of the two habitats. At 1⅜ miles you veer right, entering the dunes. You soon turn north and head toward high dunes ahead. European beach grass, coyote brush, beach primrose and bush lupine grow along the path. A deflation plain, or water catch basin, is on the right.

Soon your trail bends right and dips, wrapping around the base of a high dune. A Krummholzy Douglas fir struggles to survive on the leeward side of the dune. You start a gradual climb, winding north through the dunes. Around 1⅝ mile you head toward the tallest dunes on the peninsula. They rise on your left at 1¾ miles, the tallest 161 feet above sea level. As you pass by tall dunes, clusters of paintbrush thrive in their shelter.

Before 2 miles you pass through a stile and enter state park land. Descend to the base of a dune, then head north along its base. Before 2⅛ miles you meet a junction with Trail #23 (at its 2-mile point). You can go right to follow that trail for a longer, more arduous hike.

The shortest route to the beach lies straight ahead, still marked by the green posts. It tops a saddle overlooking the meeting of the dunes and the Pacific (assuming it is not too foggy, a slightly risky proposition in this part of Sonoma County). Then your trail makes a gradual winding descent over varying dune terrain to a junction at 2⅝ miles. Another ⅛ mile brings you to South Salmon Creek Beach.

Return by the same trail. Bypassing the side trip to Horseshoe Cove Overlook, you will return to the trailhead at 5⅛ miles.

OTHER SUGGESTION: This trail combines nicely with either Trail #23 or #25 for a longer hike.

25.

BODEGA HEAD LOOP
GRANITE IMMIGRANT FROM THE SOUTH

Bodega Head sprawls seaward from the Sonoma Coast, its sandy arm like a giant crab's claw reaching out to sea. On this hike you will see the granitic underpinnings of this peninsula. The Head is composed of quartz diorite, a light, coarse-grained igneous rock similar to granite. The rocks of Bodega Head are thought to have originated near the Tehachapi Mountains at the southern end of the Sierra Nevada. For the past 40 million years, Bodega Head has been riding the Pacific Plate north along the coast, traveling 350 miles in relation to the Coast Range to the east. Tagging along on this cataclysmic yet snail's-pace ride are Point Reyes and the Farallon Islands to

the south and Point Arena to the north. The San Andreas Fault bisects the Head just south of Bodega Dunes Campground.

It is best to save this hike for a clear day when you can see all the rugged convolutions of this dramatic coastline. For a longer excursion, you can combine this loop with the trail north along the west side of the Head (Trail #24).

Just north of the trailhead for this hike is the world's most expensive duck pond, site of one of California's first environmental struggles. Now called "Hole in the Head," the name aptly describes the states of mind of the people who planned to build a large nuclear power plant virtually atop the San Andreas Fault. The "Hole" that was to become the plant's foundation was dug without public hearings, creating a great clamor of frightened and outraged citizens who effectively organized to scuttle the project.

Your trail starts from the east parking lot overlooking Bodega Harbor. Take the path that heads east, passing to the left of the restrooms. The level trail winds through coastal scrub of bush lupine, California poppy, coyote brush and cow parsnip. A spur soon forks left, descending to the mouth of Bodega Harbor below you. The sand spit of Doran Beach stretches east of the mouth for nearly two miles. You take the level right fork, heading southeast.

Beyond ⅛ mile the gentle green rise of Tomales Bluff lies straight ahead, five miles across Bodega Bay. The San Andreas Fault underlies Tomales Bay, to the left of the bluff. Your trail turns south and descends slightly, passing a picnic table. Another spur forks left, descending toward the shore. You wind through head-high bush lupine, some with stalks four inches in diameter.

At ¼ mile you pass the top of a lush gulch. Continue south, soon coming to the steep bluff's edge above the sea. Coast buckwheat and yarrow join the lupine here. Less than ½

BODEGA HEAD LOOP:

DISTANCE: 1½-mile loop, plus optional ¼ mile round trip to top of the Head.

TIME: One hour.

TERRAIN: Circle the high headlands of Bodega Head following a rugged, convoluted shore.

ELEVATION GAIN/LOSS: 280 feet+/280 feet–.

BEST TIME: Any clear day. Spring or summer for wildflowers.

WARNINGS: Stay back from steep cliffs.

HOW TO GET THERE: Turn west off Highway 1 in the town of Bodega Bay at M.11.05 onto East Shore Road. Go .3 mile to stop sign, then right on Bay Flat Road for 3 miles, then take the left fork to east parking lot.

FURTHER INFO: Sonoma Coast State Beach (707) 875-3483.

mile offshore lies Bodega Rock, a breeding site for Brandt's cormorants and western gulls. You may hear the barking of California sea lions on the rock.

Your trail climbs southwest following the rim of the Head. Sea fig grows on the steep slopes below the trail. At ½ mile you pass the Bodega Head Beacon and your trail levels. To the east the mainland coast is cut by Pinnacle Gulch (see Trail #26), Shorttail Gulch and the deep canyon of the Estero Americano, the Sonoma-Marin County line. Due south lies the rugged outcrop of Point Reyes.

Your trail climbs west through sparse vegetation, buttercups, poppies and coast buckwheat scattered in the grass. Climb to the highest point on the rim at ⅝ mile, nearly 160 feet above the sea. A side trail branches right, climbing gently in ⅛ mile to the 204-foot summit of Bodega Head. Rounded granite rocks protrude from the grasslands at the summit, where you have a 360 degree view.

Returning to the main trail, you descend along the Head's rim with breathtaking views of the jagged cliff and an inaccessible pocket beach below. At ¾ mile your descent ends at a grassy promontory just 100 feet above the shore. You will get no closer to Point Reyes on foot today. Notice that sandstone from old marine deposits overlays the granite bedrock of Bodega Head here, though the granite is visible at tideline.

Climb west, then northwest along the bluff's edge. As you climb, the path becomes broader and you pass some hardy paintbrush. Before ⅞ mile your grassy path levels atop a sculpted granite outcrop with a convoluted shore. The invasive bush lupine doesn't grow here, but you may see miniature lupine, taller sky lupine, cream cups and goldfields.

The described route continues along the rim. You descend gradually, heading northwest. Before one mile a granite ridge juts south, providing fine views. On a very clear day you can see 18 miles up the coast to Northwest Cape beyond Fort Ross. Continue along the rim, passing highly eroded sandstone. Soon fields of purple seaside daisies line the trail.

At 1⅛ miles you overlook the blond sand of a tiny, pristine pocket beach between you and the west parking lot. Your trail wraps inland, heading for the cypress trees at the head of the small cove.

Just before you reach the shapely cypresses, a trail branches right. From this junction you can continue straight for ⅛ mile to the west parking lot if you want to combine this hike with Trail #24. Otherwise take the right fork, heading east over level grasslands with clumps of sticky monkeyflower and Douglas iris. At 1¼ miles you descend gradually to merge with a trail from the left as you come to a gate, then the paved road before 1¼ miles.

It is ¼ mile up the road to your starting point. You return to the trailhead at 1½ miles.

OTHER SUGGESTION: A paved bike lane all along Bay Flat Road allows you to bike out to Bodega Head and back from the town of Bodega Bay (7 or 8 miles round trip).

26.

PINNACLE GULCH to SHORTTAIL GULCH

TWO CREEK CANYONS LEAD TO SECLUDED BEACHES

The new Shorttail Gulch Trail expands the options and broadens the perspective at this fine little coastal access project managed by Sonoma County Parks.

The dirt trail starts across the street from the paved parking area. Your trail descends southeast, passing bush lupine, coyote brush, yarrow and iris. As the trail descends, the coastal scrub vegetation becomes more dense. Berry vines and sticky monkeyflower join the tangle of plants.

You soon reach the head of Pinnacle Gulch where grasslands offer a view of the Pacific Ocean. Your trail descends steeply by five short switchbacks into the gulch. Before ⅛ mile you are beside the creek in the scrub-choked canyon. Willows grow along the stream where your path levels briefly. Plantain, black sage, poison oak, cow parsnip and sword fern mix with other coastal scrub plants.

Your path descends gradually along the stream, passing poppy, lupine, cow parsnip, paintbrush and beach strawberry. Native grasses grow on the steep hillside across the creek. The trail climbs briefly, then levels, with a glimpse of the ocean at the end of the gulch. Birds sing from the coastal scrub. You resume a gradual descent passing hen and chicks, coast buckwheat, checker mallow, angelica, buttercup, sticky monkeyflower, bee plant, vetch and poison oak.

At ¼ mile you see several houses perched high above on the rim of the canyon. Continue a gradual descent, soon coming to more luxuriant vegetation, with thimbleberry joining the mix. You pass under the limbs of wildly sprawling willows, where their dense vegetation hides the creek. The sound of running water rises from below.

You climb briefly to ⅜ mile as the vegetation thins, then resume a gradual descent. Soon a coffeeberry bush on the left has foliage stressed and salt-burned by its proximity to the ocean. Salmonberries crowd the creek.

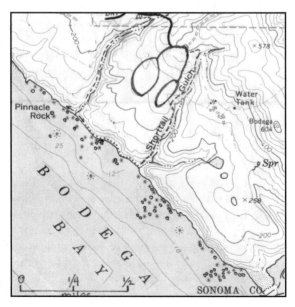

PINNACLE GULCH TO SHORTTAIL GULCH:

DISTANCE: 2-mile-loop, or 1⅛ miles round trip to beach
(at low tide you can walk south ⅜ mile or more).
TIME: One hour or more.
TERRAIN: Down a steep coastal-scrub-filled canyon to
an isolated beach, returning via a canyon to the south.
ELEVATION GAIN/LOSS: 200 feet+/200 feet−.
BEST TIME: Nice anytime. Low tide best for beach
exploring, spring and summer best for wildflowers.
WARNINGS: Stay off adjacent private property. Watch
for poison oak. Watch for rogue waves on the beach.
HOW TO GET THERE: Just south of Bodega Bay on
Highway 1 at M.8.76, turn west onto South Harbor
Way, then left on Heron Drive. In .9 mile, turn left
onto Mockingbird and come to trailhead parking area.
FEES: Day use: $5/vehicle.
FURTHER INFO: Sonoma County Regional Parks
(707) 565-2041.

Climb briefly to ½ mile, then descend past paintbrush, gum plant and poison oak to the beach on the shore of Bodega Bay. Pinnacle Rock stands just offshore to the west. The long ridge of Bodega Head reaches seaward beyond the rock. To the northwest the long low arm of Doran Beach stretches to the mouth of Bodega Harbor. A rugged and rocky, cliff-backed shoreline stretches southeast. About five miles down the coast, the shore meets the mouth of Tomales Bay, with Tomales Bluff jutting seaward on its west shore. Much closer, about 1¼ miles down the coast, you can see Estero Americano. The broad, deep canyon serves as the Sonoma-Marin County line.

The dark sand beach at Pinnacle Gulch is less than ¼ mile long at high tide. The isolation of this wild, rugged coast so close to the town of Bodega Bay merits a visit during most any tide or weather. Beware, however, that the ocean can be ferocious and unforgiving here despite being on a bay. Stay out of the water, where rip currents could carry you out to sea. Watch for oversize killer waves and stay back from the surf.

If the ocean is calm and you know the tide is ebbing, with

caution you can explore up and down the coast. You can walk ¼ mile north along the sand before you come to a rocky promontory which blocks the way to Doran Beach.

You can walk south from Pinnacle Gulch Beach whenever the seas are calm and the tide is moderate and ebbing, but the lower the tide the farther you can go. From the mouth of the gulch you walk southeast on sand for almost ⅛ mile. You then come to a rocky point that requires a tide lower than +4.5 feet to pass. If tide and surf are low enough, rock hop around the point to reach a second sandy beach that extends to ¼ mile.

You then reach another pile of rocks that provide a passage more rugged than the last, but easily traversable. You might find easier going on a volunteer trail at the base of the cliff. After 200 feet of rock hopping, a third sandy beach provides easy walking. You reach the mouth of Shorttail Gulch just beyond ⅜ mile, where you meet the new Shorttail Gulch Trail.

To proceed farther along the rugged coast you need to do some rock climbing. Most people will want to turn back here. At a tide lower than +2 feet, experienced hikers can proceed by scrambling up and down a 30-foot-high rock ledge. You reach a sandy, low-tide beach littered with big rocks. At ⅝ mile, another jumble of rocks makes passage difficult. During a minus tide on a calm day, you might pick your way all the way to Estero Americano. Be sure to start your return before the rising tide, to make certain you will not be stranded.

When you are ready to return, follow the trail up the left side of Shorttail Gulch. It quickly leads to a stairway. Climb by 131 steps to one mile. After a brief descent into a tunnel of cypress beside the creek, ascend moderately along the stream, following the nearby boundary on a straight-line course. Descend gently beyond 1⅛ miles to the cool shade of a broad cypress. Your trail bends left, then dips to cross a bridge over a side stream.

Climb 13 steps, then resume the straight-as-an-arrow bearing on a gentle climb, still following the north fork of Shorttail Gulch around 1¼ miles. At press time, this was still one of the wildest stretches on the trails of this little County Parks project.

Suddenly the path swings left and climbs steeply by 85 more steps. Expanding views reward your efforts, so take it easy and enjoy.

At 1⅜ miles your path swings left again to wind and dip as it heads west to a paved road at 1½ miles. Cross the street, turn right and walk the sidewalk of Osprey Drive north for ¼ mile, then turn right and follow Mockingbird Drive for another ¼ mile as it climbs, dips and climbs again, returning to the trailhead parking area at 2 miles.

BETWEEN HIGHWAYS 1 & 101

LAKE SONOMA
INCLUDES NEXT THREE TRAILS

Lake Sonoma provides Sonoma County's largest public recreation area. The 2700-acre lake behind Warm Springs Dam nestles in 18,000 acres of steeply rolling coastal hills that remain mostly in a natural state, offering redwood, fir and oak forests and steep grasslands. One of the best wildflower displays in this flower-rich county occurs every spring around Lake Sonoma. An 8000-acre wildlife area in the north half of the park is off limits to hikers, but fosters an abundant variety of mammal and bird species that spill over into the areas reached by 40 miles of trails.

The three trails described here offer distinctly different choices. Woodland Ridge is an easy day hike. The second trail provides the best mountain-bike loop at Lake Sonoma, with chances for fishing and primitive camping. The third and most difficult trail offers several choices of secluded backcountry camps along the wooded south shore of Warm Springs Arm.

Altogether, the area offers about 100 quiet, pretty primitive camps, mostly on the lake shore, in 15 separate areas. These can be reached only by hiking or boating, but are open year-round, unless closed following major rains. A large campground for vehicles, also open year-round, overlooks the lake. Lake Sonoma offers great fishing for bass and channel catfish, and many quiet, out-of-the-way inlets ideal for canoeing. Ask the Corps of Engineers for more information.

27.

WOODLAND RIDGE LOOP
SHORT, INVIGORATING NATURE LOOP

This pleasant loop provides an introduction to the varied habitats of the Lake Sonoma area. While the longer Lake Sonoma trails may be more rewarding, this hike is ideal for families and people not inclined to explore the longer trails.

From the gravel parking lot south of the visitor center, you cross a wooden bridge over a concrete culvert and come to a

112

picnic area. Turn left and parallel the culvert and Stewarts Point Road.

You soon enter a small grove of redwoods where your trail turns right. Climb 63 wooden steps, leaving the redwoods for a forest of large bay laurel trees. Their pungent leaves and nuts had many uses for the Southern Pomo, who called these lands home long before white settlers arrived.

At the top of the steps, you enter a forest of young redwoods growing beside weathered stumps. Your trail turns left as the climb eases. Descend briefly, then contour the hillside through mixed forest of oak, bay, madrone, redwood and Douglas fir.

Beyond ⅛ mile more steps signal the resumption of a steady climb. Switchback right, then left, then right again through mixed forest. At ¼ mile your climb steepens, passing Douglas firs to four feet in diameter. Poison oak vines climb some of the trunks. After you switchback left, your climb eases and the forest thins.

The trail swings right, climbing along a bald ridge lined with oak, madrone and manzanita. In spring many wildflowers grow in the grassy clearings, including California poppy, Indian warrior, Indian pink, blue dicks and grass nut.

Beyond ⅜ mile you have an excellent view of the Mayacmas Mountains to the east. The prominent peak on the left is Geyser Peak. On cool days you may see white plumes of steam rising from its geysers. Rocky Mt. St. Helena rises on the right, at the head of the Napa Valley 20 miles away.

Ascend along the open ridge. Four kinds of oak grow here: evergreen coast live oak, canyon live oak, interior live oak and deciduous black oak. They all produce acorns, a staple of the Pomo diet. At ½ mile madrones shade your otherwise sunny climb. Another short climb leads to the summit of this hike, where you have more views of the Mayacmas Range and Alexander and Dry Creek Valleys.

You descend to parallel Stewarts Point Road briefly, then swing right and continue a winding descent through mixed hardwood forest. Near ⅝ mile you get a glimpse of Lake Sonoma to the northwest.

Before ¾ mile you descend steps. The side trail to the overlook has been closed due to unstable soils. Descend gradually through oak forest with scattered young Douglas firs. Before ⅞ mile your trail turns right and descends into a dark, dense madrone forest, a twisting tangle of shiny-barked branches. In winter, birds come to feed on the madrone berries. Descend along a steep gully that feeds Dry Creek after rains. Sticky monkeyflower grows beside the trail.

DISTANCE: 1¼-mile loop.

TIME: One hour.

TERRAIN: Climb from grasslands through redwood forest into oak forest with scenic views, then descend through madrone/oak woodlands.

ELEVATION GAIN/LOSS: 140 feet+/140 feet–.

BEST TIME: Spring for wildflowers. Nice anytime.

WARNINGS: Watch for poison oak. Take your time on the steep first section of trail. Trails close after major rains in winter.

HOW TO GET THERE: Exit Highway 101 onto Canyon Road (M.43.6 from the north, M.43.05 from south). Go west on Canyon Road for 2.1 miles. Then go right 3.2 miles on Dry Creek Road to Lake Sonoma Visitor Center. Trail starts at small gravel parking lot south of main parking area.

FURTHER INFO: Lake Sonoma Visitor Center (707) 433-9483, extension 27.

Your descent steepens. In autumn the path is littered with slippery black oak leaves. Your trail bends left, coming to a view of the parking lot and visitor center below. You wind down through the oak woodlands, passing native bunch grasses around one mile.

Descend four dozen steps, then pass a large water tank. A few more steps bring you to the bottom of the hill. Turn right and wind through a cleared area and over a bridge to return to the picnic grounds and parking area at 1¼ miles.

OTHER SUGGESTIONS: A short, wheelchair-accessible walk (¼ mile round trip) leads through the visitor center (open Wednesday-Sunday 9–5 in winter, 8–5 in summer) to the FISH HATCHERY. An exhibit in the visitor center shows local birds including hawks, owls, ducks, loons, pheasants and many smaller birds.

114

28

HALF-A-CANOE LOOP
ROLLER COASTER TRAIL OVERLOOKING LAKE

Your trail descends from No Name Flat parking area into oak woodlands, crossing a bridge in 150 feet. Make a winding climb through grasslands with scattered oaks and buckeyes. At ⅛ mile you can glimpse a corner of Lake Sonoma. Your climb soon eases, then levels heading west.

Climb gently through oak-studded grasslands. The climb steepens and winds beyond ¼ mile, then turns west and descends. At ⅜ mile you meet the broad Half-a-Canoe Trail.

Turn left and head southeast along the dirt road. The path levels, then climbs east onto a ridgetop with grand views of the surrounding countryside and a picture of the elevation changes that lie ahead. On the left, alternating canyons, ridges and valleys stretch all the way to Mt. St. Helena, 23 miles east. To the northeast, you may see the plumes of the Geysers on a cool day. On your right, an immense, steep grassland plunges to the shore of the Warm Springs Arm 700 feet below. If you complete this loop, you will descend to that shore.

The next section of trail climbs up and down roller coaster hills along the ridgetop, a great run for mountain bikers. (Bikers: please slow and watch at blind corners for horse and foot traffic; if you speed, you are responsible for accidents!)

At ⅞ mile you descend to a junction with Little Flat Trail on the left (1⅝ miles, mostly down, to Little Flat Trailhead). From the junction, continue the roller coaster run, a short up followed by a long descent.

At 1⅛ miles you leave oak woodlands for grasslands with golden fairy lanterns in spring. Gray pines and toyons are scattered along the dry ridge. You pass outcrops of serpentine rock as the road climbs, dips and climbs along the ridgetop, with more grand views of steep canyon country.

Around 1⅜ miles you enter a grove of large black oaks. After 1½ miles you meet the Bummer Peak spur on your left. The faint spur climbs ⅛ mile to the top of the 1150-foot peak, where blue-eyed grass, star lily and Douglas iris sparkle in grasslands. The views from the summit are limited by trees. They open up on the south face, which plunges steeply to a narrow spot on the Warm Springs Arm.

From the Bummer Peak saddle, the fire road descends 300 feet to Bummer Peak Camp, then turns south through the heart of the pretty camp where the glassy lake shimmers through the leaves of live oaks and madrones.

Beyond 1⅝ miles your trail descends, swinging right to return to steep glades overlooking the sparkling waters of the lake. You make a winding descent west, looking toward wooded Picnic Creek and mossy Buzzard Rock across the lake. You level briefly then continue your winding descent.

At 1⅞ miles your descent steepens into a twisting plunge, passing buttercup, tarweed and iris. Make a big bend left and continue your steep descent. Beside the trail in spring and early summer grows a dense carpet of tiny star-shaped flowers with a pleasant, piny fragrance. False baby stars, of the phlox family, range in color from deep pink or lilac to white to yellow, often all in one patch. Here it occurs with rattlesnake grass and woodland star. As you descend, you pass black sage and golden fairy lanterns.

Around 2⅛ miles your trail levels and meets a spur 100 feet from the shore. The spur goes left for ⅛ mile to Lone Pine Camp, along the shore beneath black and live oaks.

The main trail turns north, paralleling the shore. Vine maple twines in the trees near the junction. Around 2¼ miles cross a gulch where a seasonal stream may provide water into late spring. The trail turns west along the shore. You soon pass elegant brodiaea growing at the base of an oak.

At 2⅜ miles your trail turns northwest. You soon climb gradually away from the shore. Around 2⅝ miles your trail winds along the contours of the shore, considerably higher above the water now. You come to a muddy creek crossing where mimulus grow, then wind west to cross two smaller creeks. After the third creek at 2¾ miles, you climb west. Your trail soon levels in a large glade.

At 2⅞ miles you meet a junction. The spur on the left goes ½ mile to Madrone Point Camp. The bike loop goes right, climbing to parallel a singing creek on your left. Descend briefly beyond 3 miles, then resume a steady climb up the creek canyon, winding through glades and oak woodlands. Around 3⅜ miles you pass the inspiration for the trail name on the right.

At 3½ miles you level briefly, with a glade on your left where thousands of wildflowers grow in spring. False baby stars and blue-eyed grass are the most abundant. You may hear the gobble-gobble of wild turkeys in this area or see the big birds if you are lucky. Grouse and quail also live nearby. Your climb continues, winding through another glade, then through a gully.

The climb eases, then bends right, climbing to a junction around 3¾ miles. The left fork climbs ¼ mile to the Liberty

HALF-A-CANOE LOOP:

DISTANCE: 4⅞-mile loop; or 3⅛ miles round trip to
Bummer Peak Camp.

TIME: Three hour hike, one hour bike.

TERRAIN: Roller coaster descent along rolling ridge to
Bummer Peak Camp. Then steep descent to lake and
Lone Pine Camp. Along shore to Madrone Point Spur,
then climb up creek canyon.

ELEVATION GAIN/LOSS: Loop: 1120 feet+/1120 feet−;
920 feet+/920 feet− round trip to Bummer Peak Camp.

BEST TIME: Spring.

WARNINGS: Ticks, rattlesnakes and scorpions live in
the area. Steep trail; take it easy. Mountain bikes must
slow for blind corners. Trail may be closed in winter
when slippery and muddy.

HOW TO GET THERE: Exit Highway 101 onto Dry
Creek Road (M.36.1 from south, M.36.5 from north).
Go northwest on Dry Creek Road for 10½ miles to
Lake Sonoma Visitor Center. Go west from there
1.7 miles to junction with Stewarts Point Road. Go
straight at junction (on Rockpile Road) for 1.9 miles,
then left into No Name Flat parking lot.

FURTHER INFO: Lake Sonoma Visitor Center
(707) 433-9483, extension 27.

Glen Campground kiosk. Go right, making a winding ascent
through grasslands. At 4⅛ miles, meet Rockpile Road at the
Lone Rock Trailhead (no parking allowed).

From Lone Rock your dirt road climbs south into oak forest. The road soon levels beside an immense coast live oak,
with blue dicks and poppies in the surrounding grasslands.
You descend briefly, then level, traversing steeply rolling
grasslands with scattered oaks and madrones. The flannel
leaves of wooly mullein line the path.

You pass a large manzanita on the left around 4⅜ miles, then
descend to meet the spur from No Name Flat Trailhead. Go left,
retracing your route to reach the trailhead at 4⅞ miles.

LAKE SONOMA

29

SOUTH SHORE to
OLD SAWMILL CAMP
DOWN, UP AND AROUND TO OLD SAWMILL CAMP

As Lake Sonoma increases in popularity, you can find solitude and wilderness by backpacking (also by boating, horseback riding, day hike, and—when trails are dry—mountain biking) into the beautiful backcountry camps along the lake's steep, wooded south shore. Every spring the steep forests and grasslands of the north-facing terrain burst into color with one of Sonoma County's finest wildflower displays. After the flowers have faded in summer, the sparkling waters of the lake warm to swimming temperature.

The campsites offer shade, seclusion and fine views of steep, rugged country. The camps provide a touch of civilization with tables, trash cans and fire pits with adjustable grills. Wildlife abounds, so with a little luck you will see hawks, ospreys, wild turkeys, coyotes, perhaps even a bear. Though the trail never climbs more than 400 feet in one stretch, the continuous ups and downs following the convoluted shore add up, making this one of the more difficult trails in the book, especially for backpacking.

From Skaggs Springs Vista Trailhead, you overlook the Warm Springs Arm of Lake Sonoma. The confluence of Warm Springs Creek and Little Warm Springs Creek now lies 100 feet below the lake surface, buried with its rich history. A band of the Southern Pomo called this valley home. The village of Kahowani was located near the confluence. Another village, Takoton, was on Dry Creek about a mile upstream from where the dam is today. Cawako, the principal village, was three miles downstream from Takoton.

Near Kahowani, hot springs bubbled from the ground at 135 degrees. In the late 1800s Skaggs Springs Resort tapped the springs, becoming a popular destination. When the waters began to fill behind the dam in 1982, nothing remained of the resort, but the hot springs were still used.

Your broad trail descends gradually south through hardwood forest alternating with grasslands. In spring the trail is lined with buttercups (most common flower on this hike), blue dicks, blue-eyed grass, lupine, bedstraw, poppies and vetch. Lake Sonoma's blue waters shimmer below.

Before ¼ mile you leave the broad path, veering right to descend steeply through grasslands with iris. Switchback three times, descending along a grassy ridge. At ⅜ mile you switchback right and descend into forest where soap plant, shooting stars, milkmaids and poison oak grow beneath oaks, bay laurels and California buckeyes. Forget-me-nots and maidenhair ferns grow in shady spots.

At ⅝ mile you reach a junction. The trail on the right leads to Quicksilver Camp and South Lake Trailhead. Straight ahead a spur descends to the lake. You go left, climbing and descending with the contour of the land.

Beyond ¾ mile you descend moderately to cross Little Warm Springs Creek, then climb steeply by switchbacks to gain a ridge at 1⅛ miles. Then ascend more switchbacks through oak woodlands. At 1⅜ miles you cross a small gully where native bunch grass grows beside tiny white flowers called woodland star. Descend gradually to 1½ miles, where you cross a deep gulch.

Your trail makes a winding ascent, then descends gradually, following the shore. At 1¾ miles an unmarked spur descends to the shore. Continue your descent to another spur at 1⅞ miles. This side trail, marked "Island View Camp," descends ¼ mile to a pleasant camp beside the lake.

The main trail climbs northwest, then west. At 2 miles you switchback left and climb into a large meadow, where a few young redwoods mix with oaks and buckeyes. You soon return to oak forest, then pick up an old road at 2¼ miles. Ascend it gradually through steep terrain, passing lupine and flowering currant. In a steep, rocky spot, star-shaped cream fawn lilies grow in profusion.

Climb southwest to cross a tiny creek in a deep canyon at 2½ miles, where bay laurel, big leaf maple and redwood grow. Your trail ascends briefly, then descends across sunny slopes dappled with wildflowers. At 2⅝ miles a large live oak overhangs the steep slope on the right.

You descend to a glade bordered by madrones, with grand views of the lake. Watch the tops of snags along the shore for ospreys. The fish-eating, hawklike birds perch atop a snag, then dive for fish, carrying the catch in powerful talons. In winter they migrate to South America.

At 2¾ miles your trail makes a winding descent, then levels, near the lake. After your trail turns west, start a gradual climb through black oak forest. Beyond 3 miles you wind around the Picnic Creek inlet of the lake. The trail rolls with the terrain, passing baby blue eyes and shooting stars as you cross several dry gullies.

At 3⅜ miles you ascend to a meadow. Descend briefly to an old road, then follow it on a winding ascent into rugged Picnic Creek Canyon. The rocky terrain supports redwoods, oaks

SOUTH SHORE to OLD SAWMILL CAMP:

DISTANCE: 16 miles round trip to Old Sawmill Camp (difficult); 4 miles round trip to Island View Camp, 8 miles round trip to Picnic Creek (moderate).

TIME: Overnight to Old Sawmill Camp, any portion as day hike.

TERRAIN: Descend to lake's south shore, then many short up and down stretches, crossing creek canyons and rounding points to camp near head of Warm Springs Arm of Lake Sonoma.

ELEVATION GAIN/LOSS: 720 feet+/720 feet– to Island View Camp; 1700 feet+/1700 feet– to Picnic Creek; 3160 feet+/3160 feet– to Black Mountain Camp; 3360 feet+/3360 feet– to Old Sawmill Camp. All round trip.

BEST TIME: Spring for wildflowers, early summer and autumn for swimming.

WARNINGS: Watch for rattlesnakes, ticks, scorpions and poison oak. Stay away from wild pigs. Steep country, take it easy, especially in hot weather. Purify water before drinking. Camping permits required. Trails may be slippery or impassable after major storms. Hunting sometimes allowed; check before going. Bikes allowed in dry season. Cyclists must slow to walking speed on blind corners. Other users watch for bikes.

HOW TO GET THERE: See directions for Trail #27. From visitor center (permits available), go south on Stewarts Point Road for 1.7 miles to junction. Go left for another 2.8 miles, then turn right to Skaggs Springs Vista Trailhead.

FEES: Backcountry camps: $10-14/night. Car camping at Liberty Glen: $10/night (no water available).

FURTHER INFO: Lake Sonoma (707) 433-9483.

and ferns. Beyond 3¾ miles, the road levels, then descends across more gullies.

At 3⅞ miles you leave the old road for a winding descent to the creek, passing trail plant and star lily. Toyon, wood rose, honeysuckle, poison oak, baby blue eyes, hound's tongue and hazel grow in the moist habitat between trail and

121

creek. At 4 miles you come to redwood-lined Picnic Creek, a pleasant place for a break.

Second-growth redwoods grow along the creek. The big stumps with springboard cuts were logged by hand before the advent of chainsaws. Shade-loving plants carpet the forest floor. Ferns include woodwardia, sword, coastal wood, leather, maidenhair, and the bird's foot. Tiny Pacific starflowers grow abundantly. You may also find alum root, miners lettuce, fairy bell, fat and slim Solomon's seal, twisted stalk, calypso orchid and wood strawberry.

Your trail winds steeply out of the canyon bottom, a view of a small waterfall upstream. At 4⅛ miles you enter drier habitat where large bays and oaks grow. A rocky, sunny slope on the left supports paintbrush, sticky monkeyflower, chamise, blue dick, and a carpet of low-growing, tiny white to lilac flowers with a delightful fragrance, false baby stars. Traverse the steep wall of Picnic Creek Canyon, climbing across a shady slope overlooking the lake.

At 4¾ miles you crest a steep ridge and descend west, leaving Picnic Creek behind. The trail levels along a shady slope, passing beneath gracefully arching madrones. Soon a fern- and moss-covered cliff is on your left, while the spiny needles of young California nutmeg grow on your right. Then a sunnier rocky slope supports the deep red flowers of Indian warriors. You ascend an easy grade.

At 5 miles your trail veers left around the Bear Creek inlet. Descend steep switchbacks to ford fern-lined Bear Creek, which cascades along a series of rocky pools. Then climb sunny slopes where poppies grow. At 5¼ miles you ascend steeply through chamise, toyon and manzanita. Your trail bends left to a grassy hill with a view of the lake.

Climb west to 5⅜ miles, returning to hardwood forest, then contour a steep, shady slope. Your level trail winds through a cool gully, then climbs west across a steep gulch. Your path soon levels again.

At 5¾ miles a clearing affords a grand view of the upper Warm Springs Arm. Make a winding descent to a cool seep with big woodwardia ferns. Ascend steeply away from the lake, soon coming to a view of the moss-covered outcrop called Buzzard Rock. Descend to the base of the rock at 6 miles. Red larkspur and monkeyflower grow beside seeps. The trees here are draped with lichen.

You climb steadily to 6¼ miles, then veer left around the inlet of Seven Oaks Creek. Descend to a pleasant creek crossing, then climb north to overlook the lake. A spur on the right descends to Black Mountain Camp. The main trail turns left through a large glade. Ascend gradually, passing through an old fence line at 6¾ miles, then into a large meadow. Your trail becomes vague as it winds, then descends to ford a small creek where pioneer eucalyptus grow beside native bays and black oaks.

Cross another big meadow as your trail heads northeast, then picks up an old ranch road to descend through the largest meadow yet, Buck Pasture. At 7 miles your trail turns left as the spur to Buck Pasture Camp descends 300 feet to the prettiest camp along the trail, nestled among rocks and large oaks overlooking the lake.

Continuing to Old Sawmill Camp, your trail contours through the meadow. At 7¼ miles climb moderately through hardwood forest for ⅛ mile. Then cross a small gully before ascending through grasslands. Pass through another fence before 7½ miles, then climb a ridge.

Where the trail descends southwest, I flushed a wild turkey. The twenty-pound tom burst from the chaparral, frantically beating its four-foot wingspan, taking off like an cargo plane on a bee line toward the lake. Quite a thrill!

The trail soon levels in grasslands, a popular rooting spot for wild or feral pigs. They do considerable damage to native plants, feeding on bulbs, corms and tubers that would otherwise produce wildflowers.

Beyond 7¾ miles your trail makes a gradual, winding descent, then descends steeply, passing an old springhouse beneath immense black oaks. After a dry gully ascend gradually through grasslands alternating with oak woodlands.

Around 8 miles from your trailhead, descend briefly to the spur to Old Sawmill Camp. It descends north for ⅛ mile to five pleasant sites in a rolling grassland surrounded by immense black oaks, healthy Bishop pines and a few young redwoods. Old fig, apple and plum trees remain from a small community once supported by the sawmill by the creek (now underwater). The old Skaggs Springs Road is between the camp and the lake. Periwinkle, cultivated Oregon grape, blackberry vines and other escaped domestic plants sprinkle the hillside above the winding arm of the lake. A spring box southeast of the outhouses provides drinking water and watercress if it has not dried up. Be sure to purify the water whether from there or the lake.

Many birds visit the clearing at Old Sawmill Camp. You may see quail, jays, hawks, ospreys, golden eagles, wood ducks and woodpeckers. Before sunset we heard the distinct gobble-gobble of wild tom turkeys calling back and forth across the canyon. At night, alternating silence and the symphonic croaking of frogs were pierced by the calls of

great horned, barn and screech owls. The howl of a distant coyote wafted down the canyon from the west.

At dawn the turkeys were at it again. The gobbling came closer, nature's alarm clock for the decadent backpackers trying to sleep past dawn. When we finally awoke, unable to ignore the incredible racket any longer, tom and hen were strolling along the road below our camp, turkeys on parade. His bright red wattles sparkled in the rising sun. Their body feathers shimmered in bronze iridescence.

The trail continues west from the camp turn-off, ascending and descending for short stretches, following the lake shore to the inlet of Warm Springs Creek. The trail fords the large creek at 9⅛ miles, then climbs ⅛ mile to a junction. To continue around the lake go right, trekking through more ups and downs along the rugged shore.

At 11 miles you come to Rancheria Creek where a maze of trails may be confusing (map and compass handy here). Head east to follow the Warm Springs Arm's dry north shore staying high above the shore. Madrone Point Camp is 16 miles from the Skaggs Springs Vista Trailhead, a reasonable hike from Old Sawmill Camp.

If you wish to return the shortest way from Old Sawmill or one of the other south shore camps, you head east along the shore, retracing your steps. Do remember that the final ¾ mile entails a long uphill pull. If the day is hot, it is best to climb out either early or very late in the day.

OTHER SUGGESTION: If you prefer a longer backpack, you can start at SOUTH LAKE TRAILHEAD, ½ mile beyond the left turn, adding 5¼ miles to total distance. Quicksilver Camp is on that trail segment.

124

30

ARMSTRONG WOODS LOOP
THROUGH THE DEEP, DARK VIRGIN FOREST

The Southern Pomo had dozens of villages along the Russian River east and north of the present park. They hunted and foraged in the rolling hills to the west of their settlements. But they referred to the grove of giant redwoods along Fife Creek as "the dark hole." They stayed out of this dark, cool forest, believing it was inhabited by evil spirits.

In 1874 Colonel James Armstrong came to California to invest. Working in the logging industry, he became fascinated by the redwoods and sought to save the ancient grove along Fife Creek near Guerneville (then known as Stumptown). After his death in 1900, his family continued the effort for preservation. Armstrong Woods became a county park in 1917, then joined the State Park system in 1934.

This hike starts at the main parking area beside the park entrance. Kids especially might want to follow the white bear tracks from the visitor center that lead toward the crosswalk and trailhead. Walk north past the entrance kiosk and carefully use the crosswalk to cross the road west to pick up Pioneer Trail, following it northwest into the forest. Your trail soon turns north, paralleling Fife Creek past redwoods to 12 feet in diameter.

After ⅛ mile you cross a road where the Parson Jones Tree towers on your right. This 310-foot-giant is the tallest tree in the park. Just ahead a six-foot cross section of a redwood shows that the tree lived about 1100 years. The Parson Jones Tree is estimated to be 1300 years old.

Continue north along Pioneer Trail, walking the level trail through redwood forest with trees of many sizes. Scattered Douglas firs, bay laurels, tanoaks and big leaf maples also grow in the forest. In autumn the maples add bright splashes of color, catching sunlight filtering through the dark forest. Plants in the understory include hazel, redwood sorrel, trillium, sword ferns, twisted stalk and poison oak. You pass numbered posts keyed to the nature trail (brochures available at kiosk).

At ¼ mile you come to an upended redwood root on the left, worn smooth by many hands over time. Your trail winds around a gnarled giant, then comes to another paved road. Our described hike crosses the road, veering left across Fife Creek to pick up Discovery Trail. (Pioneer Nature Trail continues north on the right. We'll return to it soon.)

Head toward the Armstrong Tree on Discovery Trail paralleling the road. The path has a guide rope and braille interpretive text designed for the visually impaired. Many hazels here radiate a lovely green glow as they catch the filtered light. Redwoods along the path are among the largest trees you have passed. Wood rose and bracken fern join the understory. On the left a platform protects the roots of a giant beside the trail. The deck allows you to get close to the ancient tree without hurting its shallow root system.

As your path curves right, then curves right again before ½ mile, look up for a good perspective on the immense Armstrong Tree 150 feet ahead. Estimated to be 1400 years old, it is only two feet shorter than the Parson Jones Tree. With its 14.6-foot diameter, the Armstrong Tree is the most massive tree in the grove.

Your trail forks at ½ mile as you come to the base of the colossus. The left fork connects with Pool Ridge Trail, which climbs steeply north to meet the trails in Austin Creek State Recreation Area (see Trail #31). Take the right fork, descending briefly, then curving left along the base of a hillside. Moist ground supports clintonia, trillium and slim Solomon's seal. Climb along the base of the hillside, overlooking seasonal Fife Creek.

Descend steps to return to the flood plain of the creek. The largest redwoods thrive on such flood plains, aided by rich soils, a high water table, and periodic flooding. Continue along the quieter side of the nature loop. You immediately pass a big redwood on the left with large knobby burls. The path hugs the base of the slope. You soon wind around a fire-toppled redwood giant leaning against the hill.

Your trail winds around more large redwoods, then crosses a bridge across the creek at ¾ mile. You quickly meet a circle around a gnarled, burl-encrusted giant, the Icicle Tree. Its burls have grown stalactite-like formations that reach toward the ground, a very uncommon growth form. After the circle, huckleberry (edible dark blue berries in late summer and fall) grows on the left.

The path soon ends as you meet Pioneer Trail. For the easiest loop of 1¼ miles, go right on the broad path, heading south paralleling the road. (See next paragraph for a longer option). Redwood violets grow abundantly along the trail. Soon a triple-topped giant on the right is 11 feet in diameter. Around ⅞ mile look for trillium, trail plant, inside-out flower and redwood sorrel growing on the forest floor. Continue south, passing the Burbank Circle to complete the loop. Cross the paved road and continue another ¼ mile back to the parking lot.

ARMSTRONG WOODS LOOP:

DISTANCE: 1¼-mile loop or 2¾-mile loop.

TIME: One or two hours.

TERRAIN: Level flood plain filled with virgin redwoods, with optional climb to ridge.

ELEVATION GAIN/LOSS: Negligible for short loop, 440 feet+/440 feet- for long loop.

BEST TIME: Spring for wildflowers. Nice anytime.

WARNINGS: Watch for poison oak. May be muddy after rains. Park open 8 a.m. to one hour after sunset.

HOW TO GET THERE: The town of Guerneville (silent E's) is on Highway 116, 13 miles east of Jenner on the coast, about 20 miles west of Santa Rosa. At the stoplight in Guerneville, turn north onto Armstrong Woods Road and go 2.2 miles to main parking area and park entrance.

FEES: It's now free to park in the main parking lot. Beyond the kiosk,day use/parking: $6/vehicle.

FURTHER INFO: Armstrong Redwoods State Reserve (707) 869-2015 or 865-2391.

For a longer, more arduous loop, go left on the broad path at ¾ mile. At ⅞ mile a 100-year-old redwood grows atop an old stump on the left, beside two virgin trees. Notice how the roots of the young tree reached six feet to find soil after sprouting atop the stump. Redwoods are survivors! Parallel the creek as you walk the flood plain. Before one mile a goosepen redwood stands on the left. Early settlers used hollow redwoods like this to cage their poultry. You promptly come to a fork. Stay left to cross two small bridges to reach the picnic area and the end of Pioneer Trail before 1⅛ miles.

Veer right and walk the paved road past the group picnic area, then veer right again onto a paved fork, passing a restroom on your left, and the top of the picnic area on your right. You promptly come to a parking lot on the edge of a large clearing. Veer right to the east end of the lot and head up East Ridge Trail.

Cross a bridge over the east fork of Fife Creek. You might

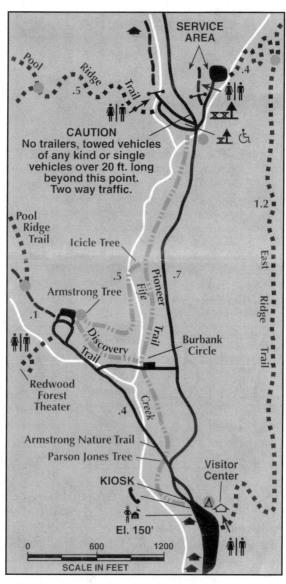

SERVICE AREA

.4

CAUTION
No trailers, towed vehicles
of any kind or single
vehicles over 20 ft. long
beyond this point.
Two way traffic.

Pool Ridge Trail

.5

Pool Ridge Trail

Icicle Tree

.5

Pioneer Trail

.7

Fife

Armstrong Tree

.1

Discovery Trail

Burbank Circle

Redwood Forest Theater

Creek

.4

1.2

East Ridge Trail

Armstrong Nature Trail

Parson Jones Tree

KIOSK

Visitor Center

El. 150'

0   600   1200

SCALE IN FEET

notice that the creek often flows here even when it's entirely underground down on the redwood flood plain. Follow the trail climbing northeast. At 1¼ miles your climb steepens in a mixed forest of redwoods, firs and hardwoods. You wind around two venerable old giants, then pass a huge, hollow stump. Ascend switchbacks through hardwood forest to a junction on the ridge at 1½ miles. On the left the trail climbs north to Bullfrog Pond in 3 miles.

Turn right and climb along the ridge. The thin soil here is very different from the canyon floor, supporting a variety of hardwoods with scattered Douglas firs. As-

128

cend to a top at 1⅝ miles, th[...]
knob at 1¾ miles, where you l[...]
surrounding forest.

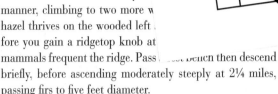

More such views unfold as you [...]
manner, climbing to two more w[...]
hazel thrives on the wooded left [...]
fore you gain a ridgetop knob at [...]
mammals frequent the ridge. Pass [...] bench then descend
briefly, before ascending moderately steeply at 2¼ miles,
passing firs to five feet diameter.

You soon leave the ridge to descend its west slope. Descend
steeply at 2⅜ miles, then switchback left for a gradual winding descent to return to redwood forest with an abundant
huckleberry understory around 2½ miles. As your trail
descends moderately, you may glimpse the dense grove of
giants on the canyon floor. As you make a well graded descent
west and southwest, the redwood giants' towering tops are
suddenly above you. Soon a drift of cool air indicates you are
nearly there. Descend to the parking lot at 2¾ miles.

OTHER SUGGESTIONS: A ridge loop of about 5 miles
climbs to overlook the virgin forest on POOL RIDGE and
EAST RIDGE TRAILS, linking with trails to the camp-
ground and trail system at Austin Creek (see Trail #31).
You can arrange guided day and overnight HORSEBACK
TRAIL RIDES by calling (707) 887-2939.

31.

AUSTIN CREEK
GENTLE, SECLUDED WILDERNESS

*Austin Creek State Recreation Area, recently expanded
to about 6200 acres, offers a steep but gentle wilderness nestled in the remote canyons of East Austin Creek.
Two pleasant backcountry camps allow hikers, mountain
bikers and equestrians the opportunity to camp in this placid
hill country, where immense glades alternate with dark green
forests. Elevations range from 150 feet along the creek to 1940
feet at McCray Mountain on the park's eastern boundary.*

*Spring offers the best exploring here. Oregon ash, red
alder, big leaf maple, western azalea and myriad oaks display verdant new foliage in the canyons, while wildflowers
sparkle among the fresh green grass. Winter can be pleasant
between storms, when mild, sunny days of solitude may ac-
centuate the rushing, brimming creeks. If you go in summer,*

AUSTIN CREEK:

DISTANCE: 10⅜-mile loop, with shorter options of a
4- or 9-mile loop.

TIME: Five hours to overnight.

TERRAIN: Descend through glades and forest, then
along Schoolhouse and Gilliam Creeks to East Austin
Creek. Ascend along creek, then return steeply up and
down one ridge and up another to trailhead.

ELEVATION GAIN/LOSS: 1720 feet +/1720 feet-.

BEST TIME: Spring for wildflowers, winter for solitude.
Summer is hot and dry.

WARNINGS: Watch for poison oak, rattlesnakes, ticks
and scorpions. Backcountry camping requires permit
before entry; camp only in designated camps. Fires
allowed only in fire pits.

HOW TO GET THERE: From Guerneville, go north on
Armstrong Redwoods Road for 3 miles to the picnic
area (parking for equestrians). Hikers drive the steep,
narrow winding road (impassable to trailers) climbing
for another 2.2 miles until the road forks. Go left to
signed Gilliam Creek Trail.

FEES: Day use: $6/vehicle. Car camping:$15/night.
Backcountry camps: $15/night.

FURTHER INFO: Austin Creek State Recreation Area
(707) 869-2015 or 865-2391.

*be forewarned that it gets very hot. Dry conditions may ban
fires or close the camps for a while. It is always advisable to
purify your drinking water.*

*Mountain bikers are not allowed on the single-track trails,
so if you are biking here use the fire road that begins just
before the Vista Point on the road to Bullfrog Campground.
You can bike into Tom King and Mannings Flat Camps. Gilliam Creek Camp has been closed. Cyclists, please remember
to yield to equestrians and announce your presence when
overtaking hikers from behind.*

The Gilliam Creek Trail descends north into the headwaters of
Schoolhouse Creek. Your trail quickly enters mixed forest of
canyon and coast live oak, white oak, bay laurel, redwood and

Douglas fir. Contour along the bottom of a glade, then descend. Watch for poison oak vining up trees and over rocks.

At ⅛ mile you traverse the bottom of another glade on your right, with a steep, wooded slope on your left. Descend steeply into forest with madrone and toyon. Your path levels at ¼ mile, then climbs briefly. Descend toward a towering rock outcrop, then cross a seasonal brook.

At ⅜ mile, climb into an expansive glade, with grand views west to the many ridges and canyons between you and the coast, 14 miles away. Traverse the lower glade, passing blue-eyed grass and blue dicks in spring, then fording another seasonal creek at ½ mile. As you leave the glade, your trail contours along the base of a rocky slope where poppies, dudleya and phacelia grow. Pass through chaparral with chamise, manzanita and sticky monkeyflower.

At ⅝ mile you ascend into a glade with views northwest to the stark serpentine slopes of Red Slide, the high ridge called The Cedars rising beyond it. Austin Creek drains virtually all the country before you.

Your trail turns west to descend Gilliam Ridge, at ¾ mile passing beneath large oaks. Look for silverleaf lotus, woodland star, baby blue eyes, a delicate blue lupine, bird's-eye gilia and pink Hartweg's sidalcea in spring. Leave the ridge, descending to cross a fork of Schoolhouse Creek at ⅞ mile. The trail drops west through woods and glades to cross another tributary at one mile, then descends through rolling grasslands.

Your descent steepens as you follow the winding creek at

1⅛ miles. The descent eases as the quickening waters of the creek drop away on the left. You pass several veins of dark brown, then blue-green serpentine rock.

The descent steepens again at 1¼ miles. Round a big bend left to ford a fork of Schoolhouse Creek, lined with moss-draped rocks, soap plants, leather ferns and wildflowers. Then descend south, following the stream into forest with strawberry, honeysuckle, maidenhair fern and oceanspray in the understory. At 1⅝ miles you ford Schoolhouse Creek at its confluence with the tributary. Moss and lichen thickly coat everything in this deep, dark canyon. Lady and sword ferns thrive beneath Douglas firs, bay laurels, maples and oaks.

Your trail descends northwest along the pretty creek. At 1⅞ miles you ford the creek, then ford it again in 200 feet. At 2 miles you climb past a gnarled black oak four feet in diameter, then descend along the creek past evergreen and two-eyed violets, hazel, Oregon ash, starflower and elderberry.

At 2⅛ miles you reach a junction near the confluence with Gilliam Creek. (For the shortest loop, go right, fording Schoolhouse Creek, then follow Gilliam Creek upstream to the fire road where you go right for a 4-mile loop.) Our described trail stays left. You follow larger Gilliam Creek as it flows west.

Pass through a sunny clearing before 2⅜ miles, then return to dense, dark hardwood forest. Wood rose, trillium, star lily and red larkspur grow along the creek. Beyond 2½ miles you follow Gilliam Creek on a particularly pretty stretch of alternating rapids and still, glassy pools. Woodwardia ferns thrive on the banks.

Descend to a ford of Gilliam Creek at 2⅝ miles. Wildflowers grow on the sunny north bank in spring, including baby blue eyes, milkmaids, wild geranium, golden fairy lantern and bedstraw. In 400 feet the trail, which used to ford back to the south side of the creek, now follows along the north bank.

At 2¾ miles the tread improves along the north bank. But the canyon, steeper and narrower downstream, requires frequent fords. In dry season you may be able to keep your feet dry, but in winter and spring the likelihood of dry feet greatly diminishes. In 200 feet the trail returns to the south side of Gilliam Creek. Immense bay laurels sprout leather ferns on their trunks. You pass the first redwoods since near the trailhead.

Just before a ford at 2⅞ miles, the trail has slid out, forcing a detour uphill. Ford to the north bank where wild grape grows and traverse a lovely glade with blue-eyed Mary, white iris and western bistort. Cross a rocky tributary at 3 miles, then ford Gilliam Creek below a pleasant pool. Follow the south bank briefly, then ford the creek three more times in the next ⅛ mile. The last ford is beside a beautiful pool where the canyon turns steep.

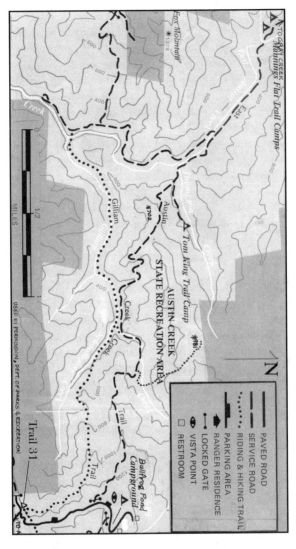

Your trail ascends steadily along sunny hillsides where lovely clarkia grow above the creek's dark canyon. You pass many fir stumps in an area once heavily logged. At 3⅜ miles you climb through a clearing where manzanita and coffee-berry compete with young firs. Your path contours high above the creek, then descends. Level again beyond 3½ miles, still 100 feet above Gilliam Creek.

Descend to the creek at 3¾ miles. Gilliam Creek Camp was once nearby, but it has been closed. In spring the blossoms of purple milkweed and golden fairy lantern brighten this pretty spot.

You have no way to go but up from this deep hole near the confluence of Gilliam and East Austin Creeks. Head west to a wet ford of East Austin Creek, where Sargent cypress, mimulus and valley lupine grow along the stream. After the ford your trail climbs to a broad fire road. Turn right and ascend gradually north following East Austin Creek upstream.

At 4 miles your road dips, descending near the creek, then climbs past the Fox Mountain Trail. Continue up canyon, winding with the creek, with occasional views of its pristine waters. The trail passes through mixed forest of fir, bay, canyon live oak, white oak and madrone with scattered woodwardia ferns, manzanita and toyon. Maidenhair fern, mint, watercress, yellow woodland madia, blue flax and crimson columbine line the road in spring.

At 4¼ miles an immense, decaying fir stump stands on your left, leather ferns and milkmaids growing beside it. At a big bend you cross a seasonal creek where it recently washed out the road. At 4⅜ miles you have grand views along the winding creek. I saw a herd of wild pigs in this area, retreating from the scent of a human. Climb over a rise at 4½ miles, then the grade eases. Look for the brodiaea called wally basket here in spring.

At 4¾ miles a large bay laurel overhangs the road. You climb high above East Austin Creek. Descend through a glade into forest. You soon have a view east up the canyon of Thompson Creek. Your path turns northwest above East Austin Creek, contouring through cool forest. At an unnamed tributary you cross a mudslide.

At 5⅛ miles you descend to a wet ford of the creek surrounded by large redwoods. As I forded the icy waters on a warm February day, a brown rock with black spots wriggled and moved out to the center of the creek. Two large steelhead were spawning, migrating to their birthplace upstream. Austin Creek is currently closed to fishing.

Across the creek you meet the East Austin Creek Trail. (If you turn right here, deduct 1⅜ miles from the total distance.) Our described route turns left. The road climbs gradually northwest up the broad canyon carved by East Austin Creek. Hardwoods and grasslands dominate the floor, while conifers mix with hardwoods on the slopes. Beyond 5⅜ miles the creek stays in view.

At 5⅝ miles you overlook the creek as creek, canyon and road bend left into undisturbed forest. Climb slightly, then descend to a ford at 5⅞ miles, where cypress, Douglas fir, willow, bay laurel and oak grow. Lower Mannings Flat Camp has nice sites nestled beneath trees on the west bank, overlooking the creek and a beautiful meadow with wildflowers in spring.

The road north leads in ⅛ mile to Upper Mannings Flat Camp, shaded by an immense white oak and an even bigger Douglas fir. The track crosses a creek in 250 feet, then continues north along East Austin Creek, passing Chinese houses on a rocky cutbank. Pond turtles and lilies reside along a broad, calm span of the stream.

A downed oak urges a detour right to creek side, where two-eyed violets inhabit a mossy bank. You begin to see mule ears and birchleaf California mountain mahogany.

Around ½ mile from the ford, the creek turns to sparkling whitewater over gray-green rock. A family of majestic redwoods rises from the bank. The track continues up the west bank another ¼ mile to a junction near the northern park boundary. The right fork there follows Gray Creek about ¾ mile to the park boundary.

Our loop hike retraces your steps down East Austin Creek, returning to the junction at 6½ miles. Go straight on the fire road. At 6⅝ miles you climb a slight hill. Soon the park's largest swimming hole snuggles in a bend of the creek. The waters are slowed by clusters of large, light-colored rocks, great for basking on a warm day.

The road descends from the knoll, returning to creek level, an 8-foot diameter redwood on the left. Honeysuckle, milkmaid and leather fern grow nearby. At 6⅞ miles you cross a bridge over Thompson Creek, overlooking its confluence with the larger stream. Just before the bridge, a spur on the right leads to another pristine swimming hole.

Your road climbs steeply away from East Austin Creek, overlooking the deep canyon of Thompson Creek. Swing right at 7 miles, then left to meet a spur on the left. The spur heads ¼ mile upstream to Tom King Camp in a pretty spot beside the creek.

On the main trail, take your time and enjoy the views on a steep ascent to the summit at 7½ miles. You rise through an oak-dappled glade where wally basket and ookow abound in spring. Then make a steady, winding descent through a glade to 8 miles, then along a tiny stream.

At 8⅛ miles you parallel Gilliam Creek. An easy ½ mile brings you to the lateral to the Gilliam Creek Trail. You can turn right and ascend to the trailhead by the same trail you came down. Our described route stays on the fire road to ascend Panorama Grade, a nice name for a 1000-foot climb with grand views. Backpackers climbing out have been known to call it faintly worse names. Bring on the horses!

Your steady ascent starts immediately, following Gilliam Creek as it tumbles on your left. At 8½ miles large twin redwoods stand beside the creek. Your road bends away from the creek at 8⅝ miles, climbing steeply. Your ascent eases briefly in a large glade around 8⅞ miles. You quickly resume your steep climb, overlooking Schoolhouse Creek Canyon. Take a break to enjoy the view.

Ascend into forest at 9⅜ miles, then return to rolling grasslands. At 9½ miles a footpath forks left, climbing to Bullfrog Pond Campground. Continue steeply up the dirt road to a gate near the Vista Point on the paved road at 9¾ miles.

Turn right and follow the road shoulder for ½ mile, contouring, then descending to a footpath on the right at 10¼ miles. Descend the path less than ⅛ mile to Gilliam Creek Trailhead and hike's end.

OTHER SUGGESTIONS: The road's right fork leads to a wonderful, wooded campground. A spur trail links the campground with the described loop. McCRAY MOUNTAIN TRAIL climbs from the campground to the flank of the 1940-foot-high peak. POOL RIDGE and EAST RIDGE TRAILS descend from near Gilliam Creek Trailhead into Armstrong Redwoods State Reserve.

32.

RIVERFRONT REGIONAL PARK
PONDS, BIRDS, PICNICS & FOREST AT OLD QUARRY SITE

Riverfront Park opened in early 2005 after the old gravel quarry site was purchased jointly by the Sonoma County Water Agency and the Sonoma County Agricultural Preservation and Open Space District. The property was owned, farmed and ranched by the Wilson family from the 1850s until the 1970s, when they sold it to a gravel mining company. The three manmade ponds, which cover one third of the property, were created after the pits from the gravel mining operations filled with water because of their proximity to the Russian River, on the property's west boundary. The 305-acre park offers trails past one quarry pond and circling another. The park's trail system will eventually be expanded to offer more hiking options, including access to the Russian River and a trail through marshlands.

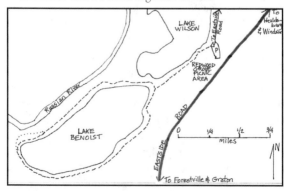

RIVERFRONT REGIONAL PARK:

DISTANCE: 2⅛-mile loop.

TIME: One or two hours.

TERRAIN: Mostly level path passes one lake and circles another through riparian habitat.

BEST TIME: Spring for wildflowers.

WARNINGS: No swimming allowed. Watch for poison oak. Park closes at sunset.

HOW TO GET THERE: Exit Highway 101 at Central Windsor exit (M,29.7 from north, M29.2 from south). Go west on Windsor River Road for 2.1 miles, then go left on Eastside Road for 1.8 miles and turn right to enter park.

FURTHER INFO: Sonoma County Parks (707)565-2041

FEE: $5/vehicle, day use.

The trail heads west from the trailhead parking area on a broad dirt road. On your left is a lovely forest of large redwoods that shade the park's picnic area. Oregon ash and California bay trees grow along the grove's perimeter.

As your broad, level track bends left, Lake Wilson is on your right. Beyond ¼ mile you come to Lake Benoist (pronounced Benwah) on your left. At 68 acres, Lake Benoist is nearly as large as Santa Rosa's Spring Lake. Go left to circle the lake in a clockwise direction. You pass popular fishing spots for both people and birds. Great blue herons build their penthouse nests in tall trees beside the ponds, providing ideal spots to survey the fish action below.

Lake Trail follows the shoreline past fennel, mugwort, wax myrtle, coyote brush, wild grape, red alder, Hinds walnut, coast live oak, California boxelder and its cousin, big leaf maple. Before ½ mile you cross a seasonal stream that flows into the lake. Beyond ⅝ mile redwoods grow on the right side of your path, between you and the lake. Watch also for poison oak, willow, mint, plus both native California and Himalaya blackberry vines.

At ¾ mile, native spicebush grows on the left at the base of a steep hill. Look for its red or pink blossoms, which have

137

a spicy scent, in late spring. Before ⅞ mile your trail crosses another small stream.

Around one mile, look northeast across the lake of a view of Mount St. Helena. Cross another stream flowing into the lake around 1⅛ miles. Soon soon come to the west shore of the lake which is much drier than the shaded east shore, with fewer kinds of plants. The next section of trail may flood at high water, but an alternate trail climbs around the low spot.

Climb a hill to 1⅜ miles where your trail merges with the high path. The Russian River lies not far to the west. Among the abundant willows grow elderberry, poison hemlock and wild rose. Around 1⅝ miles Lake Trail bends to the right. The closed area on the left may one day be added to the park's trail system. The Russian River flows by Lake Benoist within about ⅛ mile, but the area between has a dense tangle of plants.

At 1⅞ miles Lake Wilson appears on the left. You soon come to the end of the loop trail. Stay to the left, heading east to return to the parking lot at 2⅛ miles.

33.

RAGLE RANCH REGIONAL PARK
A COUNTRY FEELING IN A CITY PARK

Ragle Ranch Regional Park has a split personality. The lush green lawns of the eastern portion of the park have softball and soccer fields, a playground, picnic areas, a dog park and paved jogging and bike paths. But west of the manicured lawns lies the wild beauty of the park's natural side, where oak woodlands, creeks and wetlands support a diverse bird population and provide walker and equestrian with soothing country vistas.

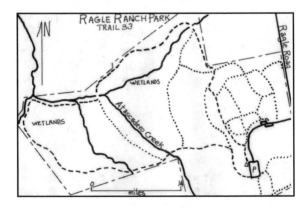

RAGLE RANCH REGIONAL PARK:

DISTANCE: 1⅝-mile loop.

TIME: One hour.

TERRAIN: Through oak woodlands, grasslands and
wetlands along several forks of Atascadero Creek.

BEST TIME: Spring for wildflowers, winter for birds.

WARNINGS: Trail will be wet in rainy season; waterproof
boots recommended.

HOW TO GET THERE: Take Highway 116 or 12 to
Sebastopol. From center of town, go west on Bodega
Highway for 1.1 miles, then go right on Ragle Road for
.5 mile to park entrance on left.

FEES: Day use: $5/vehicle.

FURTHER INFO: Sonoma County Parks (707) 565-2041.

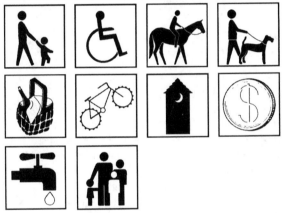

These 157 acres were once the ranch of the pioneer Ragle family, who came to Sebastopol in 1856. When the county parks department acquired the land in 1976, they had the foresight to leave most of the acreage in its natural state. Meanwhile, Sebastopol has grown to encompass the former ranch. A checklist of birds spotted in the park is posted near the entrance.

From the northwest corner of the parking area, walk north on the paved trail. After 200 feet, your trail veers left on a broad paved track. The pavement bends to head north at ⅛ mile.

Continue to a trail sign before ¼ mile. You walk through oak woodlands with a tangle of berry vines and willows, with an orchard on your right.

Before ⅜ mile you cross a bridge over a creek. Your trail swings left to follow the slow-moving creek southwest. Big Oregon oaks along the trail support the parasite mistletoe. Coast live oaks also grow here. Blue-eyed grass and dwarf brodiaea sparkle in the grasslands in spring. At ½ mile the creek fans out into wetlands on your left. White brodiaea and

139

wood rose grow on your right. Your trail passes a eucalyptus grove, then a vineyard beyond the park boundary.

At ⅝ mile you cross a bridge over Atascadero Creek. The trail forks, the left fork heading south up the creek. (If you take the left fork, you cut ½ mile off the total distance.) Take the right fork, following the creek downstream. Dense willows and berry thickets grow along the creek. You may also see poison hemlock. Scan the marshlands on the left for birds.

Ford a tributary before ¾ mile. The crossing can be wet in winter. Your trail bends right, returning to the banks of Atascadero Creek. The creek soon turns to leave the park.

Around ⅞ mile your trail turns left to follow the park's western boundary. This section of trail can be very wet in winter and spring. Scattered oaks line the trail until one mile, where you start a gradual climb beneath Oregon ash trees, still following the boundary. Soon your trail turns east. To the northeast Mount Saint Helena rises above the plain.

You descend slightly at 1⅛ miles, passing a bay laurel. An apple orchard grows beyond the fence on your right. You pass weeping willows at 1¼ miles. In 300 feet the Atascadero Creek trail merges from the left. You cross a bridge over the creek, then continue east. At 1⅜ miles you enter an area that is very muddy in the rainy season. Redwood timbers span some of the wet area. Then a bridge traverses the worst of the wetlands.

After crossing the fourth bridge, climb east through an old pear orchard at 1½ miles, heading toward a gazebo. At the top of the hill, pass through a gate to return to the city side of the park. The gazebo is straight ahead, but veer right to walk through a small community garden. The garden has been designated as a National Peace Site. A post has "May peace prevail in the world" written in four languages. Your starting/finishing point lies to the east.

OTHER SUGGESTIONS: Many PAVED PATHS wind through the eastern part of the park, ideal for jogging and cycling. JOE RODOTA/WEST COUNTY TRAIL, offer 5 miles of level, paved trail along a former railway across the Laguna and through farmlands. The western trailhead is in Sebastopol on Petaluma Avenue between Fannan and Abbott Avenues. Eastern trailhead: turn south off Highway 12 at M.12.2 onto Merced Avenue, meet trail immediately, parking on right. The new LAGUNA DE SANTA ROSA LOOP explores the wetlands with a ½-mile all season trail which links with a 2-mile loop when the seasonal bridge is installed. Find it behind the Sebastopol Community Center on Morris Street off Highway 12 west of downtown.

34.

HELEN PUTNAM REGIONAL PARK
ROLLING OAK WOODLANDS AND GRASSLANDS

A maze of trails meanders all over the 216 acres of this pastoral park near the Sonoma-Marin County border. The park's steep, rolling grasslands and oak woodlands provide a pristine backdrop for an aerobic workout, whether you are a casual walker, a cyclist or a serious runner. One of the best things about these paths is that you can take a different route on the crisscrossing trails every time you visit, yet never fear getting lost. The marvelous views of the surrounding country-side from the steep hills and ridges provide an added bonus. Recently a short segment of the 400-mile Bay Area Ridge Trail has been designated in Putnam Regional Park. When the Ridge Trail is completed, hikers will be able to follow it along ridges through eight Bay Area counties.

From the parking lot, follow the paved service road beyond the gate. In 150 feet you come to restrooms and a park map. (The paved Ridge Trail on the right also goes to the pond, about ⅛ mile longer than the described route.) From the map and bulletin board, our described route goes right on the pavement for 50 feet, then veers left on the dirt version of Ridge Trail. Your dirt trail climbs moderately east and southeast into grassy pasture where previous grazing has denuded the land of many of its native plants.

141

HELEN PUTNAM REGIONAL PARK:

DISTANCE: 2-mile loop or 2⅞-mile loop.

TIME: One or two hours.

TERRAIN: Steep, rolling coastal hills.

ELEVATION GAIN/LOSS: 360 feet+/360 feet−.

BEST TIME: Spring for wildflowers. Clear day for views.

WARNINGS: Stay off adjacent private property. Park closes at sunset. Watch for poison oak.

HOW TO GET THERE: Exit Highway 101 at Washington Street (M.4.9 from north, M.4.6 from south) and go west to the center of town. Go left on Petaluma Blvd., then take first right. Take Western Avenue for 1.9 miles to Chileno Valley Road. Go left for .8 mile, then left into park.

FEES: Day use: $5/vehicle.

FURTHER INFO: Sonoma County Parks (707) 565-2041.

Before ⅛ mile your climb eases, overlooking gently rolling, grass-covered coastal hills with California poppy, rattlesnake grass, coyote brush and checker mallow. The hills, sprinkled with oaks, stretch in all directions—the classic Sonoma County rural landscape. Savannah Trail forks left but you climb gradually through open grasslands on Ridge Trail, a part of the Bay Area Ridge Trail (BART).

At ¼ mile your path levels overlooking a ranch just beyond the park boundary. An old ranch house and its outbuildings are clustered in the shelter of a canyon. Your trail quickly merges with a broader path on the right, then climbs to a pond, where a junction and rest bench are beside a wooden water tank. The narrow, steeper Cattail Trail goes around the pond's left side.

Turn right and cross the earthen dam of the pond to meet the paved Ridge Trail along the east shore. Go left on the pavement, climbing north. At ⅜ mile daffodils, a scrubby coast live oak and poppies grow between the trail and the pond while chamise grows on the right. Climb a bit farther to overlook healthy young oaks, the result of a native oak reforestation project.

You climb away from the pond. Beyond ½ mile the trail angles

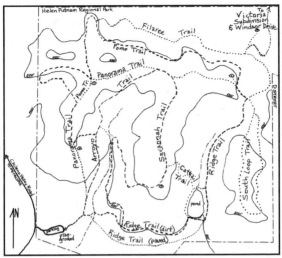

right. Many oaks grow along the park boundary on your right. You soon reach the top of the hill where you meet a knot of trails at a big junction. The paved Ridge Trail (BART) descends through the eastern part of the park, then descends to Victoria Subdivision, connecting with Oxford Court and Windsor Drive to town. On the right is South Loop Trail—mostly in the shade of oaks, but with views over Marin's rolling hills—which you can use to add ½ mile to the described hike. One redwood post on the left marks Panorama Trail. To its right is Pomo Trail. Follow narrow Pomo Trail north, climbing for 200 feet. It soon approaches the paved path, then veers left to follow the edge of oak woodlands where checker mallow and sun cups grow in spring. To the east you glimpse sprawling suburbia through the trees, rolling Sonoma hills beyond.

Your trail enters the oak forest, following the contour of a rolling hillside. Where a bench sits on the left at ¾ mile, the view reveals Mt. St. Helena to the north and Sonoma Mountain to the northeast. In the foreground, residential Petaluma reaches right to the park boundary.

Continue on Pomo Trail as it contours north. A large California buckeye stands on your left, with fragrant, showy flower spikes in late spring. Its chestnutlike fruit is inedible before leaching (like acorns). The Indians used the toxic nuts to stupefy fish, making them easier to catch.

Your trail rolls into the oak forest. Soap plants, brodiaea, Mariposa lily and profuse poison oak border the trail. You enter a grassy clearing, then return to the forest. Watch out for the low, spreading branches of the live oaks. The vines of hairy honeysuckle climb the trees along the trail. Annuals along the trail include milkmaids, vetch and buttercups.

At ⅞ mile your trail dips briefly, then climbs. Another view

143

opens to the north. On clear winter days you may see the steam plumes of The Geysers to the left of Mt. St. Helena. Between St. Helena and Sonoma Mountain is Bennett Mountain in Annadel State Park. All three peaks and the geysers are remnants of this area's volcanic past.

Your trail bends left through a glade surrounded by oak woodlands, where you meet the west end of Filaree Trail. Climb moderately on Pomo Trail, coming to its summit around 1⅛ mile. You meet a steep northeast slope where miners lettuce grows large along with bedstraw beside the trail.

Your level trail turns south, wandering through more beautiful oak woodlands. At 1¼ miles you climb to the junction with Panorama Trail, where a bench sits beneath live oaks with views over the western hills of Sonoma and Marin counties. Turn right to follow Panorama Trail, which climbs gradually, then levels on the ridge. At 1⅜ miles you meet the western park boundary, where your trail bends left and descends south, then east, then climbs southeast past godetia and yarrow.

Around 1½ miles you meet the west end of Pomo Trail. Turn right and climb gradually southwest. When you start to descend, you have an excellent view west. Your trail descends along the ridge to 1⅝ miles, where your path splits at a view-rich bench beside a live oak. The right fork provides the quickest return to the trailhead. Take the left fork, which makes a long bend left, then a gradual descent northeast into an oak-filled canyon.

At 1¾ miles you meet Arroyo Trail. For the shortest route, turn right and head south down the canyon, a long oak-filled gully. It descends to the trailhead at 2 miles.

To prolong your hike, turn left and climb north on Arroyo Trail. Continue straight at the next junction to ascend back to the ridgetop. When you reach Panorama Trail, turn right and follow it for 150 feet, then go right on Savannah Trail. It contours south along a ridgetop to 2 miles, then climbs to around 2⅛ miles, where you return to oak woodlands. After meeting the unmarked top end of Cattail Trail, climb briefly through grasslands with a view of the pond, then descend through oak woodlands.

By 2⅜ miles you leave the shade of oaks and pass a spur on the right that crosses a small bridge to meet Arroyo Trail. Continue straight, descending Savannah Trail. It continues down the oak-filled canyon on occasionally rough tread.

Beyond 2½ miles the creek swings to the west and drops away. You burst into grasslands with a vista over the parking lot to rolling hills. From 2⅝ miles you wind left through a gully on a steady descent. When Savannah Trail ends at dirt Ridge Trail, turn right and retrace your route to the parking lot at 2⅞ miles.

144

EAST OF HIGHWAY 101

35.
CLOVERDALE RIVER PARK
PAVED PATH THROUGH RIPARIAN ZONE TO RIVER

Cloverdale not only has a new 73-acre county park, but that park also provides the only public land with access to the Russian River between Mendocino County and Healdsburg. Cloverdale River Park, which opened in 2001, has been great news for Cloverdale, which essentially re-created itself after the Highway 101 freeway bypassed the former highway bottleneck town. But the park was severely damaged during the Christmas-New Years storms of 2005-2006, with an acre of riverbank land in the park washed away, several hundred feet of fencing destroyed, about ⅛ mile of paved trail ruined, and the park's main parking lot and picnic area partially undermined by the floods. The havoc closed the park's northern section for six months, and while repairs have made the park usable at press time, estimates are that finishing repairs and restoring the land will cost $1.3 million.

If you want to use the picnic facilities or launch a canoe or kayak, you're probably better off driving into the northern entrance to the park and paying the day use fee. We describe River Trail from the park's south entrance because it was created with the Cloverdale community in mind.

From the south parking area, follow the First Street sidewalk east for 250 feet to the park entrance. Turn left and follow the paved path on the right as it descends north with a Russian River view. You pass a picnic table where an unmarked spur trail forks right to descend to the river.

Continue north on the main trail, passing a vault toilet, another picnic table and a bench. The paved track contours above the river and below a cliff where toyon and poison oak grow, passing wild grape, willow and various oaks.

At ¼ mile from the parking area, veer right to find the actual start of Mahkahmo Trail, which this description follows to its north end. Continue past madrone, cottonwood, walnut and fennel on your right, with Cloverdale's sewage treatment plant on your left.

From ½ mile your paved trail winds, descending to the river terrace where lush riverine woodlands grow. Look for Oregon ash, California bay and California boxelder among the dense tangle of greenery. Several volunteer paths on the right descend to the nearby river.

Cross a seasonal creek beyond ⅝ mile, then the larger Oat

CLOVERDALE RIVER PARK:

DISTANCE: 2¼ miles round trip.

TIME: One or two hours.

TERRAIN: Mostly level path follows the Russian River through riparian and riverine habitats.

BEST TIME: Spring for wildflowers.

WARNINGS: Watch for poison oak. Park closes at sunset.

HOW TO GET THERE: Exit Highway 101 at Central Cloverdale/Citrus Fair Drive exit (M.52.0 from north, M51.4 from south). Turn right on Citrus Fair Drive and go north to First Street downtown. Turn east on East First Street for .4 mile, then turn left just before Russian River bridge onto Crocker Road and park in one of the 10 designated, paved parking spots. Or, for picnic and other facilities in the main part of the park, exit Highway 101 at North Cloverdale/Highway 128 exit (M.53.4 from south), then turn right on McCray Road and go .8 mile to park entrance (fee charged).

FURTHER INFO: Sonoma County Parks (707)565-2041.

FEE: $5/vehicle, day use at north end. Free from south end.

Valley Creek on a sturdy bridge around ¾ mile. Mahkahmo Trail winds closer to the river. As you pass a small rock pile on your right, you near the river as it tumbles over a small rapid below, a very pretty spot.

Around ⅞ mile your trail exits the woods for a grassy clearing. Follow the trail upriver. Beyond one mile, several volunteer trails descend to the river. Your view suddenly expands to include a historic red water tower, the freeway, a sawmill and some houses, with a tall wooded ridge to the west towering over all. Mahkahmo Trail continues, swinging right to approach the Russian River again.

You come to a gate and the main part of the county park around 1⅛ miles, with the main parking lot just ahead. Continue past more picnic tables and a restroom.

On your right, you can find your way down to the river. I managed to follow its west shore upstream to about 1¼ miles, gaining a view of a larger rapid just upstream, backed by golden hills draped with dark green oaks. Ducks floated by while turkey vultures circled in their tottering flight overhead. A great blue heron perched beside the rapids looking for a fish. The rushing water and the dense riparian woodlands all around almost muted the city and freeway noise. In the coolest parts of the day, songbirds add their various melodies to the soothing sounds.

When you've had your fill, retrace your steps back through the gate and follow Mahkahmo Trail south through the woods to your starting point. Remember that the park closes at sunset.

36.

FOOTHILL REGIONAL PARK
PONDS & WILDFLOWERS GLIMMER IN OAK WOODLANDS

This addition to Sonoma County's excellent regional park system was dedicated in September 1990. Foothill Park's 211 acres were preserved in the nick of time, as the former farm town called Windsor boomed into a large bedroom community for nearby Santa Rosa. The park's mostly gentle trails explore the boundary where wild and rolling Sonoma hills meet the sea of suburbia so rapidly filling the once fertile Santa Rosa Plain. Three small lakes nestle in the canyons below the park's view-rich ridge lines, creating a haven for wildlife and walkers, and fishing opportunities for those with a license.

From the parking area, go through the main gate where Three Lakes Trail climbs east. Our described route returns by that trail, so veer left and go north on Westside Trail which ascends along the ridgetop, traversing grasslands where rattlesnake grass and soap plant grow beneath coast live oaks. In spring you will likely see the blooms of brodiaeas, mule ears, Mariposa lilies, sun cups, buttercups, yarrow, vetch and the delicate yellow owl's clover called butter and eggs.

Your path soon turns northwest, climbing past manzanita and poison oak. A small lake lies hidden in the canyon on your right. Pond A Trail descends to it. You reach the top of a hill around ¼ mile, where vistas open south over the Santa Rosa Plain, with the green belt anchored by Shiloh Ranch and Annadel parks to the southeast.

The trail veers right to contour east along the ridgetop. Bobcat Trail forks right at ⅜ mile. Continue on Westside Trail. Stay left at two forks before ½ mile and head northeast along the ridge on Oakwood Trail. You ascend a rocky hill with a glimpse of the park's largest lake to the south. Your

FOOTHILL REGIONAL PARK:

DISTANCE: 3-mile easy loop or steeper 2¾-mile loop with peak climb.
TERRAIN: Rolling hills of grasslands and oak woodlands.
ELEVATION GAIN/LOSS: 325 feet+/325 feet- for easy loop, 650 feet+/650 feet- for full hike.
BEST TIME: Spring for wildflowers.
WARNINGS: Watch for poison oak and rattlesnakes. Stay off adjacent private property. Yield to horses. No swimming or boating in the ponds. Park closes at sunset.
HOW TO GET THERE: Exit Highway 101 at Windsor (M.29.7 from north, M.29.2 from south). Go east on Lakewood Drive for .1 mile, then left on Brook Road South for .6 mile. Turn right on Foothill Drive., go .6 mile, then left on Hembree Lane .1 mile to park.
FEES: Day use: $5/vehicle.
FURTHER INFO: Sonoma County Parks (707) 565-2041.

path turns east at the top and contours through oak-dotted grasslands with abundant Douglas iris.

Around ⅝ mile you pass picnic tables as you begin to parallel the park's north boundary. The track turns narrow, descending beside cypress trees marking the property line. The wooden water bars crossing your path prevent erosion but create a hazard for mountain bikers. The terrain is steeper on this quiet side of the park where lupine join the wildflower array and black oaks rule the forest. Views expand toward the west and south. Miners lettuce thrives where your trail switchbacks sharply left and ascends briefly.

Descend north at one mile with views over the rolling, grassy hills beyond the park boundary. You descend gradually, then moderately by three more switchbacks.

You cross a gully at 1⅛ miles, then ascend moderately along the top edge of the gully's deepening canyon. Toyon beside the path presents drooping white flowers in July, bright red berries for Christmas. The native Pomo roasted the berries to make them palatable.

Contour south around 1¼ miles, soon meeting a junction

with Ravine Trail, which descends on the right. Contour south on Oakwood Trail, passing a lake on your left lying just beyond the park boundary. You soon turn southwest away from the lake on a gradual descent where madrones mingle with oaks.

Before 1½ miles a spur on your left leads 200 feet to two picnic tables in a pleasant spot overlooking Windsor and the wooded Russian River canyon beyond. Follow Oakwood Trail, descending northwest, then southwest along a ridgetop. By 1¾ miles it overlooks the large lake in the park's center on your right, then another small lake on your left.

The easiest trek follows Oakwood Trail as it descends to end at a junction with Three Lakes Trail beyond 1⅞ miles. Turn right to follow the broad path 1⅛ miles to the trailhead.

For a longer loop, our revised description climbs southeast on Alta Vista Trail. Follow a power line past larkspur, blue-eyed grass and Mariposa lily. Shards of chipped obsidian indicate traditional Pomo presence around the park; please leave them in place. At 1¾ miles you reach the park's highest point, a 600-foot-high hilltop in the extreme southeast corner of the park.

From this high knob surrounded by black oaks and buckeyes, you have the best view yet over the Santa Rosa Plain and west over the wooded Russian River Canyon. If you look east-southeast beyond the nearby fence, Hood Mountain's craggy face rises above the Valley of the Moon.

Descend north-northwest along an oak-shaded ridge with views on the left. Descend steeply to a junction with Soap Plant Trail on the right before 2⅛ miles, then descend moderately through grasslands to soon meet the junction with Three Lakes Trail. Follow it west along the park boundary, soon passing along the south shore of Pond C. After you cross the spillway of the rather barren pond, climb to meet Oakwood

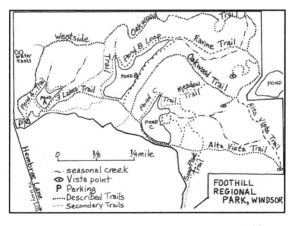

Trail on the right. Continue along Three Lakes Trail, passing Pond B and climbing over a small ridge to the junction with Westside Trail, before descending past Pond A to return to the trailhead and parking lot at 2¾ miles.

37.

SHILOH RANCH REGIONAL PARK

LITTLE SLICE OF WILDERNESS IN WINDSOR HILLS

Shiloh Park, dedicated in March 1990, shelters 850 acres of steeply rolling oak woodlands. The wild park is home or feeding ground to black-tailed deer, bobcats, mountain lions, gray foxes, coyotes, wild pigs and rattlesnakes. Many raptors hunt here, especially red-tailed hawks and kestrels. Please leave your dog home because of the wildlife. The county eventually plans to extend the park boundary east to Mark West Creek. In the meantime, new trails built here recently expand the options, allowing for a an easier, more diverse hike. This description explores both the new Canyon Trail and the park's newest trail, Creekside Trail.

Take Big Leaf Trail heading northeast opposite the park entrance, climbing a grassy hill for 250 feet to a fork. The left fork connects with your return trail. Go right, climbing southeast through oak woodlands, mostly coast live oak with scattered madrones and manzanitas. The understory is dense with poison oak and sticky monkeyflower.

Ascend gradually through woodlands with scattered grasslands where many wildflowers grow in spring. You may see blue dicks, poppies, blue lupines, blue-eyed grass and buttercups in the first ⅛ mile. Then look for elegant brodiaea growing in a shady spot on the left.

Your trail stays mostly level to ⅜ mile. On your right you overlook acres of vineyards crowded by a residential neighborhood. Pass a water tank at the top of a vineyard as you begin climbing gradually southeast along the park boundary. Your trail turns away from the boundary to climb east into woodlands. You are soon in the shade of young Douglas firs, the understory dense with soap plants, poison oak, wood strawberries, hairy honeysuckle vines and young maples. Descend briefly, then resume a gentle climb paralleling a redwood split-rail picket fence.

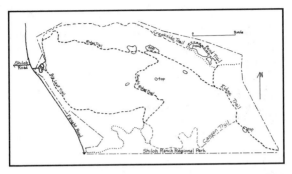

Your ascent steepens around ⅝ mile, passing morning glory vines and bracken ferns. You meet a gulch at ¾ mile, then switchback right to cross it. Maidenhair ferns grow on your left. Stay to the right and contour briefly before resuming a gentle ascent. Climb through a glade with more brodiaea, blue-eyed grass and buttercups.

Big Leaf Trail ends beside a rest bench before one mile as you meet South Ridge Trail. (A right turn, descends to Faught Road.) Go left, climbing northeast, then southeast to a junction where the spur on the right is closed by a huge washout. Continue northeast for 150 feet to meet Canyon Trail. (You can continue up South Ridge Trail, as our original description did, for a steeper hike.)

Climb briefly south on broad Canyon Trail, then descend along a grassy ridge with views across the park on your left and across the Santa Rosa Plain on your right. From 1⅛ miles you descend gradually east.

Around 1¼ miles your descent turns moderate, soon encountering a rutted and water-barred hill. Swing left and descend to cross two forks of a canyon beyond 1⅜ miles, then contour east before climbing to cross another canyon where toyon and soap plant grow beneath oaks and madrone. Canyon Trail continues as a narrow track, generally contouring along a south slope.

Come to an unmarked junction beside a lichen-encrusted manzanita before 1⅝ miles. Stay right to soon switchback left, descending to another finger of the canyon. Climb steeply out of the canyon, then gradually north across wildflower-dappled grasslands beneath oaks, following the canyon upstream. Bend right to ascend steeply east before 1⅞ miles, veering away from the canyon.

By 2 miles your ascent eases, climbing to Canyon Trail's end at Ridge Trail in 400 feet. A right turn ascends to the park boundary in ¼ mile (½ mile round trip). Our described loop turns left to contour generally north, then bends left and descends to the junction with Pond Trail just beyond 2¼ miles.

SHILOH RANCH REGIONAL PARK:

DISTANCE: 3¾-mile loop, 4¼ miles with side trip to east ridge.

TIME: Two or three hours.

TERRAIN: Alternating steep and gradual climb to ridge, then descend to ponds and down canyon.

ELEVATION GAIN/LOSS: Full hike: 840 feet+/840 feet-. Short loop: 520 feet+/520 feet-.

BEST TIME: Spring for wildflowers. Early or late in day for wildlife.

WARNINGS: Watch for poison oak, ticks and rattlesnakes. Stay off adjacent private property. Park closes at sunset.

HOW TO GET THERE: Exit Highway 101 onto Shiloh Road (M.27.9 from north, M.27.4 from south). Go 1.5 miles east to end of Shiloh Road, then go right on Faught Road for .1 mile to park entrance on left.

FEES: Day use: $5/vehicle.

FURTHER INFO: Sonoma County Parks (707) 565-2041.

Go right, descending a dirt road to a fence line with a now missing gate. Veer left on a grassy path that soon comes to a pond at 2½ miles, where a picnic table overlooks the placid scene. The ponds (no swimming or wading), somewhat bare except for a few willows along the bank, are in a pretty spot rimmed with grassy hills. In spring it is a little green valley (golden by summer) where blue dicks, blue-eyed grass, yarrow and sun cups sparkle in the grass and hawks and buzzards soar.

Pond Trail continues to the right of the pond, passing a rest bench on the earthen dam. Continue across the dam to a junction with the new Creekside Trail. A left turn here follows the south shore of the ponds, then returns quickly to Ridge Trail.

Our described loop heads west on Creekside Trail from the junction near the dam, following the canyon's shady south slope beneath oaks. Descend sporadically from 2¾ miles. By 2⅞ miles your descent begins in earnest as your trail stays near the creek. Lush moss and ferns thrive beneath the oaks,

152

draped in old man's beard lichen. Soon bay laurels, madrones, and abundant young Douglas firs join the forest. Continue a gradual descent, passing a seat carved from a stump.

Beyond 3⅛ miles, the creek descends more quickly than the gradually descending trail. Birds here often sing their appreciation of the quiet green forest. By 3¼ miles, the shady descent turns moderate. By 3⅜ miles the canyon opens up, with more gradual slopes. Descend to a bridge across a narrow side canyon, then contour along the slope before climbing to trail's end and a junction with Ridge Trail. Turn right and descend, crossing a rocky gully. Your track soon forks. Go left for ⅛ mile, then watch on your right for a short path to the trailhead and parking lot at 3¾ miles.

38.

MOUNT SAINT HELENA
ROBERT LOUIS STEVENSON'S "SPYGLASS HILL"

Mount Saint Helena towers over the rolling hills and valleys of northern Sonoma County. At 4339 feet, the rugged peak serves as a landmark from the Bay Area to Mendocino County. The mountain was in the territory of the Wappo, a tribe who called themselves "woods people" and resisted attempts by Spanish missionaries to include them in mission life. The natives hallowed the mountain, going to its top for days to fast and pray, waiting for a song from its deity.

Composed of ancient lava, the mountain was formed by folding and uplifting of the earth's crust rather than as a volcanic cone. The peak and the rugged Palisades to the south form an igneous rock island distinct from the surrounding sedimentary rock and the much younger Clear Lake volcanic region to the north.

In 1841 Russians from Fort Ross scaled the summit, planting a cross and naming the peak for the empress of Russia. In 1872 the discovery of a quartz vein rich with silver launched a mining boom here. By 1874 Silverado City, on a flat near the present highway's summit, had 1500 residents. Only a year later boom turned to bust, the rich vein cut off by a fault and never relocated. Most of the buildings were hauled off to other mines in the area.

By 1868 the Lawley Toll Road crossed the flank of the mountain. A stagecoach transported vacationers to Lake County resorts and supplies to quicksilver mines. Black Bart and other highwaymen often robbed the stage of its mining payrolls, escaping into the surrounding wilderness. The Toll House Hotel stood at the road's summit, providing refreshments and shelter for weary travelers.

In May of 1880 Robert Louis Stevenson, on tour from his native Scotland, came to the ghost town of Silverado with his new bride, seeking a dry, healthy climate to recuperate from tuberculosis. They spent two idyllic months in an abandoned bunkhouse on the flank of the mountain. After leaving, Stevenson wrote numerous articles about the region, including The Silverado Squatters. *The mountain made a lasting impression on Stevenson during his brief stay. He called it Spyglass Hill in his most famous work* Treasure Island.

Her great bald summit, clear of trees and pasture, a
cairn of quartz and cinnabar, rejected kinship with
the dark and shaggy wilderness of lesser hilltops.

Robert Louis Stevenson State Park today consists of 5272 acres on all sides of the mountain. Other than the trail, the park is undeveloped. It is open during daylight hours.

From the parking area on the west side of the summit of Highway 29, the unmarked trail climbs twelve steps, then turns northwest. After 200 feet, you reach a level clearing, the site of the Toll House Hotel. Picnic tables mark the spot today. You can see the old stage road descending north.

Just west of the flat, a sign marks the mountain trail. You climb into a forest of Douglas fir, tanoak, canyon live oak, black oak, bay laurel, madrone and big leaf maple. In spring you may see the white flowers of dogwood trees near the start

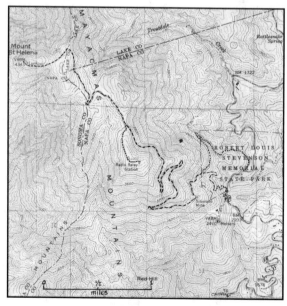

DISTANCE: 10 miles round trip to summit, 1½ miles
round trip to Stevenson Memorial.

TIME: Four hours to all day.

TERRAIN: Steady climb through forest and chaparral to
the top of Sonoma County's highest peak.

ELEVATION GAIN/LOSS: 2400 feet+/2400 feet−.

BEST TIME: A clear day in spring, fall or winter.

WARNINGS: South-facing trail very hot in summer. No
water on trail. Watch for rattlesnakes and ticks.

HOW TO GET THERE: Go east to Calistoga (via Highway 128, Mark West Springs Road or Calistoga Road).
From Calistoga, take Highway 29 north for 7 winding
miles to parking area at summit, M.45.43.

FURTHER INFO: Napa State Parks (707) 942-4575.

of your climb. Other understory plants include hazel, wood
rose, California nutmeg and hairy honeysuckle.

Beyond ⅛ mile your trail bends left, the first of many
switchbacks. You reach the next switchback at ¼ mile. Then
your climb eases a bit. Two more switchbacks bring you to
⅜ mile, where the trail gets rockier.

You switch left, then right to ½ mile, then climb north as
the forest thins to reveal views of the rugged countryside.
The habitat becomes drier as manzanita and knobcone pine
appear along the trail. Now you switchback more frequently,
climbing steadily. Soon the trail bends right and descends
briefly, passing left of a rock outcrop.

At ¾ mile you come to the Robert Louis Stevenson Memorial. The plaque sits in a shady flat between two rocky
ridges, marking the site of the three-story bunkhouse where
the Stevensons sojourned in June and July of 1880. Although
little sunlight reaches the spot today, Stevenson's writings
indicate that it was sunnier then. A spur on the left climbs
toward the old mine.

The main trail climbs briefly, then switchbacks right and
climbs steeply. You soon gain a ridge with views north into
Lake County and west toward the bulk of the mountain. Your
trail climbs steeply to a broad gravel road at ⅞ mile. Turn
left onto the road, your route to the summit.

From here it is 4⅛ miles to the North (main) Peak, about
3 miles to South Peak. The nature of the hike changes radi-
cally. You exchange the intimacy and the steepness of the

trail for the broad views and easy grade of the road. The road climbs west, then south. At one mile you overlook the deep, shady canyon that holds the Silverado mine and the site of the Stevenson cabin. In 400 feet you round a big bend, revealing views south into the Napa Valley.

The road turns right and climbs southwest through chaparral with scattered knobcone pines. As you climb gradually along the peak's south face, notice that bay laurel is a prominent member of the chaparral plant community.

At 1½ miles you approach the first big switchback to the right. A few gray pines tower above the road and surrounding brush. These pines with long, gray-green needles, have large cones that produce delicious nuts. The road switchbacks below large, igneous Bubble Rock and climbs east. Knobcone pine and manzanita dominate the chaparral, which also includes blueblossom, whitethorn and creeping ceanothus, canyon live oak and Douglas fir.

At 1⅞ miles your route turns northwest. Your steady, easy climb rounds a big switchback left at 2¼ miles, where you can see 7056-foot Snow Mountain to the north. You head south for ⅛ mile before switchbacking right and heading north, a large rock outcrop above on your left.

At 2⅞ miles your road passes under power lines and continues its winding path. Beyond 3 miles, the road bends left and climbs for ½ mile to meet South Peak Trail. The spur climbs ⅜ mile to the 4003-foot lesser summit.

The route to the main peak heads north. At 3⅝ miles the

chaparral consists of dense chinquapin and scattered coffeeberry bushes. Descend slightly for ¼ mile, then climb.

At 4 miles you round a switchback where the road gains the main ridge of the mountain. You are in Napa County, climbing northeast with the Sonoma County line on the ridge to your left. Beyond 4⅛ miles you make the steepest climb yet.

Pass under the power lines again at 4⅜ miles as your climb eases. Fir and nutmeg are the dominant species here. You soon gain a ridge where your route turns sharply left to enter Sonoma County. You head west, the main peak visible ahead. Sugar pines appear along the route.

The road passes through a forest of large Douglas firs and sugar pines. At 4⅝ miles you leave the forest and begin the final climb to the peak. The generator of a television station on your right makes a terrible racket. You reach the top of the world just short of 5 miles from the trailhead.

Although the generator detracts from the wilderness feeling at the summit, you can escape it by walking a few paces down the rock shelves of the Giant's Causeway on the north face. You overlook many miles of wild Coast Ranges. To the north, Anthony Peak and Snow Mountain rise prominently in the Yolla Bollys. To their left, Mt. Konocti hides Clear Lake from view, Cobb Mountain and the Geysers mark the northern Mayacmas Range, and Lake Sonoma nestles in hills beyond Alexander Valley, the Pacific Ocean near Gualala beyond. If the day is clear enough, you see Mt. Shasta nearly 200 miles north-northeast, with Lassen Peak to its right. Pyramid Peak in Desolation Wilderness and the high country north of Yosemite are to the east.

As you retrace your steps south on the trail from the summit, the whole North Bay Area sprawls before you. Santa Rosa is due south, with Sonoma Mountain, San Francisco and the Bay, Carquinez Straits and Mt. Diablo to the left. Point Reyes and the Farallon Islands are south-southwest. You may see these landmarks even more clearly if you take the side trip to South Peak. You will find that the descent takes about half as long as your trip up.

OTHER SUGGESTIONS: The pleasant campground at Bothe-Napa Valley State Park provides a good staging point for hikers who live outside the area. You may also stay at one of the hot springs resorts in Calistoga, where you can soak your weary muscles after a trip to the peak. THE SILVERADO MUSEUM in Saint Helena provides more information about Stevenson's stay in the area. PALISADES TRAIL east of the summit descends 8⅛ spectacular miles below the Palisades to meet OAT HILL MINE TRAIL (starts at junction of Highway 29 and Silverado Trail) which also provides a great hike. For details, see Ken Stanton's *Great Day Hikes in & around Napa Valley*.

157

39

RITCHEY CANYON
REDWOOD CREEK CANYON TO OLD HOMESTEAD

Bothe-Napa Valley State Park lies in a side canyon at the northern end of the Napa Valley. The park's 2000 acres reach west up the canyons of Ritchey and Mill Creeks, sheltering some cool stands of coast redwoods. The park's attractive campground rambles through mixed conifer forest and blue oak woodland overlooking the second growth redwoods of Ritchey Creek.

This area was originally home to the Wappo tribe. In the early 1870s, the socially prominent Hitchcock family of San Francisco acquired these lands as a country retreat. They dubbed it "Lonely." Their daughter, Lillie Hitchcock Coit, came here to rest when she wasn't stirring controversy. An early feminist, Lillie challenged social standards by riding horses astride and forcing her way into an exclusive San Francisco men's club.

From the horse trailer parking area just beyond the campground turnoff, take the dirt path heading west beneath oaks, madrones, big leaf maples and Douglas firs. In 200 feet your trail crosses a paved path and parallels the road. Before ⅛ mile the trail veers left to follow Ritchey Creek behind a park residence. You merge with a broad path and continue up the creek, passing redwoods and firs to four feet in diameter. Hazel, wood rose, snowberry, trail plant, ferns, bay laurel, poison oak and wild grape tangle in the understory.

At ¼ mile pass a drinking fountain and ascend gradually along the creek. Soon a small waterfall tumbles over a concrete dam. The next section of trail suffered much storm damage in a recent winter. At ½ mile a fork on the right leads to the campground and Ritchey Canyon Trail on the north side of the creek. Continue straight on Redwood Trail, climbing southwest.

Your trail levels briefly beside a five-foot-diameter Douglas fir on the left. Examine its trunk to see conks, the fruiting bodies of a parasitic fungus that decays the tree from within. Resume your climb through the forest.

Redwoods become sparse at ⅝ mile, where you pass a fire-scarred fir. California buckeye grows nearby. At the top of a moderately steep hill at ¾ mile, the forest thins as annual grasses, iris and manzanitas encroach. Before ⅞ mile you top another hill and meet Coyote Peak Trail on the left. Mule

RITCHEY CANYON:

DISTANCE: 3½ miles round trip to cascade, 6½ miles to homestead. Add ¾ mile to climb Coyote Peak.

TIME: Two hours for cascade, four for homestead.

TERRAIN: Lush, gentle lower canyon leading to steeper upper canyon, homestead site and views of Napa Valley.

ELEVATION GAIN/LOSS: Cascade: 450 feet+/450 feet-. Homestead site: 1200 feet+/1200 feet-. Coyote Peak: add 500 feet+/500 feet-.

BEST TIME: Spring. Late summer or early fall next best.

WARNINGS: Poison oak is prevalent in the park. Rattlesnakes, ticks, scorpions live here.

HOW TO GET THERE: Park is west of Highway 29, 4 miles north of St. Helena, 5 miles south of Calistoga. Turn west at M.33.47 (Napa). Go past entrance station and Visitor Center, then continue straight .2 mile to trailhead.

FEES: Day use: $6/vehicle. Camping: $25/night.

FURTHER INFO: Bothe-Napa State Park (707) 942-4575.

ears grow at the junction. The site of the Hitchcock family's Lonely lies north of the junction.

Your trail continues on the right, passing purple larkspurs in spring and descending briefly before climbing into dense mixed forest. You pass a lateral (seasonal bridge) to Ritchey Canyon Trail north of the creek. (Equestrians and cyclists must turn right.) Hikers continue up canyon on Redwood Trail. Before one mile dogwoods grow on the left, presenting white flowers in spring and red leaves in fall.

Descend briefly, passing a circle of redwoods with two of the biggest trees to this point along the trail. A six-foot-diameter fir grows just beyond. You pass more big redwoods and firs to 1⅛ mile. Then the forest thins as you ascend along the creek. Near 1¼ miles a grove of young redwoods grows between trail and creek, a nice blanket-picnic spot on warm days. Star Solomon's seal carpets the ground around the grove. The canyon narrows as your trail steepens, hugging the hillside above the creek.

You return to creek side, cross a recent slide, then pass woodwardia ferns at 1⅜ miles. In 250 feet you reach a ford where you may be turned back at high water (winter and early spring). The ford is usually easy, so let's assume you made it. On the north side of the creek you meet the Spring and Upper Ritchey Canyon Trails. You can turn right to return down the north side of the creek for the easiest loop (3 miles). The greatest rewards lie ahead. Equestrians must go left to recross the creek and follow Spring Trail.

Hikers go straight on Upper Ritchey Canyon Trail to reach the cascade. Climb moderately to 1⅝ miles, where you're 100 feet above the creek. Thimbleberry mixes with the other understory plants. Your trail soon descends, coming to the gently cascading creek by 1¾ miles. Ford the creek again where elk clover grows, then ascend to cross a side stream cascading over mossy rocks. Trilliums and honeysuckle thrive in the moist air along with maidenhair and woodwardia ferns.

Your path climbs a steep hill, then ascends moderately up the canyon. At 1⅞ miles you cross another seasonal cascade with a redwood hanging over it. Ascend steeply, then wind away from Ritchey Canyon, climbing south to 2 miles. Your ascent eases, passing toyon and star lily, then ends at a junction around 2⅛ miles.

From here you can return the way you came for a 4¼-mile hike. Or you can ascend southeast, returning via Spring Trail (and South Fork and Coyote Peak trails if you wish) for a longer, steeper loop. Our described hike goes right on Upper Ritchey Canyon Trail. It contours west up the canyon through tall chaparral to 2¼ miles.

Your path descends steeply, then gradually, returning to redwoods near the creek. Around 2⅜ miles you cross a rock-choked side stream. Big white alders and lush elk clover grow in the creek bed.

The trail climbs, then levels and winds through mixed scrub and redwood forest. Around 2½ miles redwoods grow to four feet in diameter. You ford another tributary and ascend gradually. At 2⅝ miles a redwood grove beside the creek provides another good picnic spot.

Then climb steeply for 300 feet to cross another side stream where woodwardia ferns and heart-shaped wild ginger grow. Your trail turns southwest, continuing its ascent. Beyond 2¾ miles the path levels, then fords another tributary. Ascend to drier habitat at 2⅞ miles, where you have a clear view of volcanic cliffs across the canyon to the northwest.

Continue a winding climb, conifer forest alternating with oak woodlands. Begin a long ascent on eroded tread at 3⅛ miles. You descend briefly, then climb again.

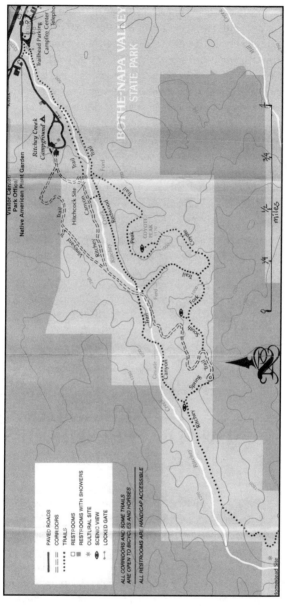

Just beyond 3¼ miles, the main trail veers left and climbs
south. Take the path that forks right. It descends to cross a
dilapidated bridge near a grassy clearing. In 100 feet you pass
a memorial stone beneath large redwoods. In another 75 feet
you reach a homestead site, a beautiful grassy clearing on
an east-facing slope, overlooking the redwood-filled canyon
of Ritchey Creek. Although no trace of a house remains,
many fruit trees grow in the clearing, as well as rose bushes,
grapevines and a walnut tree. Among the fruit trees are pear,

161

plum, fig, peach and at least three varieties of apple. Rocky volcanic cliffs rise above the brushy slope to the north.

Take a break to enjoy this idyllic spot, homesteaded by the Traverso family in 1884. If the fruits are ripe, pick yourself a snack. Otherwise leave the place as you find it. If you sit quietly listening to the birds singing, you may see deer, fox, coyote or other mammals crossing the clearing.

The main trail continues south for ¾ mile to the park boundary. I prefer to return from the homestead, perhaps taking a side trip on Spring Trail or to the top of Coyote Peak, each of which adds about ¾ mile to the total distance of 6½ miles. Or take Ritchey Canyon Trail east from the junction below the cascade, following the north side of the creek for a different perspective.

> **OTHER SUGGESTIONS:** HISTORY TRAIL starts at the end of the park road, passes a pioneer cemetery and climbs over a ridge to Bale Grist Mill, a partially restored 1846 flour mill (2.4 miles round trip). Ten pleasant WALK-IN CAMPS at the top end of the campground offer seclusion. You can arrange guided HORSEBACK TRAIL RIDES in the park by calling (707) 887-8700.

40.

SPRING LAKE/ LAKE RALPHINE LOOPS
GENTLE TRIPLE LOOP IN POPULAR PARKS

The 358 acres of Spring Lake Regional Park are bordered on three sides by city. On weekends and holidays these trails bustle with users young and old, with every kind of human-powered locomotion. But if you travel the park's trails during a quiet time, or camp there at night, you will find an expansive natural area snuggling in green hills where city noise intrudes very little. Spring Lake Park is bordered on the southwest by 152-acre Howarth City Park and on the northeast by 5200-acre Annadel State Park, forming an eight-mile-long natural refuge encircled by city. Spring Lake also offers non-motorized boating, fishing, and a swimming lagoon fed by warm springs.

The hike described here begins at the parking lot at Oak Knolls Picnic Area, near the Newanga Avenue entrance. You can walk into the park and join the loop at a dozen other locations. The described hike follows the mostly unpaved equestrian loop around Spring Lake, but you

can just as easily follow the paved bike/joggers path or mix portions of the two intertwining trails. Cyclists are asked to use the paved trails only.

From the north end of the parking lot, take the paved bike path north along the Spring Creek Diversion Channel for 400 feet, then go right on the paved path to cross the channel. Go right at the next fork to head northeast past the swimming lagoon. Buttercups and sun cups grow in the grasslands. Where the pavement ends, a dirt trail continues into oak woodlands, heading north. A dirt path with a bridge enters from the right, heading south.(Cyclists please stay on paved paths.) Hikers continue into oak woodlands on a broad gravel path. Soon, wooden steps on the right climb northeast to meet a dirt path at ¼ mile. Take the path as it generally contours north along a steep hillside, with filtered views of the swimming lagoon on your left.

Climb a short hill into oak woodlands. Your footpath parallels a broad path on your left. The forest is mostly coast live oak with bay laurel and buckeye. Soap plant and poison oak grow abundantly in the understory.

Your trail starts a series of short ups and downs, passing hairy honeysuckle and toyon. Continue on the high path, overlooking the swimming lagoon and the lake.

When your path forks, take the left fork (right fork to Shady Oak Picnic Area) and descend to cross a road around ⅜ mile (where a symbol indicates you are on the horse path). Head north toward the dam, passing fennel, coyote brush, berry vines and vetch. You overlook a cottonwood tree grow-

SPRING LAKE/LAKE RALPHINE LOOPS:

DISTANCE: 2¼-mile loop, 3¾-mile double loop or 6¼-mile triple loop.

TIME: One to three hours.

TERRAIN: Mostly level around Spring Lake, easy climb to Lake Ralphine.

BEST TIME: Spring for wildflowers, but nice anytime.

WARNINGS: You must yield to horses. Watch for poison oak.

HOW TO GET THERE: Exit Highway 101 onto Highway 12 West (M.20.05 from north, M.19.35 from south). In 2 miles go right on Hoen Avenue for 1.5 miles, then left on Newanga Avenue for .6 mile to park entrance. Then go right to parking.

FEES: Day use: $5/vehicle in off-season, $6 in summer. Car camping: $18/night (hot showers for campers!).

FURTHER INFO: Spring Lake Park (707) 539-8092.

ing on the left down by the paved path before ½ mile. Stay on the horse trail, soon descending with the Santa Rosa Creek Diversion Channel on your right.

You soon join the paved path, following it across an inlet of the lake at ⅝ mile. Then stay left on a paved path along the shore beside cottonwoods, alders and willows with scattered acacias and pines. Another paved path runs atop the dam on your right. Continue along the shore passing tules, horsetail ferns and yellow water iris. Before ¾ mile, near the end of the dam, hikers take the dirt trail that forks left along the shore. offering close-up views of Spring Lake and its bird life.

Beyond one mile a faint trail forks right to cross the paved path near a bench and climb northwest into woodlands. Go right to take the Howarth Park loop (continue straight to finish the loop around Spring Lake, as described at the end of this report). Beyond 1⅛ miles your dirt path descends to join a broader trail at a sign for Howarth Park (no horses), then climbs west up a rocky hill.

Your trail levels at 1¼ miles, then descends through oak woodlands. Beyond 1⅜ miles you pass houses on your right. Climb a short hill at 1½ miles then contour west.

After ascending another short hill at 1⅝ miles, the path winds through the woods. Another easy grade brings you to 1¾ miles, where you overlook Lake Ralphine through the trees on your left. Descend along a redwood fence, then past toyon and manzanita to a junction at 2 miles. Take the left fork, descending east on a narrow path to the dam of Lake Ralphine. Cross the dam, a popular fishing spot. Pass the boat house and come to the parking and picnic area around 2⅛ miles. Walk past the picnic area to a paved path with a park map beside it.

Take the paved trail northeast around Lake Ralphine, watching for ducks, geese and egrets that frequent the shore. In 300 feet go left on the dirt Fisherman's Trail paralleling the paved route. You follow a section of the long-distance Bay Area Ridge Trail (BART) for the rest of this hike. Pass through oak woodlands with scattered willows, manzanitas, bays and madrones. Snowberry, honeysuckle, toyon and

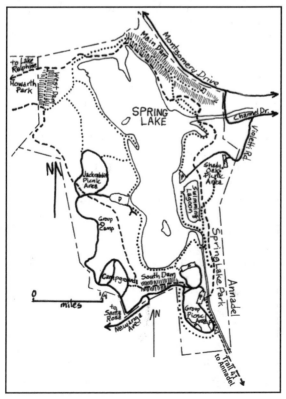

Scotch broom grow in the understory. Beyond 2⅜ miles firs and pines mix with the hardwoods.

At 2½ miles you reach the end of the lake. Eagle Scout Trail forks left to return to the dam, but stay to the right to join the paved path briefly, passing lush vegetation with poison oak, elderberry, vetch and mule ears. Our newly revised route soon forks right to climb southeast on the dirt tread of the BART (Bob Whiting Trail segment). Beyond 2⅝ miles your madrone-lined path levels, heading east-northeast. At 2¾ miles Whiting Trail ends at a paved path. Go right, ascending the pavement briefly to a junction just south of West Dam, where you meet Spring Lake dirt trail. (The junction where you left that trail is ¼ mile to the left.)

From the south end of the west dam, head south on the gravel horse path (still BART but not signed). At 2⅞ miles veer left, wrapping around giant water tanks past unsigned junctions until a trail sign before 3 miles indicates a right turn for BART. Follow BART, climbing south through open oak woodlands in rocky terrain.

At 3 miles your trail turns vague near a cinder block building. Follow the gravel road on the right for 200 feet, then veer right again on the signed horse trail (and BART) heading south. Parallel a fence briefly until 3⅛ miles, then wind southeast among oaks.

You cross a paved road and continue southeast on the dirt path through a rocky area. Your trail turns east briefly, then descends to merge with another path near Jackrabbit Picnic Area. You head east paralleling the paved road at 3¼ miles. Pass the boat ramp parking, then veer right to climb southeast, then descend south.

Around 3½ miles several paths fork right into the Group Camping Area. You continue on the horse loop passing poppies, lupine and blue-eyed grass. In 250 feet you reach the South Dam, where a fork on the right leads to Sonoma County Campground. Go left across the dam to complete your loop at 3¾ miles. You can extend your hike by walking the paved loop for another trip around Spring Lake. Or you can go south from the parking area to connect with Trail #41.

OTHER SUGGESTIONS: You can join the loop from the campground on a short trail from campsite #5, meeting the loop ¼ mile west of the trailhead. PRINCE MEMORIAL GREENWAY Multi-Use Trail follows Santa Rosa Creek west from downtown for about 7 miles, linking with Joe Rodota Trail. Get on PRINCE GREENWAY at Railroad Avenue off West Third Street where a bridge spans Santa Rosa Creek.

ANNADEL STATE PARK
INCLUDES THE NEXT FOUR TRAILS

Annadel is a wilderness refuge surrounded by city. The park offers 5200 acres of hills, creeks, woodlands and meadows reached by more than 40 miles of trails. You can fish at 26-acre Lake Ilsanjo and go birding at Ledson Marsh. More than 130 bird species visit the park. Annadel became a state park in 1971 after Sonoma County residents raised over a million dollars to match state and federal funding.

The park recently completed a five-year restoration, resulting in improvements to many trails and closures of others. Hike #41 changed the least, but most other trails in the park have been thoroughly reworked and rerouted, with many old fire roads being replaced by single-track trails. Many believe that the mountain bikers benefitted most from this restoration, but hikers and equestrians who venture out on all but the busiest days at Annadel will find their trail experiences here to have improved markedly.

The Southern Pomo and Southern Wappo tribes lived in the area around today's park. They and the Coast Miwoks, who lived just south, gathered obsidian and food in these rolling hills.

In 1837 the Mexican government gave sea captain John Wilson a land grant of 19,000 acres including these hills. Wilson, captain of the Ayacucho, *the ship made famous by the book* Two Years Before the Mast, *built a home at his Rancho Los Guilicos but seldom stayed there. William Hood owned the land from 1849 to the 1870s. Samuel Hutchinson acquired the land in the late 1870s. He established a home, farm and cobblestone quarry. He may have named the place "Annie's Dell" for his first daughter. In 1888 Southern Pacific named the train station near Hutchinson's home Annadel.*

In the 1930s Hutchinson's son sold the land to young entrepreneur Joe Coney, who used the land for ranching, farming and hunting into the 1960s. In 1956 Coney dammed Spring Creek, naming the resulting lake for his wife Ilsa and himself—Ilsanjo. Coney often invited the public, including area Boy Scouts and Girl Scouts, to his Annadel property.

The dozens of trails in the park interconnect, offering a maze of choices. The next four loops explore most of the trails and mention the others. But don't feel bound to limit your explorations to the described hikes. An 8½-mile stretch of the 400-mile Bay Area Ridge Trail traverses Annadel. All the trails offer abundant diversity of native plants and wilderness in the populated heart of Sonoma County.

41

ROUGH GO/CANYON/ SPRING CREEK LOOP

VIEW-LINED ROUTE TO LAKE ILSANJO

From the horse trailer parking area at the southeast corner of Spring Lake Park, head south on Spring Creek Trail, a broad gravel road behind the gate at the south end of the lot. Your road winds along channelized Spring Creek through grasslands. In ¼ mile the Stonehedge spur enters on the right. Continue along the road with city on the right, Spring Creek and the green or golden hills of Annadel on the left.

At ½ mile cross a bridge and meet a fork. Go left, climbing on Rough Go Trail. Climb steadily on the road's rocky tread. Coast live, black and Oregon oaks are scattered in the grasslands beside the path. Chinese houses, buttercups, blue-eyed grass and vetch grow on the shoulders. Pass several unmarked spurs. Please stay on named trails.

Your climbing road bends left at ¾ mile, then right at ⅞ mile. At one mile you pass big rocks on your steady climb. At 1⅜ miles, as the road makes a big bend left, you have views on the right of wooded Spring Creek Canyon. Your steady climb continues, passing Cobblestone Trail on the left around 1½ miles. Rough Go Trail ascends to meet Orchard Trail on the left at 1⅝ miles. (Both side trails descend to Channel Drive at the northwest corner of the park.)

Continue on mostly level Rough Go Trail. You soon overlook immense False Lake Meadow on your left. Then Mt. St. Helena rises beyond the meadow. Poppies, dwarf lupine and blue-eyed grass add color in spring.

At 1⅞ miles you meet a junction and a picnic table. On the left, Live Oak Trail descends to link with North Burma Trail. Continue on Rough Go Trail, which climbs south, then levels with views over a big meadow to Hood Mountain.

At 2 miles you start a gradual descent toward hidden Lake Ilsanjo. At 2⅜ miles your trail bends left and the 26-acre lake is suddenly before you. You may see ducks in the tules along the shore. Lake Ilsanjo is one of the most popular places in the park, offering picnic tables, toilets and fishing.

Walk 200 feet to find a picnic table overlooking the lake beside the dam across Spring Creek. Spring Creek Trail is on the right. It offers the shortest return, 2⅛ miles to the trailhead. Shadier than Rough Go or Canyon Trails, Spring Creek Trail is a good choice on a hot day.

ROUGH GO/CANYON/SPRING CREEK LOOP:

DISTANCE: 5½-mile loop.

TIME: Two or three hours.

TERRAIN: Level trail along creek, then climb to large meadows. Descend to Lake Ilsanjo, then climb and descend Canyon Trail to complete loop.

ELEVATION GAIN/LOSS: 700 feet+/700 feet–.

BEST TIME: Spring for wildflowers.

WARNINGS: Mountain bikers must yield to hikers and horses and announce presence when passing. Stay on marked trails. Watch for poison oak and rattlesnakes.

HOW TO GET THERE: Same as Trail #40.

FEES: Day use at Spring Lake: $6/vehicle in summer, $5/vehicle in off-season.

FURTHER INFO: Annadel State Park (707) 539-3911.

Our description follows Rough Go Trail across the dam, meeting Canyon Trail at 2⅝ miles. You can go left to connect with Trail #42, but the described hike turns right on Canyon Trail, climbing away from the lake and through a meadow.

At 2¾ miles your trail climbs gradually through grasslands and scattered oak woodlands with blue dicks, buttercups and blue-eyed grass. At 2⅞ miles the dirt road bends left and makes a winding descent into mixed forest with firs, oaks and bays. At 3 miles Hunter Spring is on the left. A sign says the water is unsafe to drink, but the flowing water feels cool and fresh on your face on a hot day. In the forest understory near the spring grow woodwardia ferns, hazel and coffeeberry. Your trail descends to meet Marsh Trail before 3⅛ miles. Marsh Trail climbs east, then meanders southeast to Ledson Marsh in 3⅜ miles. Both Marsh Trail and the part of Canyon Trail you follow from here are designated segments of Annadel's 8½-mile link in the Bay Area Ridge Trail.

Canyon Trail descends gradually with grand views, first north to Mt. St. Helena beyond the rolling hills of Annadel, then west to the Santa Rosa Plain, the Russian River and the hills toward the coast. Around 3½ miles you can see Spring Lake to the north.

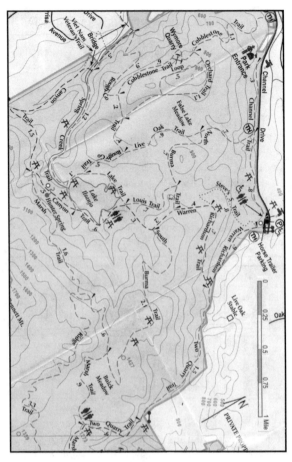

Poppies and dwarf lupine grow along the road.

At 3⅝ miles your descent steepens, then makes a big bend right, where elegant brodiaeas grow in spring. The descent eases around 4 miles, where you look east into Spring Creek Canyon. Then resume a steady descent through woodlands, crossing a small creek at 4¼ miles.

Your fire road climbs briefly, passing yarrow, soap plant, blue dick and blue-eyed grass. You soon descend again, the trail cooler now under oaks. At 4½ miles cross a bridge over the creek and meet Spring Creek Trail. Go left and descend gradually down the canyon. At 5 miles you close the loop, meeting Rough Go Trail on your right. Continue down Spring Creek Trail to the trailhead at 5½ miles.

OTHER SUGGESTION: You can join the loop at the ¼ mile-point from a no fee access off Stonehedge Road.

42

NORTH BURMA/LOUIS/CANYON/
MARSH/SOUTH BURMA LOOP
LONG LOOP THROUGH MEADOWS AND FORESTS

North Burma Trail climbs south beneath oaks, bays and madrones. Rocky single-track tread ascends along a seasonal creek on your left as Douglas firs start to mix with the hardwood forest. Beyond ⅛ mile mossy boulders and ferns thrive in the creekbed. Your trail bends left to cross the creek, then bends right to climb southwest along a ridge. By ⅜ mile your trail climbs west through mixed forest. Beyond ½ mile the ascent eases, paralleling the same seasonal creek. Around ⅝ mile North Burma Trail bends away from the creekbed.

You soon meet Live Oak Trail, which forks right to head south. (It climbs to meet Rough Go Trail in ⅞ mile.) Follow North Burma Trail as it makes a gentle, then a gradual ascent through mixed forest with scattered grasslands. Your climb eases beyond one mile, soon coming to a summit. Descend along a brushy slope, then along the border between brushy hardwood forest on your left and grasslands on the right with views west to the Santa Rosa Plain. Bennett Peak rises to the south, beyond the valley where Lake Ilsanjo hides. Around 1¼ miles North Burma Trail contours through hardwood forest, with a glimpse of Lake Ilsanjo to the south.

Before 1⅜ miles, turn right on Louis Trail to descend east (junction was unmarked when I hiked it in November 2005). It soon crosses a seasonal creek and contours south. Climb southeast around 1½ miles, then descend moderately on rough tread. The tread improves beyond 1⅝ miles (where you meet the old Steve's S route descending from left). Continue a winding, fitful descent through oak woodlands with a big meadow on your right. At 1⅞ miles your trail levels in the grassland.

At 2 miles Louis Trail ends at W.P. Richardson Trail, with a sign for Lake Ilsanjo just ahead. You can go either left or right around the lake. Our described route goes left around the lake on the broad Canyon Trail. Beyond 2⅛ miles a spur trail on the right loops quickly to the lakeshore. Stay on Canyon Trail, which before 2¼ miles meets the other end of the spur/loop, where you'll find picnic tables, horse ties, and an outhouse.

At 2½ miles Canyon Trail comes to a junction at the south end of the lake. Lake Trail is on the right. Turn left and climb south on Canyon Trail, a broad track that soon climbs gently southwest. Beyond 2⅝ miles you may hear Spring Creek on the right when it's flowing amply from the lake. Mount St. Helena rises beyond the lake. Beyond 2¾ miles Canyon Trail makes a winding descent through forest, passing Hunter Spring at 2⅞ miles.

Ascend to a junction at 3 miles, where the start of Marsh Trail is on the left. Turn left on the single-track Marsh Trail (also the Bay Area Ridge Trail) climbing moderately. The ascent eases around 3¼ miles, where you gain filtered views of Lake Ilsanjo with Mount St. Helena towering beyond. Make a winding climb through a gully at 3⅝ miles, then continue a moderate ascent.

Your climb eases at 3¾ miles, coming to a picnic table. These upper sections of Marsh Trail are graced by cool forests of mature hardwoods and Douglas firs with native bunch grasses liberally sprinkled through the understory, and punctuated by ferns and mossy rocks. Marsh Trail soon resumes a moderate ascent, winding through a gully at 3⅞ miles where oceanspray, also known as cream bush, and native bunch grasses thrive.

At 4 miles you climb along a lush gully where redwoods grow above the trail, then wind through the gully at a grove of redwoods. Continue through forest on Marsh Trail, winding through a larger grove of redwoods beyond 4⅛ miles. You also pass Douglas firs to four feet in diameter and some large madrones, with many trunks in this area scarred by fire.

Around 4¼ miles you pass the most redwoods yet along Marsh Trail, then wind through another gully. Then make a winding ascent into mature conifer forest surrounding a junction with Ridge Trail on the right. (BART leaves Marsh Trail here to climb along Ridge Trail, described in Trail #44.)

Continue southeast on Marsh Trail as it descends. At 4½ miles single track turns to double briefly at a rough sloughing spot. Marsh Trail ascends along the right edge of a larger canyon with abundant redwoods. Where you cross the canyon, redwoods grow to five feet diameter. Continue a winding, gradual ascent to 4⅝ miles, then generally contour to a junction beside Buick Meadow at 5 miles, where a rest bench overlooks the placid scene.

You go left on South Burma Trail, following the left edge of the big meadow. Around 5¼ miles your broad trail bends left to climb west. You soon overlook Buick Meadow, Sonoma Mountain and Bennett Peak. At 5½ miles your trail levels. Star lilies, blue dicks and elegant brodiaeas grow beneath manzanitas. Soon a dense carpet of fragrant Sonoma sage

DISTANCE: 8⅞-mile loop.

TIME: Three to five hours.

TERRAIN: Climb through forest, then descend through chaparral, grasslands and oak woodlands to lakeshore. Climb through forest, dense in places, then contour to Buick Meadow. Climb along a wildflower-dappled ridge, then descend through forest and grasslands before retracing your steps over the final summit to descend through forest.

ELEVATION GAIN/LOSS: 1280 feet+/1280 feet -.

BEST TIME: Spring for wildflowers.

WARNINGS: Watch for rattlesnakes, especially in warm weather. Watch for poison oak along trail. No fires or camping. Carry drinking water. Park closes at sunset. Hikers should watch for cyclists and equestrians. Cyclists should announce their presence when passing, slow to walking speed on blind corners.

HOW TO GET THERE: Turn south off Highway 12 at M.18.9 (3.9 miles from Highway 101) onto Mission Blvd. Go left at stoplight onto Montgomery Drive. Follow Montgomery for 1.5 miles, then turn right onto Channel Drive and follow it for 1.5 miles, where North Burma Trail is on right.

FEES: Day use: $4/vehicle at this entrance. Park map available for free near iron ranger.

FURTHER INFO: Annadel State Park (707) 539-3911.

grows along the trail. The sage has delicate purple flowers in spring. It grows in patches, this one covering about an acre. Amidst the sage is narrowleaf buckbrush, chamise and blueblossom, and hairy star tulips and scarlet fritillaries in spring. Before you leave the sage patch, a picnic table is on the right.

The main trail winds, levels, then descends rocky tread to 5¾ miles, where it contours along the ridgetop. South Burma Trail continues, making a winding descent through forest of Douglas firs with scattered oaks. By 5⅞ miles your descent steepens, soon coming to a picnic table in a shady spot, with Valley of the Moon visible far below. Descend steeply to 6 miles, then gradually through dense forest. By 6¼ miles the dense woods give way to open forest with a grassy understory. Continue winding down the ridge, then contouring along it to 6⅜ miles. Resume descending through forest, soon making a big bend right. At 6⅝ miles you ascend a small rise into dense forest, then resume your descent, following rough tread to South Burma Trail's end, meeting W.P. Richardson Trail at 7 miles.

Turn right on Richardson Trail, ascending the broad, eroded track through grasslands with scattered oaks, then contouring north. Suddenly the vista expands beyond Annadel's rolling, wooded hills to include the Santa Rosa Plain and the coastal hills beyond. When you reach a junction beyond 7⅛ miles (unsigned at press time), turn left on North Burma Trail. It descends gradually, dropping along the left edge of a sloping meadow, then bends left to descend through forest.

Return to North Burma's junction with Louis Trail at 7½ miles. Retrace your steps on North Burma Trail, climbing to the summit around 7⅞ miles, then descending to the trailhead at 8⅞ miles.

OTHER SUGGESTIONS: Many more trails traverse the wild, rolling hills of Annadel. Channel Drive offers three other choices. COBBLESTONE TRAIL, near park entrance, climbs 2 miles, meeting Orchard and Rough Go Trails. W. P. RICHARDSON TRAIL (bikes, horses OK) climbs 2½ miles to Lake Ilsanjo.

43.
STEVE'S S/SOUTH BURMA/ MARSH/TWO QUARRY LOOP
VARIED, WILDFLOWER-RICH LOOP

Take W. P. Richardson Trail, a broad road that climbs southeast through forest of Douglas firs and oaks. In 500 feet take the narrow Steve's S Trail on the right, which offers hikers solitude and a more direct (and steeper) route to Lake Ilsanjo. (Bikers and equestrians: use Richardson Trail.)

Hikers ascend steps and climb southwest through tall fir forest, with scattered spindly bay laurels. Understory plants include soap plant, hedge nettle and poison oak.

By ⅛ mile obsidian chips litter the ground. The Southern Pomo gathered obsidian here for arrowheads and spear points. It is illegal to take obsidian or plants from state park lands.

Climb steadily through the forest, crunching on obsidian chips. Your trail bends left, then right around ¼ mile. Pass bracken, maidenhair and wood ferns. At ⅜ mile snowberry (inedible white berries in summer), miners lettuce and sword ferns join the understory, soon followed by lady ferns, fat Solomon's seal, twisted stalk and wood rose.

At ½ mile you approach a ridge where many large firs grow. The tiny white flowers of woodland star grow from the duff. Your path soon levels, passing firs to five feet in diameter. At ⅝ mile many oaks and bays grow with the firs in mixed forest. The trail winds, then resumes its climb. Cross a seasonal creek, then bend left and climb to Steve's S Trail's end at Richardson Trail, where a picnic table sits beside the junction.

Turn right on Richardson Trail at ¾ mile, descending through forest to ⅞ mile, then gently climbing into grasslands with scattered oaks. Climb to meet North Burma Trail (see Trail #42) on your right beyond 1⅛ miles. Continue on the broad Richardson Trail as the verdant face of 1887-foot Bennett Mountain shimmers in the sun before you. Climb gradually, then descend briefly to meet South Burma Trail at 1⅜ miles. You can see nearby Lake Ilsanjo from the junction.

Turn left to climb east on South Burma Trail (signed no horses). Ascend gradually through forest on rutted, rocky tread to 1⅝ miles. Then your trail bends left and climbs on better tread through deep forest to the first summit. The trail bends right and descends briefly, then resumes climbing, gaining a wooded ridgetop around 2 miles. Climb fitfully along the ridgetop to 2⅛ miles, then moderately on a cool sidehill around 2¼ miles, passing raspberry before gaining a higher ridgetop with occasional views of Hood Mountain's craggy face across Valley of the Moon.

Pass a picnic table in a shady spot beside the trail at 2½ miles and continue climbing on occasionally rough tread. By 2⅝ miles you gain the higher ridgetop and follow it southeast, then south past sticky monkeyflower, ceanothus, coyote brush, madrone and manzanita. Dense patches of fragrant, low-growing Sonoma sage also thrive along the ridge.

Just beyond a high-point on the ridgetop at 2¾ miles, a shaded picnic table sits beneath a large Douglas fir on the left. Dip and rise to a third ridgetop summit at 2⅞ miles.

South Burma Trail begins its descent to Buick Meadow, soon visible below. Descend by rocky tread, making a big bend right beyond 3⅛ miles. Your trail soon levels in Buick

Meadow, where white and other brodiaeas grow in spring. South Burma Trail ends at the junction with Marsh Trail at 3⅜ miles.

Turn left on the shady, narrow Marsh Trail (open to mountain bikes) which contours south with Buick Meadow on the left. Climb slightly to ford a seasonal creek at 3⅝ miles. You soon begin a gentle descent, crossing another seasonal creek beyond 3¾ miles, where you leave fir forest for oak woodlands. Contour to 4 miles, then descend gently past raspberry patches.

Descend to the junction with Two Quarry Trail beyond 4¼ miles. You'll find an outhouse, two tables, and horse ties here beside an often wet ford of a seasonal creek. You can turn right here, continuing on Marsh Trail to reach Ledson Marsh (see Trail #44). Our described hike turns left on Two Quarry Trail to head northeast, climbing briefly before descending gently past another raspberry patch.

From 4½ miles Two Quarry Trail descends moderately through forest. After you pass a big slide around 4¾ miles, redwoods join the forest mix. Descend to a confusing junction at 4⅞ miles, the confusion due to the adjacent boundary with private property. A picnic table has pleasant views if you can ignore the nearby modern house.

Turn left to follow a narrow section of Two Quarry Trail.. It descends through a forest of Douglas firs, bays and oaks. You quickly come to a ford of the seasonal creek that flows from Buick Meadow. Redwoods grow to three feet in diameter here. Descend past California hazel, big leaf maple, variable-leaf snowberry and more raspberry, following the creek briefly before climbing a small rise to begin a steady descent.

STEVE'S S/SOUTH BURMA/MARSH/ TWO QUARRY LOOP:

DISTANCE: 7⅛-mile loop.

TIME: Three or four hours.

TERRAIN: Climb through forest, then contour through grasslands before climbing to flower-studded ridgetop. Descend to Marsh Trail and contour to Two Quarry Trail, which you ascend and descend past views, meadows and quarries.

ELEVATION GAIN/LOSS: Full loop: 1080 feet+/1080 feet−. Short loop: 480 feet+/480 feet−.

BEST TIME: Spring for wildflowers.

WARNINGS: Watch for rattlesnakes, especially in warm weather. Extensive poison oak along trail. No fires or camping. Carry drinking water. No bikes or horses allowed on Steve's S Trail. Park closes at sunset.

HOW TO GET THERE: Turn south off Highway 12 at M.18.9 (3.9 miles from Highway 101) onto Mission Blvd. Go left at stoplight onto Montgomery Drive. Follow Montgomery for 1.5 miles, then turn right onto Channel Drive and follow it for 2.3 miles to end. Trail is on right as you enter parking lot.

FEES: Day use: $4/vehicle at this entrance. Park map available for free near iron ranger.

FURTHER INFO: Annadel State Park (707) 539-3911.

Cross two small seasonal creeks before 5¼ miles, then break out into grasslands as the descent continues, the clearing offering a vista of Hood Mountain's craggy face. The steady descent continues on rocky tread in and out of the forest.

Pass the first of the quarries, where three adjacent sites on the left have been relieved of much rock. Continue a moderate descent on rocky tread, passing more borrow pits. Soon the trail bends left, descending past more quarry pits, with that seasonal creek again on your right. The descent soon turns gentle past oceanspray, crossing more seasonal tributaries.

Soon the main creek descends immediately on the right of your trail. It has many rocks, but little water except after storms. After crossing another rocky seasonal stream, the

177

trail bends to the left and the creekbed drops away. Smooth track contours through another gully, then climbs slightly to 6⅜ miles, crossing one more gully before ending at W.P. Richardson Trail. A picnic table and rest bench sit beside the junction.

Turn right and follow the broad Richardson Trail, descending gently along the edge of forest and grasslands, with a sweet rolling meadow on your right. By 6⅝ miles the descent increases to gradual as you leave the meadow behind. More obsidian chips sparkle on your path. Descend moderately by 6¾ miles. Beyond 7 miles you complete the loop, meeting the bottom of Steve's S Trail. Continue down the Richardson Trail to your trailhead at 7⅛ miles.

OTHER SUGGESTIONS: Many more trails traverse the wild, rolling hills of Annadel. Channel Drive offers three other choices. COBBLESTONE TRAIL, near park entrance, climbs 2 miles, meeting Orchard and Rough Go Trails. NORTH BURMA TRAIL, east of park office, climbs 1.7 miles to link with Live Oak, Louis, W. P. Richardson and South Burma Trails. W. P. RICHARDSON TRAIL (bikes, horses OK) climbs 2½ miles to Lake Ilsanjo.

44.

LAWNDALE/MARSH/ RIDGE LOOP
EXPLORING THE QUIET SIDE OF ANNADEL

It seems that the number of people you see on an excursion in Annadel State Park diminishes proportionate to the distance of the trailhead from Santa Rosa. So Schultz and Lawndale trailheads on the park's eastern edge provide seclusion as well as the shortest routes to Ledson Marsh, where dozens of bird species have been sighted. Lawndale Trail was changed dramatically in Annadel's recent trail restoration, becoming longer and more pleasant. The habitat along Lawndale also changed greatly because of the removal of the many invasive eucalyptus trees in this part of the park. The eastern trails are very close to Sugarloaf Ridge State Park, which has an excellent campground. Lawndale Trail and portions of Ridge and Marsh trails are now designated sections of the 400-mile Bay Area Ridge Trail.

Our first edition described Schultz Trail, but since parking is extremely limited at Schultz Trailhead, this loop through the eastern half of Annadel State Park starts out by ascending

LAWNDALE/MARSH/RIDGE LOOP:

DISTANCE: 5¾ miles round trip to marsh, 6¾ miles round trip to Trail #43, 11⅞-mile loop with Marsh and Ridge Trails.

TIME: Three to six hours.

TERRAIN: Easy climb through forest and meadows to Ledson Marsh. Easy climb on Marsh Trail. Easy climb along Ridge Trail to flank of Bennett Peak, then descend through forest and grasslands.

ELEVATION GAIN/LOSS: Full loop: 1350 feet+/1350 feet-, 900 feet+/900 feet- for short loop.

BEST TIME: Spring for wildflowers. Winter for best birding at marsh.

WARNINGS: Watch for poison oak and rattlesnakes. Carry water. Mountain bikers must slow to walking speed at blind corners, yield to horses. May be closed to bikes and horses in winter.

HOW TO GET THERE: Take Highway 12 east of Santa Rosa to M.25.6, where you turn south on Lawndale Road. Go 1.2 miles to Lawndale Trailhead.

FURTHER INFO: Annadel State Park (707) 539-3911.

Lawndale Trail. Mountain bikers might actually loop back on Schultz Trail. If you do, be sure to use extreme caution on the narrow, winding 1.4 miles of pavement between Schultz and Lawndale trailheads.

Starting near a pioneer home, Lawndale Trail climbs southwest behind a big green gate. Ascend moderately on a broad road lined with black oaks, California buckeyes, madrones and Douglas firs. Around ⅛ mile you climb through a rolling meadow where poison oak, blue-eyed grass, buttercup and woodland star abound.

Where your road bends left, you get a glimpse of the Valley of the Moon between you and Sugarloaf Ridge to the northeast. Ascend moderately through mixed forest where toyon, wood rose, honeysuckle, iris and hound's tongue grow in the understory. As your road switchbacks left, crossing a seasonal creek at ¼ mile, California hazel grows beneath a oak/Douglas fir canopy. You might see Chinese houses, yarrow, maidenhair fern and wood rose in the understory.

As you climb, look for oceanspray and big leaf maple. Soon fragrant mugwort lines the left shoulder. A clearing provides

179

a view of Mount Hood across the valley as your trail bends to the right around ½ mile, ascending moderately. Look for blue dicks in the grassy understory.

Continue your climb, leaving forest for grasslands with scattered oaks around ⅝ mile, with more views of Hood Mountain. After passing a picnic table and horse tether, your trail bends left, returning to forest by ¾ mile, where variable-leaf snowberry and lady ferns thrive in the understory. Douglas firs to four feet diameter dominate the forest around one mile, with abundant California bay, but you soon see the first redwoods on the hike. Bend right to cross a rocky seasonal creek around 1⅛ miles. Beyond 1¼ miles redwoods dominate the forest while hazel, twisted stalk, then bear grass join the understory. You pass beneath big power lines before 1½ miles, where your trail switchbacks left to climb moderately through forest. You might see mule ears and phlox. Around 1⅝ miles, brush replaces the forest. Look for sticky monkeyflowers, sun cups, shooting stars and poison oak. You approach power lines again, but your track bends left, returning to forest without crossing them. Douglas firs grow to six feet diameter here.

By 1¾ miles many fire-scarred redwoods grow below the trail on the left. Soon these young redwoods surround the trail. By

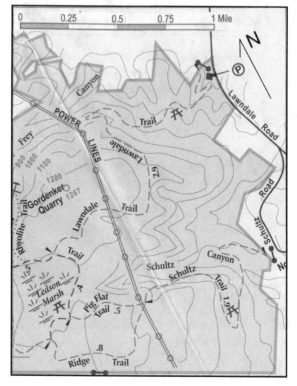

1⅞ miles the redwoods are no longer charred. Continue through forest where the redwoods give way to Douglas firs.

Around 2 miles your trail contours through forest as a canyon deepens on the left. Beyond 2¼ miles the forest parts for grasslands. Climb briefly around 2⅜ miles to cross under the power lines, where mule ears and blue-eyed grass grow beneath oaks and manzanitas. Come to an apparent junction, but it's only power line access. Continue straight on Lawndale Trail on a gentle climb through scattered forest and chaparral. Descend slightly on rocky tread from 2⅝ miles, meeting a junction with a hikers only trail at 2¾ miles.

Lawndale Trail soon ends as it meets Marsh Trail beyond 2⅞ miles. You can see Ledson Marsh from the junction. For the shortest option retrace your steps to complete a 5¾-mile hike. This description continues straight on Marsh Trail, following the marsh's shore. In the marsh, you may see ducks, grebes and other water-loving birds. Quail inhabit the surrounding forest and grasslands.

Continue along the shore of the marsh, passing the yellow flowers of poppy, sweet clover, tarweed and narrow-leaved mule ears. Marsh Trail meets hikers-only Rhyolite Trail on the right at 3⅛ miles. It no longer loops back to Lawndale Trail, but deadends before ½ mile. The northwest corner of Ledson Marsh is on your left. An interpretive sign explains how removal of non-native eucalyptus is saving the marsh and restoring the park's native habitats. Sonoma Mountain rises beyond the marsh.

Broad Marsh Trail continues northwest on a gentle climb, followed by a gentle descent around 3⅜ miles, where you cross the remains of an old stone wall. About 450 feet beyond, you ford a seasonal creek and reach the junction of Marsh Trail and Two Quarry Trail (see Trail #43), where two picnic table, horse tethers and an outhouse offer a break.

Go left to follow the restored, now narrow Marsh Trail, heading west on a gentle ascent through grasslands. Your trail soon bends right to ascend through forest where red larkspur and raspberries grow. By 3¾ miles Marsh Trail descends a bit, then contours with a big meadow on your left.Cross a seasonal creek before 4 miles, leaving the meadow to climb through forest. After a summit, a gentle descent brings you to a vista over vast Buick Meadow around 4¼ miles. Descend to a junction with South Burma Trail (see Trails #42 and 43) and a rest bench before 4⅜ miles.

Our described route continues on Marsh Trail on a gentle descent through forest to 4½ miles, then a gentle climb. Before 4⅞ miles you ford a seasonal creek where large redwoods grow, with more redwoods beyond the ford.

Turn left on Ridge Trail around 5 miles, climbing gradually. Around 5¼ miles you pass purple larkspur above a rocky gully. Ridge Trail switchbacks left to climb briefly, then descends gently to 5⅜ miles, then a gradual ascent resumes.

At 5½ miles Ridge Trail bends left to cross the gully you've been climbing along, then continues a gentle ascent through forest. From 6 miles, Ridge Trail descends slightly, then resumes a gentle ascent. You reach the trail's summit before 6½ miles, where oaks, madrones and Douglas firs grow on a grassy hillside. Filtered vistas look south to Sonoma Mountain and southeast to Mount Veeder. The summit of Bennett Peak is ⅝ mile southwest and about 450 feet above you.

Dip across a rocky gully, then climb slightly to another summit around 6¾ miles. A gentle descent leads to a picnic table on a big bend of Ridge Trail around 6⅞ miles. Ridge Trail makes a winding, gradual descent through forest with a grassy understory. By 7⅛ miles you leave the forest for grasslands with scattered black and coast live oaks. Continue a gentle, winding descent in and out of shady woodlands. Beyond 7⅜ miles a huge meadow lies below on your left, with Hood Mountain rising beyond.

Beyond 7⅝ miles Ridge Trail crosses an old stone wall. Climb briefly, then descend. Around 7⅞ miles vistas expand to include Sonoma Mountain to the south. Look east for a glimpse of Ledson Marsh. Beyond 8 miles Ridge Trail bends left, offering a great view of the marsh, which looks much larger from here than when you first saw it.

Ridge Trail descends to its end at the junction with Marsh Trail. Turn left and descend north, then east on Marsh Trail. Around 8⅝ miles you pass a picnic table on your left with a view of the marsh, then come to a junction with Pig Flat Trail (connects with Schultz Trail). Bear left to continue on Marsh Trail. From around 8¾ miles Ledson Marsh is directly on the left of the trail. You soon cross a bridge over the Schultz Canyon outlet of the marsh, then come to a marsh interpretive area, where you might get an even closer look at the marsh's cattails, reeds, rushes and bird life.

At 9 miles you return to Marsh Trail's Y intersection with Lawndale Trail, completing the big loop. Turn right on Lawndale Trail and retrace your route from the start of this hike, descending to the trailhead at 11⅞ miles.

OTHER SUGGESTION: You can also climb to Ledson Marsh from TRAILS #42 or 43 via MARSH TRAIL, or take SCHULTZ TRAIL (officially no parking at trailhead) 2⅜ miles to marsh.

45.

SANTA ROSA CREEK HEADWATERS to HOOD MOUNTAIN

EXPLORE HOOD MOUNTAIN REGIONAL PARK ON NEXT THREE TRAILS

When you turn off Highway 12 onto Los Alamos Road, suburbia surrounds you. But as Los Alamos winds up the steep walls of Santa Rosa Creek Canyon, you quickly leave subdivisions for steep grazing lands with scattered homes. Then the road loses its stripe and narrows enough to give even the most confident driver a case of white-knuckle-itis. It is time to slow to a crawl, even to pull into a turnout to give the countryside a good look. As you wind around the flank of towering Castle Rock, you gain a ridge surrounded by steep, untrammeled mountainsides. As the ridge leads you to the parking area for Hood Mountain Regional Park, congratulate yourself for making a quick escape from the urban blight below.

In 2004 County Parks finally was able to reopen the road descending to the heart of the park's facilities only to have the road closed again when the very wet Christmas-New Years storms of 2005-2006 caused a huge landslide that closed the park for the next six months. So for now you'll need to hike or bike the .6 mile road downhill to the park's main parking lot and trailhead, then climb out the same way at the end

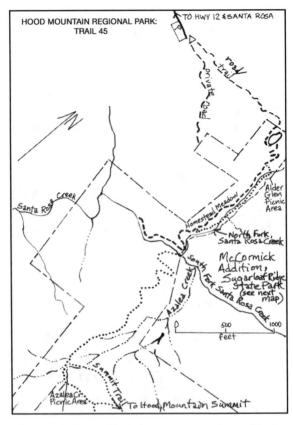

*of your trek. County Parks hopes to reopen the road by late
2007. If that happens, you can deduct 1¼ miles from the
length of the next two trail reports.*

From the parking area, take the paved road on the left. You
descend east through steep grasslands scattered with oaks
toward the headwaters of Santa Rosa Creek. Use caution
on the narrow portion of trail that passes to the right of the
landslide. After ⅛ mile your road narrows and steepens. (Be
sure to save energy to climb this steep hill at the end of your
hike.) Coyote brush lines the road.

At ¼ mile two old apple trees overhang the right side of
the road with a bushy fig on the left, marking the site of
an old homestead. Continue your steady plunge into the
canyon, passing madrone, bay laurel, young Douglas fir and
oak on the right. Beyond ⅜ mile the forest becomes dense,
with evergreen interior live oaks and deciduous black oaks.
Native bunch grasses grow on the steep cut bank. Ferns and
mosses cover the rocky ground.

At ½ mile your road makes a big bend right and steepens.
Several canyons ahead shelter various forks of Santa Rosa

SANTA ROSA CREEK HEADWATERS:

DISTANCE: 3½ miles round trip for described hike,
   10¾ to Hood Mountain summit.
TIME: One or two hours (all day to climb peak).
TERRAIN: From ridge down into deep canyon at head-
   waters of Santa Rosa Creek, then back up.
ELEVATION GAIN/LOSS: 650 feet+/650 feet–.
BEST TIME: Spring.
WARNINGS: May be closed during fire season in summer
   or fall. Call first. Be sure you are fit enough to climb
   back up the steep hill. Watch for poison oak. Park
   closes at sunset.
HOW TO GET THERE: On Highway 12, (at M.21.3),
   6 miles east of Highway 101, turn north onto Los
   Alamos Road and go 5 steep, winding miles to park.
FEES: Day use: $5/vehicle.
FURTHER INFO: Sonoma County Parks (707) 565-2041.

Creek. Sticky monkeyflowers grow along the shoulder.

After a side trail branches right (hikers only), you reach
the park's main parking area at ⅝ mile, with several picnic
tables. Take the next trail on the right (OK for horses and
bikes). Descend steeply through a big S curve bending left,
then right. You pass a water faucet and horse trough, then
more picnic tables. These overlook a grassy glade sloping
down to Santa Rosa Creek within a mile of its source.

Just beyond, at ¾ mile, Alder Glen Trail (hikers only) forks
left, descending to Alder Glen Picnic Area on the creek. California hazel grows beside the junction. Our description follows the main trail on its winding descent south, accompanied
by the burbling of the creek. Cross a small tributary, climb
briefly, then descend again, with wild rose on the right.

The trail climbs to ⅞ mile, then draws near the creek. Your
trail levels as Alder Glen Trail descends on the left. Climb
gradually, then descend again following the twists of the
canyon. You pass California buckeye. Local Indians used its
fruits to stupefy fish, making them easier to catch.

At 1⅛ miles you enter Homestead Meadow, where deer
often graze. The trail makes a gradual descent to 1¼ miles,

185

where it joins a broad road. The ruins of a small shed stand beside a rock outcrop nearby.

Take Santa Rosa Creek Trail to the right of the rock. The narrow trail contours through grasslands briefly, then descends near Santa Rosa Creek, where moss-draped alders and bays grow. Follow the trail west alongside the beautiful creek. Before 1½ miles dense woodwardia ferns drape over the opposite bank. In another ⅛ mile your trail veers left and descends briefly, crossing a bridge over a tributary. Soon your path narrows and passes a rock outcrop where leather ferns grow from the stone. At 1¾ miles your trail descends to the creek. This shady spot provides a pleasant resting place on a warm day. Santa Rosa Creek tumbles west, plunging 400 feet in the next two miles only to be channeled through suburban sprawl. But from here, the creek appears much as it has for centuries, showing no signs of human tampering with its joyously gurgling, meandering course.

You can easily continue down the creek another 250 feet to where a side stream pours from a deep canyon and tumbles over a small waterfall into Santa Rosa Creek. Retrace your steps to the junction when you're ready. You can return to the trailhead from here for a 3⅝-mile hike. If it's still early, you have time to explore more of this spacious wilderness. Keep in mind that the park closes at sunset.

Take the trail that descends east to a often wet concrete ford of North Fork Santa Rosa Creek right beside its confluence with the South Fork. Two trails climb from the ford. On the left is the trail into the 1200-acre McCormick Addition to Sugarloaf Ridge State Park (see Trail #46, no dogs). On the right 100 feet downstream, Hood Mountain Trail climbs west, then southwest, rising above the creek. It climbs 1⅛ miles to an intriguing botanical area along Azalea Creek, then continues to the summit of Hood Mountain, 7¼ miles or 8⅝ miles round trip from here, depending on your route. For clarity sake, we ignore the side trip down Santa Rosa Creek for mileage figures beyond here.

Hood Mountain Trail continues climbing past maple, bay laurel, maidenhair fern and poison oak. Before 1½ miles the trail makes a sharp and steep bend left to climb moderately east beneath tall hardwoods. It bends to the right around 1⅝ miles and climbs gradually past California hazel beneath Douglas firs. Continue past red larkspur, miners lettuce, more maidenhair, then huge woodwardia ferns on the left. Your fire road trail bends left before 1¾ miles to climb steeply. The ascent eases before a big bend right, then resumes a steep ascent. Beyond 1⅞ miles, your climb eases past toyon.

By 2 miles you have a steep drop on the left into Azalea

186

Creek Canyon. Climb to 2¼ miles, then come to a wooden two-holed outhouse on the right, with a trail to reservation-only Azalea Creek Camps on the left. Continue straight on multiple-use Hood Mountain Trail to 2⅜ miles.

Our described hike turns left on signed Summit Trail (hikers only), descending through grasslands to ford Azalea Creek, lined with fragrant azaleas which bloom in spring. Cypress grows along the creek with bay and Douglas fir. Your trail makes a winding climb above the creek, passing more cypress, leather oak, ceanothus, toyon, manzanita, madrone and a few Bishop pines, with blue-eyed grass and golden fairy lanterns in the understory. Beyond 2½ miles look for paintbrush, a tall lily, a cream iris, soap plant and coffeeberry. The profusion of plants makes the steep ascent more pleasant.

By 2⅝ miles you come to a junction and decision time. Summit Trail continues, a hiker's best choice from here to reach Hood Mountain's top via 2.2 miles of narrow, often rocky tread, with its middle portion climbing through a serpentine-caused pygmy forest. If you're heading for the peak, you're on your own from here.

Our described hike turns right on Cypress Trail. In only thirty feet, take the left fork of Cypress Trail, passing Indian warriors in spring. You trail nears a seasonal creek, then fords it beside more azaleas and descends to end at Hood Mountain Trail before 2¾ miles. Turn right to return to the trailhead. A frog pond hides in the forest to your east. Descend to an easy ford of its outlet stream at 2¾ miles, then continue past the other fork of Cypress Trail beyond 2⅞ miles. Hood Mountain Trail descends across Azalea Creek beyond 3 miles. After fording another fork of the creek, your trail returns to the start of Summit Trail at 3⅛ miles. Retrace your route down Hood Mountain Trail to the ford of Santa Rosa Creek, then ascend back to your car, 5½ miles round trip for the described hike.

OTHER SUGGESTIONS: THIS TRAIL CONTINUES SOUTH to the summit of Hood Mountain, then to Sugarloaf Ridge State Park. For the easier ascent of Hood Mountain from the south, see Trail #41. In town, SANTA ROSA CREEK TRAIL starts at Brush Creek Road and follows the north side of the creek to Farmers Lane, providing walkers access to one mile of creek. BRUSH CREEK TRAIL heads north for about 2½ miles from the same spot.

46

MORE SANTA ROSA CREEK HEADWATERS

MCCORMICK ADDITION, SUGARLOAF STATE PARK

The Sonoma County Agricultural Preservation and Open Space District acquired 1200 acres of the old McCormick Ranch in 1995, donating the land to California State Parks to become part of Sugarloaf Ridge State Park. Ironically, the primary access to these steep, remote and pristine acres passes through Hood Mountain Regional Park, which was closed for the first six months of 2006 due to storm damage.

Follow the description in Trail #45 from Hood Mountain Regional Park's upper parking lot down the road to the lower lot at ⅝ mile, then down the fire road trail to the junction in Homestead Meadow at 1¼ miles. Go left at the junction and descend to the concrete ford of North Fork Santa Rosa Creek, directly above its confluence with the South Fork.

Stay to the left when you get to the creek, crossing the concrete ford to climb the old ranch road into the signed McCormick Addition. You do not want Hood Mountain Trail, which leaves the creek about 200 feet downstream.

Climb gradually on the broad track, heading east with the South Fork below you on the right. Around 1⅜ mile your road ascends steeply, leaving the creek far below. You'll see occasional patches of pavement on the road.

Before 1⅝ miles you come to a sign for Quercus Trail. The trail shown on some maps that continued along the South Fork no longer exists. In spring, brodiaea and farewell-to-spring grow near the trail sign. Follow Quercus Trail on a steady steep ascent, soon winding to the left. As you climb, look for sticky monkeyflower, Chinese houses, lupine and blue dick.

By 1¾ miles your ascent eases to moderate. The trail bends right to climb east and northeast past clarkia. Pass beneath a two-wire power line beyond 2⅛ miles, then make a big bend right to climb steeply, gaining a sweeping vista of the upper South Fork Santa Rosa Creek watershed. You finally get a break from the steady climb, coming to Quercus Trail's end before 2⅜ miles.

Meet Headwaters Trail. On the right it descends to a fork of the South Fork, ending in ½ mile at the park boundary. Turn left and climb steeply northwest along Headwaters Trail, passing through steeply rolling grasslands with many large coast live oaks and black oaks. Your ascent eases, turning fitful around 2½ miles.

MORE SANTA ROSA CREEK HEADWATERS:

DISTANCES: (all round trip) 2½ miles to Homestead
  Meadow junction, 5¾ miles to Grandmother Oak, 6⅜
  miles to three oak vista.
TIME: One hour to Homestead Meadow, three or four
  hours for all of described hike.
TERRAIN: From ridge down into deep canyon at headwa-
  ters of Santa Rosa Creek, then back up.
ELEVATION GAIN/LOSS: 620 feet+/620 feet- to Home-
  stead Meadow. 1450 feet+/1450 feet- to Grandmother
  Oak, 1540 feet+/1540 feet- to three oak vista.
BEST TIME: Spring for wildflowers, autumn also good.
WARNINGS: May be closed during fire season in summer or
  fall. Call first. Be sure you are fit enough and leave time
  enough to climb back up the steep hill. Watch for poison
  oak. Park closes at sunset. Dogs not allowed in McCormick.
HOW TO GET THERE: On Highway 12, (at M.21.3), 6
  miles east of Highway 101, turn north onto Los Alamos
  Road and go 5 steep, winding miles to park. If the road
  descending to the main parking area has reopened, drive
  another .6 mile.
FEES: Day use: $5/vehicle.
FURTHER INFO: Sonoma County Parks (707) 565-2041 for
  road access questions. Sugarloaf Ridge State Park (707)
  833-5712 for questions about trails on state park land.

At 2⅝ miles you climb to a saddle on the ridgetop and a
junction with hikers-only Grandmother Oak Trail. Headwaters Trail continues ½ mile, ending as it meets Wildcat
Creek Trail on the left, which descends steeply ½ mile
into a deep hole to end at North Fork Santa Rosa Creek.
Headwaters Trail also meets at its end Maple Glen Trail on
the right, which climbs, contours, descends, then climbs
again before ending at the northern park boundary after
2 miles. (It also meets the Pygmy Owl Trail.)

Our described hike turns right to follow narrow, sometimes
vague Grandmother Oak Trail, climbing moderately, then
steeply along a ridgetop past chamise, sticky monkeyflower,
soap plant, coyote brush, ceanothus and birchleaf mountain

189

mahogany. When the ridgetop forks, go right to descend slightly, then climb steeply along the ridgetop to 2¾ miles, then fitfully to 2⅞ miles, where the immense Grandmother Oak is suddenly before you. This is the world's largest known coast live oak, a species that generally grows into a much smaller mature specimen. Apparently the Grandmother Oak, about ten feet in diameter with many moss-draped limbs, was even big-

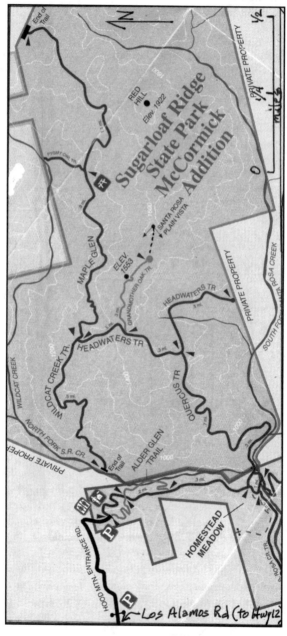

ger before it dropped some large limbs in recent winters. Still, she's an impressive specimen growing in a dramatic spot.

If you're not ready to return, you can continue east along the ridgetop (more or less), following a rudimentary use trail through the grasslands. You climb to three large white oaks on a 1600-foot elevation hilltop beyond 3⅛ miles. Look around for grand vistas: south to Hood Mountain, west down Santa Rosa Creek and out over the Santa Rosa Plain to the coastal hills beyond. Although the route becomes more vague, you could continue up this ridgetop for almost ½ mile to the top of Red Hill, elevation 1922 feet, for an even more expansive vista. Or you could explore some of the trails beyond the end of Headwaters Trail.

Whatever your plan, be sure to leave enough time and energy to complete the rugged hike out before sunset. Returning from the three oak vista makes for a 6⅜ miles round trip outing.

47.

PONDS LOOP
VERDANT NEW GATEWAY TO HOOD MTN. REGIONAL PARK

*This most recent 300-acre addition to the growing variety of Regional Parks in Sonoma County has not created an entirely new park, but instead gives a new, friendlier face to Hood Mountain Regional Park, which otherwise is the domain of avid, particularly dedicated recreationists because of its isolated location and remote wilderness nature (see Trail #45). Here at the new Pythian Road entrance to the park, access is easy and the road is paved right to the trailhead. **Please note that the trail and surrounding park lands are due to open in October 2006.** The trail, part of BART, will eventually lead down the canyon from this trailhead as well, descending to Hood House and Los Guilicos.*

From the trailhead parking area and drinking fountain, follow the trail beyond the split rail fence as it climbs northwest and north between the road and a park residence, then winds east through a small meadow before passing another park residence. Your trail then crosses the paved road, continuing on trail for several hundred yards before joining the paved road's left shoulder, climbing up Hood Creek Canyon with the creek below on your left. When the pavement ends, follow the dirt road for 150 feet, paralleling the road above the creek through riparian forest.

PONDS LOOP:

DISTANCE: (all round trip) 4¾ miles for Merganser Pond loop, 5½ miles to orchard junction with Merganser loop, 10¼ miles to Hood Mountain summit (shortest route).

TIME: Three to five hours.

TERRAIN: Climb along Hood Creek, then descend to pond surrounded by forest. Climb to views and second pond, then to a meadow with old orchard, with optional ascent to peak.

ELEVATION GAIN/LOSS: 2140 feet+/2140 feet- for Merganser Pond Loop, 2300 feet+/2300 feet- to homestead, 2710 feet+/2710 feet- to Hood summit.

BEST TIME: Any cool, clear day. Best flowers in spring.

WARNINGS: Watch for poison oak, rattlesnakes and ticks. Steep trail, often hot, usually dry: use caution. Stay off adjacent private property. No swimming or wading in ponds. Use caution on narrow access road.

HOW TO GET THERE: On Highway 12 between Santa Rosa and Kenwood, turn north onto Pythian Road at stoplight (M.24.54). Go 0.3 mile to a fork, then veer right on Pythian Road and cautiously follow the narrow, winding road another 1.1 miles to trailhead parking lot on right.

FEE: Day use, $5/vehicle.

FURTHER INFO: Sonoma County Parks (707) 565-2041.

After the road turns east, your trail climbs away from the road by switchbacks, climbing north, then northeast through mixed forest with a grassy understory. Switchback right and left around ⅝ mile on a steady ascent. A winding climb soon passes three wooden water tanks sitting atop a hill with Hood Creek now far below. Continue climbing generally northeast.

Around ¾ mile your trail meets the dirt road and parallels it briefly. Climb to a landing beneath Douglas firs where the road forks. The trail follows the left fork, soon following the bank above the road's right shoulder. Soon you descend slightly to cross Hood Creek on a concrete ford, then resume a winding climb left of the road. Soon your trail climbs away from the road and creek.

Around one mile your trail makes a winding ascent through logged over forest with an understory of glade-like grasslands.

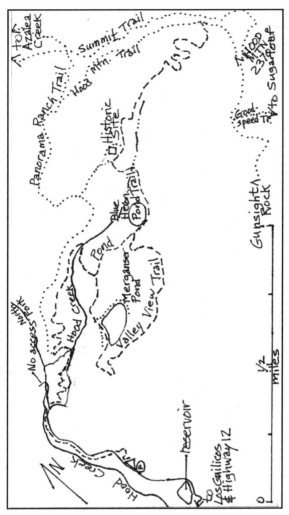

Your climb continues, winding in and out of the grasslands with occasional views down to the creek. Gain a small ridgetop around 1⅜ miles with Hood Creek burbling below on your right. Look west and northwest for a view of higher ridges. Your trail meets an old logging road on the left, Panorama Ranch Trail. It continues up to Orchard Meadow, offering the shortest route from here to Hood Mountain's summit. Our described hike stays to the right, following the trail as it veers away from the road, climbing gradually.

Beyond 1½ miles your trail bends right and contours into forest. Cross two seasonal gullies where serpentine soils support Sargent Cypress, then descend to cross a bridge over Hood Creek in a pretty spot beneath Douglas firs and California bay trees. Climb briefly, then descend west and south through grasslands with mixed, widely scattered trees.

193

At 1¾ miles your descent turns east briefly before the trail levels and comes to a junction. You can go left here for Hood Mountain's summit, but our described hike turns right to follow the Bay Area Ridge Trail (BART) on Pond Trail. Descend southwest on a broad path that winds left and right on a steady descent to Merganser Pond at 1⅞ miles, then come to a signed junction. Turn left on Valley View Trail, following the pond's western shore to 2 miles. Then Valley View Trail veers right, leaving the pond and descending to another trail sign.

Climb moderately east through grasslands with patchy forest where blue dick, sticky monkeyflower and bedstraw grow. Ascend to the valley views around 2⅛ miles. Valley of the Moon sprawls out below, with the hills of Annadel and Sonoma Mountain rising beyond. To the south on clearest days you can see San Francisco Bay. Your trail bends right to climb north. Ascend steeply to a hilltop at 2¼ miles, then descend steeply. Along the path, look for mule ears—both the broad-leaved and narrow-leaved varieties—plus ceanothus and yerba santa. Your descent ends at a ridge with views south on your right and a view of the steep, wooded slope above Merganser Pond on your left.

By 2⅜ miles you leave the views behind. Climb fitfully past many rock formations: ledges, cliffs and moss-draped outcrops. Then ascend steeply to 2½ miles, then gradually for a bit before another steep climb to 2⅝ miles, where you gain another view. This time the vista is to the west over the Santa Rosa Plain. Soon Valley View Trail descends through forest, coming to a junction where Valley View Trail meets Pond Trail at 2¾ miles. To return from here, turn left and descend ¼ mile to the Pond/Lower Johnson Ridge junction you came to before reaching Merganser Pond. Go right there, retracing your steps to the trailhead for a 4¾-mile loop.

To extend your hike, turn right on Pond Trail and climb east briefly, then descend past iris and blue dick with Blue Heron Pond on your left. The lush habitat around the pond includes big leaf maple, hazel, hedge nettle, miners lettuce, woodland star, blackberry, ferns and wood rose beneath abundant Douglas firs. The trail resumes a gradual ascent, crossing now seasonal Hood Creek around 3 miles where maidenhair ferns grow. Dip past woodwardia ferns beneath bay trees with vining poison oak, the stalks of which are three inches in diameter. Then climb again with an old walnut orchard on your left. Poppies and blue-eyed grass grow in the meadow surrounding the orchard.

Climb to a junction at 3⅛ miles. The orchard and ruins on the surrounding lands are part of the old Hendrickson homestead, settled 1875. A return from here completes a 5½-mile semi-loop hike. The trail on the left connects with Panorama Ranch Trail. The trail on the right, Upper Johnson Ridge Trail, leads past the heart of the homestead and climbs about 2½ miles to meet Hood Mountain Trail only ¼ mile from the mountain's summit, offering an 11 mile round trip route to the summit, or 10¼ miles via the shortcut bypassing Merganser Pond.

SUGARLOAF RIDGE STATE PARK
INCLUDES THE NEXT FOUR TRAILS

Only a half hour from Santa Rosa or Sonoma, you can escape to a gentle wilderness in the heart of the Mayacmas Range, nestled amidst some of the range's highest peaks. At night in the park's splendid campground, coyotes howl and owls hoot, punctuating the soft murmur of Sonoma Creek, while infinite stars glimmer in the dark sky. It is difficult to believe that cities lurk so near.

Sugarloaf Ridge State Park encompasses 2820 acres of steep, rolling hills along the headwaters of Sonoma Creek, plus about 1200 additional acres in the recent McCormick Addition along the headwaters of Santa Rosa Creek, reached via Hood Mountain Regional Park (see Trail #46). The hills shelter various habitats, including oak and conifer forests, chaparral and grasslands. About 25 miles of trails explore the main unit of the park, with some of the best described in the next four routes. Another 6 miles of trails are in the McCormick Addition.

The new Bay Area Ridge Trail (BART) currently follows nearly four miles of Sugarloaf's trails, with potential for more. The long-distance BART enters the park on the Pony Gate Trail, then traces the newly-designated Stern Trail, then the Bald Mountain Trail, ending at the top of the peak. Ongoing negotiations have not yet determined if BART will head northwest on High Ridge Trail or southeast to Brushy Peaks to enter Napa County.

The Southern Wappo village of Wilikos was located in the center of today's park long before the first Spanish settlers came to California. The Wappos lived in dome-shaped huts up to 40 feet long, made of poles and grass thatch. About 100 residents occupied roughly 40 dwellings. A large sweathouse in the village center was used exclusively by the men for smoking, steam baths and ceremonies. Members of the tribe would travel to the coast and Clear Lake to fish and trade with other

*tribes, but hunted for game locally. Resistant to exploitation by
the Spanish, many of the Wappos were killed in cholera and
smallpox epidemics in the 1830s. Most of the survivors were
moved to the Mendocino Indian Reservation around 1860.*

*Because these lands were marginal for farming, not until the
1860s did white Americans settle around Sugarloaf Ridge. The
state bought the property in 1920, planning to dam the creek
to provide water to Sonoma State Hospital. But the objections
of surrounding property owners kept the plan in limbo. In 1964
the area became part of the State Park System.*

48.

HOOD MOUNTAIN
from SUGARLOAF
GOOD CLIMB ON THE GOODSPEED TRAIL

From the parking area just inside the park boundary, the
Goodspeed Trail immediately crosses Sonoma Creek on a
sturdy bridge. Head north following Bear Creek upstream.
Bay laurel, hazel, madrone and Oregon ash trees grow beneath redwoods and firs along the stream.

Before ⅛ mile you cross a bridge over Bear Creek. Follow
the west bank briefly, then switchback left to start a long,
steady climb. The forest soon thins and chaparral species
dominate. Coyote brush, manzanita, bay laurel, chamise,
sticky monkeyflower and oaks compete for space on the dry
south slope, with abundant golden fairy lanterns in spring.

Around ¼ mile you cross a recent landslide, then switchback right, gaining the first views of the parklands up canyon.
Climb steadily on rocky tread with occasional switchbacks.
Beyond ½ mile coffeeberry and creeping ceanothus join the
tangle of brush. You overlook wooded Bear Creek Canyon to
the east. Continue a steady, well-graded climb.

As your trail levels, then descends beyond ¾ mile, you have
views southwest to the creeping suburbs in Valley of the Moon.
Cross a dirt road and descend gradually as hairy honeysuckle
and toyon mix with the chaparral. Descend four switchbacks to
cross a seasonal creek beyond one mile. At the boulder-strewn
crossing of the heavily eroded creek, the blue-green rocks indicate serpentine soils. White alders grow along the creek.

Switchback up the slope above the creek and climb generally west. Whitethorn mixes with the other chaparral. You
pass under power lines, leaving chaparral for Douglas fir

forest at 1¼ miles. Trees to four feet in diameter provide welcome shade on a warm day. Soon an understory of manzanita is dying as the taller oaks and firs steal the sunlight.

Switchback right and climb through the forest. You pass "stay on trail" signs at a spot where you might be confused by a side trail. Before 1⅝ miles the trail bends left, then right, climbing a brushy, rocky ridge.

Swing left, leaving the ridge, then cross a seasonal (usually dry) creek crowded with hardwoods at 1¾ miles. You might stop for a shady rest because the next section of trail crosses open, south-facing slopes.

Leaving the creek, you climb into grasslands. Around 1⅞ miles you traverse a brushy south slope. But you soon return to a steep grassy slope as you leave the state park for Hood Mountain Regional Park around 2 miles. Dark green Sugarloaf Ridge rises across wooded Adobe Canyon.

Ascend steadily through the large glade, a prime spot for wildflowers in spring. At 2⅛ miles a big, lone bay laurel grows above the trail. Return to chaparral briefly, but by 2¼ miles your trail ascends steeply, traversing a steep grassy hillside. By 2⅜ miles you begin a steep, hot, slow climb, an indication of the arduous ascent to the summit. The vegetation varies frequently now, from grasslands to chaparral to oak woodlands and back again.

At 2½ miles you switchback right and climb steeply through a rocky area, traversing the top of the same steep slope. At 2⅝ miles you approach the ridge of Hood Mountain, acending steep, rocky tread through an area where little grows but gnarled chamise. Top the ridge, swing left and descend briefly, then resume a gradual climb. You return to the ridgetop for a vista southwest to Annadel State Park and south to Mt. Tamalpais and San Francisco Bay. Resume climbing steeply along the ridge's wooded east face.

At 2¾ miles you climb through dwarf hardwood forest barely tall enough to provide welcome shade. This miniature forest grows on the cool north slope below the wind-pummeled ridgetop. Climb into a forest of moderately large live oaks at 2⅞ miles. Then climb steeply through a brushy area where you near the rocky ridgetop.

Your trail climbs beneath large manzanitas, then into mixed forest. The climb turns gradual beneath wind-stunted firs. You soon leave the forest for a grassy ridgetop saddle with birdseye views of Valley of the Moon. Gunsight Rock appears to the northwest. Continue your climb through more oak forest. As the steep climb eases, you see Bishop pines. Before long they dominate the forest.

At 3 miles, take the side trail on the left. You climb over the ridgetop, winding west for ⅛ mile to Gunsight Rock, 2600 feet above sea level. Although the summit of Hood Mountain is only ¼ mile farther along the main trail, Gunsight provides the best views west and south.

From the notch of Gunsight Rock, you overlook most of Sonoma County. Valley of the Moon sprawls below you, the long top of Sonoma Mountain rising beyond it. On a clear day Mt. Tamalpais juts skyward beyond Sonoma Mountain. To the south, tidal flats extend to San Francisco Bay. You may see San Francisco skyscrapers on the clearest days. Mt. Diablo is the high peak southeast. To the west lies Santa Rosa. Beyond it, green hills roll gently toward the sea. To the north stands Sulphur Peak near the Geysers and Mt. St. Helena, with 7056-foot Snow Mountain in Mendocino National Forest sometimes visible beyond its right flank. To the east, Bald Mountain, Red Mountain (with microwave towers) and pointed Brushy Peak lie within Sugarloaf Ridge State Park. To the southeast are

Little Bald Mountain, Sugarloaf Ridge and Mount Veeder. Enjoy the view from this hawk's perch where red-tailed hawks and hummingbirds soar on the wind.

Return to the main trail and turn left to head for Hood's summit. Climb north, then steeply east, passing Altar Rock, where gooseberry and yerba santa grow. You briefly continue the steep ascent before descending past a trail sign. You then climb along bleached sandstone, in and out of forest and chaparral. You finally ascend steeply north along a hot, south-facing ridge to reach the top of Hood Mountain (elevation 2730 feet) at 3½ miles.

Its flat top is cleared of brush. Although the views are not as spectacular as Gunsight Rock's, if the day is clear, look east to Bald Mountain and scan the horizon northward. You may see the snowy peaks of the Sierra Nevada glistening on the skyline. From the summit two trails head north to explore the rest of Hood Mountain Regional Park, Hood Mountain Trail (horses and mountain bikes OK) on the left and a footpath on the right, Summit Trail.

Return on the same trail you ascended. Passing through the clearings on the ridge, look for native California fuchsia. It grows in nondescript gray-green clumps when not flowering. But in late summer and fall, its bright scarlet, trumpet-shaped flowers provide one of the few native foods for hummingbirds on their southern migration.

OTHER SUGGESTIONS: See Trails #45 and #47.

49.

SONOMA CANYON/ PONY GATE LOOP
WATERFALL AND WILDFLOWERS

This hike excels in early spring, when the waterfall and creeks roar with the replenishment of recent rains. Then the deciduous trees show their new growth and wildflowers burst brightly from the meadows. The trail is also pleasant in light rain, when everything glistens with revitalizing moisture. Although you can also start the loop from the entrance kiosk, I prefer the way it unfolds from the lower end.

Park in the wide turnout just east of the trailhead. Cautiously walk downhill along the road shoulder, passing the lower

Pony Gate Trailhead across the road, the return point for this loop. In 300 feet from the parking turnout, you'll find the signed Canyon Loop Trailhead. Turn left and descend southeast into a forest of big Douglas firs and medium redwoods with scattered oaks and madrones. The trail soon levels 50 feet above Sonoma Creek. The lush understory includes wood rose, hazel, bay laurel, snowberry, twisted stalk, starflower, native bunch grasses and poison oak.

Descend again, leveling briefly at ⅛ mile where leather-leaf and lady ferns grow. Continue your descent across a bridge over Pony Gate Creek, overlooking its confluence with Sonoma Creek as it tumbles down the rocky canyon. The south bank rises steeply toward Sugarloaf Ridge, the summit of which is only a mile away, 1200 feet above.

Continue upstream on the trail. In 250 feet you get your first glimpse of the waterfall beyond cascades upstream. The trail passes under a leaning bay laurel, passing black oaks, alders and sycamores growing along the creek.

At ¼ mile you cross a small wooden bridge and meet steps climbing through a moss- and fern-draped rock garden left of the falls. Before climbing the steps, take the short spur on the right to the base of the waterfall. The falls tumble over boulders strewn along a mossy precipice, sending up spray to wet the surrounding greenery. A tiny brook cascades down the opposite bank. The pungent smell of bay laurel permeates the air.

The main trail climbs steps up a rocky side gully. You switchback right, passing maidenhair and leather ferns. Climb steeply, then moderately to ⅜ mile, where the trail broadens and bends left as you continue to climb, surrounded by mossy boulders. Oaks dominate the forest, with scattered madrones and young firs.

The trail levels as it leads away from the creek, then resumes a gradual ascent, passing sticky monkeyflower. At ½ mile you cross a seasonal side stream at a small clearing. Then the trail bends right and climbs. Soon the forest canopy parts, allowing toyon and other brush species to thrive. You cross another tributary, then swing left to climb alongside it, passing vines of Dutchman's pipe, then low growing Indian warriors.

Just beyond ⅝ mile, you climb to the paved road just below the entrance kiosk. Cross the road cautiously and start along Pony Gate Trail (horses OK). Pony Gate climbs east into a grassy clearing surrounded by oak woodlands. Then your trail winds out of the clearing, climbing through hardwood forest.

At ¾ mile your trail bends left to skirt one of the large glades that are a hallmark of Sugarloaf Ridge State Park. The trail stays in the trees here, but keep your eyes on the

SONOMA CANYON/PONY GATE LOOP:

DISTANCE: 1¾-mile loop.

TIME: One hour.

TERRAIN: Up canyon along creek to waterfall, then up and down hillside with views of canyon to return to starting point.

ELEVATION GAIN/LOSS: 560 feet+/560 feet−.

BEST TIME: Early spring when the waterfall roars. Canyon Trail nice anytime; Pony Gate can be hot on sunny days in summer.

WARNINGS: Watch for poison oak, ticks and stinging nettles. Stay off slippery rocks near waterfall. Use caution crossing road.

HOW TO GET THERE: See Trail #41 for general directions. The trailhead for this hike is 2.6 miles from Highway 12.

FEES: Day use: $6/vehicle. Car camping: $15/night.

FURTHER INFO: Sugarloaf Ridge State Park (707) 833-5712.

glade for possible sightings of wildlife. The trail contours the steep hillside, then climbs briefly to enter a small clearing that overlooks the deep, wooded canyon of Sonoma Creek. Bush lupine and bracken fern cluster along the trail.

Continue through oak forest, then pass between two gnarled oaks into a glade. Climb to meet a trail on your right before ⅞ mile. (It returns to the entrance kiosk.) Take the left fork, continuing beneath oaks. After a clearing, cross a rocky (and often dry) creekbed.

You soon come to a marked junction. Here you meet the portion of Pony Gate Trail that's designated as part of the Bay Area Ridge Trail. The right fork climbs for ⅛ mile to Stern Trail, which soon connects with Bald Mountain Trail (all BART). Take the left fork to continue on Pony Gate Trail and BART. You descend moderately over clay soil that may be slippery after rain. Around 1⅛ miles your trail bends right, then left, continuing a steady descent through oak woodlands. After a big bend right, descend across a gully and contour along the bottom of a rolling glade. At 1¼ mile you pass a stand of young Douglas firs encroaching on the glade.

You leave the glade to descend steps into a dark forest. Cross another rocky gully, then descend steeply toward the cascades of Pony Gate Creek. You ford the creek before 1⅜ miles, then climb steeply for 100 feet. Climb moderately

201

to join an old road, then resume a moderate descent. Limbs of bay and oak arch gracefully over your path.

At 1½ miles you can see the paved road far down the steep slope on your left. Your trail bends right and descends southwest. At 1⅝ miles the forest thins to allow views of the big conifers along Sonoma Creek. Chaparral grows above the trail: manzanita, chamise, scrub oak and sticky monkeyflower. Continue your descent as the trail bends right, then left to reach the paved road at 1¾ miles. Your starting point is just uphill along the road.

50.

BALD MOUNTAIN LOOP
THROUGH THE HEART OF SUGARLOAF

Bald Mountain Trail became one of the first links in Sonoma County's segment of the Bay Area Ridge Trail (BART). The completed BART will explore about 400 miles of the greater San Francisco Bay Area's high hills and skylines. Sonoma County lags behind most other bay area counties in efforts to complete BART, but progress has been made. Some of Sonoma's share of BART traverses privately held land. Slowly, more Sonoma County property owners are realizing that public trails and open space enhance property values and quality of life.

From the parking lot, climb gradually through grasslands on Lower Bald Mountain Trail. At ⅛ mile you pass a weathered phone pole, now fallen to make a low but handy seat, then switchbsack left into mixed chaparral and oak woodland. Interior live oak dominates, with bay laurel, manzanita, coffeeberry and chamise. Switchback right, passing toyon with bright red berries in winter. Then switchback left, passing creeping ceanothus.

As your trail bends right, a view of Hood Mountain opens

202

to the northwest. Return to grasslands at ¼ mile and quickly reach a junction. You will return by Bald Mountain Trail on the left. Take Meadow Trail on the right and descend to the Group Camp and Robert Ferguson Observatory beyond ⅜ mile.

Cross the gravel parking lot and veer left on the paved trail/road to cross a tributary of Sonoma Creek and head east. Pass the start of Hillside Trail on your right, continuing on the now gravel Meadow Trail. A big meadow, with a large solitary oak in its center, stretches between you and Sonoma Creek. I spotted a coyote retreating up the hill one winter morning. At ⅝ mile you cross another tributary. The road levels and heads toward Little Bald Mountain. Coyote brush and bay laurel line the path.

At ¾ mile you descend slightly and approach tree-lined Sonoma Creek. Your road winds along the creek, passing oak, bay laurel, willow, madrone and alder trees. By ⅞ mile a big meadow is on the far side of the creek. As you start a gradual climb, California rose beside the path can be distinguished from wood rose by its long curved thorns.

At one mile the creek meanders away from the road. Your road winds through a meadow where a riot of wildflowers grow in spring. Cross a seasonal creek and enter forest of oaks and young maples. Cross a bridge over Sonoma Creek, where an immense maple towers.

Your path then forks. The right fork leads to Brushy Peaks and Hillside Trails (see Trail #51). You go left on Gray Pine Trail. This narrow dirt road quickly crosses Sonoma Creek again, a ford that can be wet in winter.

Before 1⅜ miles Vista Trail (hikers only) branches left. Stay on Gray Pine Trail, climbing gradually along Sonoma Creek. As you turn toward the creek, a large California buckeye grows on the right. Ford the creek and start a steady climb along a tributary.

At 1½ miles your trail steepens briefly, crosses a culvert on the side stream and winds through mixed forest and chaparral. Climb steeply over loose tread to 1¾ miles. Then the climb eases. You parallel power lines, climbing steadily. Sticky monkeyflower and toyon line your path.

At 1⅞ miles your trail makes a big bend right and ascends under the power lines in a meadow where poppies, blue dicks and abundant bird's eye gilias grow in spring. Before 2 miles the road is covered with loose rock on a steep section that mountain bikers may have to walk. Great views lie behind you. Climb steadily on better tread, winding left. Ascend steeply from 2¼ to 2⅜ miles, passing your first gray pines amidst a manzanita thicket.

You reach 2000 feet elevation as you pass back under the power lines and climb along the ridge. The terrain on your

BALD MOUNTAIN LOOP:

DISTANCE: 6½-mile loop (hike, bike or horse) or
7¼-mile loop (hikers only).

TIME: Three to four hours.

TERRAIN: Through meadows along creek, then climb to
and along high ridge to peak with great views, then down
paved road or footpath.

ELEVATION GAIN/LOSS: 1630 feet+/1630 feet−.

BEST TIME: Spring for wildflowers. Any clear day.

WARNINGS: Carry water. Mountain bikers use caution:
slow on blind corners, yield to equestrians and hikers.
Watch for poison oak, ticks and rattlesnakes.

HOW TO GET THERE: On Highway 12 between Santa
Rosa and Kenwood, turn north onto Adobe Canyon Road
at M.26.2. Go 3.5 miles to Day-Use Parking Area (.1
mile beyond kiosk).

FEES: Day use: $6/vehicle. Car camping: $15/night.

FURTHER INFO: Sugarloaf Ridge State Park (707) 833-5712.

left drops steeply into a brushy canyon with many gray pines.
A short, steep ascent brings you to 2½ miles, where the road
levels for the best view yet. Then climb gradually through
dense chaparral with buckbrush and chamise.

Beyond 2⅝ miles the road reaches the main ridge, where
Brushy Peaks Trail (Trail #51, no bikes) forks right. Continue straight on Gray Pine Trail, climbing a steep hill with
glimpses of Napa Valley to the east. At 2¾ miles a gated road
on the right leads onto private property.

Your route promptly reaches a top, then descends west,
with Bald Mountain dead ahead. At 2⅞ miles the road
levels as brush gives way to forest of oak, bay and madrone.
Descend again, then climb steeply to 3 miles, where Red
Mountain Trail (hikers only) forks left. Continue to climb,
with another view into the lush Napa Valley. Beyond 3⅛ miles
you climb steeply again, then dip briefly, only to climb again.
At 3¼ miles a level respite soon leads to an easy climb lined
with whitethorn and bush lupine. Then climb moderately
with grasslands on the left and big black oaks on the right.

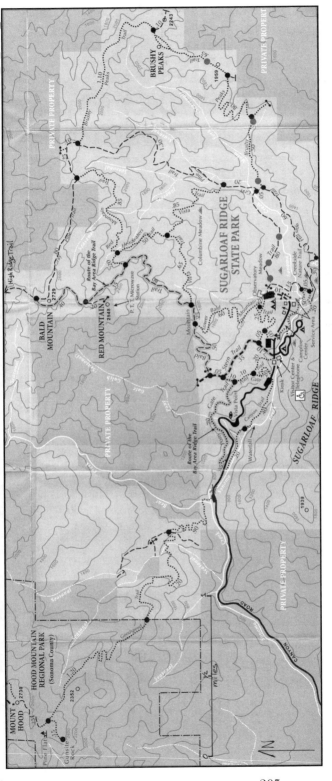

Make another steep climb to 3¾ miles where you approach the summit of Bald Mountain.

As you top the 2729-foot peak, take a rest, confident that it's all downhill from here. The summit is bald grasslands except for clumps of chamise on the south face.

The day I first climbed the peak, I arrived in sunshine and sat beside a knot of chamise for protection from a chilly wind. Soon a dense cloak of fog enveloped the peak, obscuring all views. The view described here presents what one sees on the clearest day.

To the north the Mayacmas Range sprawls northward to its highest point at Mt. St. Helena (4339'), 20 miles away. Fifty miles beyond and to the right of Mt. St. Helena, Snow Mountain (7056') marks the southern end of the Mendocino Range. To the west stands Hood Mountain, one foot higher than Bald. Beyond Hood's left flank, Valley of the Moon snuggles at the base of Sonoma Mountain (2295'). Mt. Tamalpais (2606') peaks over Sonoma's left shoulder. On the clearest day you may be able to spot the Golden Gate Bridge towers about three finger widths left of Mt. Tam (binoculars help). If it's that clear, the Transamerica Pyramid juts skyward from the city skyline. The bay lies directly south, beyond the flank of nearby Red Mountain. Mt. Diablo (3849') is the tallest peak on the southern horizon. Much closer are Little Bald Mountain (2275'), Mt. Veeder (2677') and Brushy Peak (2243'). To the east you see Napa Valley vineyards and the town of St. Helena. On the horizon east-northeast the snowy peaks of the Sierra Nevada near Lake Tahoe glisten.

The trail down heads north, quickly meeting High Ridge Trail (1⅝ miles, explores little-traveled northern extreme of Sugarloaf Park). Turn left and head west to a saddle at 3⅞ miles, then start a long descent. Your dirt road bends right and steepens, meeting a paved road at 4¼ miles. On the right the pavement ascends Red Mountain. You go left on the paved road, descending steadily.

At 4⅜ miles the descent steepens. Descend through hardwood forest with an understory of native grasses. At 4½ miles the path levels briefly, passing a picnic table. Pass under power lines and resume your descent.

Meet Red Mountain Trail on the left at 4⅝ miles. Bikers and horses must follow the paved road to descend on pavement. Weary hikers can do the same. If you're game for more exploration, turn left and descend into beautiful black oak forest. Around 4¾ miles Douglas iris line the trail. Then your descent steepens, dropping into the canyon at the headwaters of Sonoma Creek.

Before 4⅞ miles you meet Headwaters Trail, where you go right. The trail wraps around a big rock and descends near upper Sonoma Creek. The path is intermittently steep and gentle, but most always descending.

Before 5 miles the creek steepens as well. It roars down these cascades after a major storm. As the descent eases, lady ferns line the path. Then several steep sections merit caution.

Climb slightly to 5⅛ miles, then descend through live oak forest with scattered madrones, maples and firs. Around 5¼ miles you climb through a moss-covered rock garden where leather and maidenhair ferns grow, passing an immense big leaf maple on the left, known as the Ceremony Tree. Your path turns away from the creek, crosses a tributary and climbs one more short, steep hill. Then descend to meet Vista Trail before 5⅜ miles.

Turn right and climb steeply for 200 feet to an immense, beautiful glade, with poppies and other wildflowers in spring. Your trail rolls through these grasslands, grand vistas of the park unfolding with each step. Before 5½ miles the trail bends right, crossing another corner of the glade. Your view includes Sugarloaf Ridge and the hills to the west. Descend a bit to a rock outcrop on the left at 5⅝ miles.

The trail bends right to explore yet another corner of this long glade. Climb briefly to 5¾ miles, then drop through more grasslands into hardwood forest at the head of a tributary. Woodwardia ferns grow along the creek.

At 5⅞ miles you're suddenly in chaparral of twisted manzanita. Contour briefly, then descend through another glade. Soon a small seasonal pond lies on your right, where reeds, mint and wildflowers abound. At 6 miles your trail ends at the paved road.

Descend along the pavement for ¼ mile to a bench where Lower Bald Mountain Trail forks left. The side trail takes the shortest route to the trailhead. Cyclists should continue on pavement. Go left, descending into oak forest. Switchback four times as the path steepens. At 6½ miles you switchback twice more into grasslands.

At 6¾ miles complete your loop, reaching the junction where the trail on the left goes to the Group Camp. You go right, retracing your steps to the trailhead at 7¼ miles.

51.

BRUSHY PEAKS LOOP
RIDGE LOOP IN PARK'S EASTERN CORNER

From the parking area, cautiously cross the road and take the trail to the right of the picnic area. Creekside Nature Trail meanders along Sonoma Creek, with numbered signposts keyed to an interpretive text available at the park. Follow the creek upstream beneath coast live oaks, occasional white alders, Douglas firs, white and black oaks and toyon.

After passing the Campfire Center and a bridge to the campground, your trail winds through grasslands beside the creek. Cherry plums nearby are the naturalized offspring of plum trees planted by early ranchers. Ascend a short hill and return to oak woodlands.

By ⅜ mile you come to a ford of Sonoma Creek. Be careful crossing the slippery stones and logs. The trail climbs away from the creek, coming to a junction with a trail from the horse stables. Turn right and walk 300 feet to another junction where Creekside Nature Trail forks right.

Go left on Hillside Trail climbing east through a marshy area, then past a seep where blackberry vines thrive. A short spur on your left leads past a drinking fountain to a picnic table at an old homesite. The expansive view surveys the valley in the center of the park. Beyond it, Hood Mountain rises to the right of Adobe Canyon. Red Mountain is on your right, Sugarloaf Ridge on the left.

Hillside Trail continues ascending, passing water tanks around one mile. Then make a winding descent on broad tread, soon crossing a large meadow where poppies and blue-eyed Marys grow. In a wooded area you might see red larkspur and white woodland star in spring. Then your path meanders through an even larger meadow not far above Sonoma Creek.

At 1½ miles you meet a junction where Hillside Trail veers left to meet Meadow and Gray Pine Trails (Trail #50). Our described hike goes right on Brushy Peaks Trail. It soon leaves the grasslands to meander through forest along burbling Malm Fork of Sonoma Creek. Your track climbs away from the creek, soon coming to a ford of a fork of Malm Fork.

Your ascent steepens through alternating grasslands and forest. Veer left at a junction before 1⅞ miles. The path narrows and makes a winding ascent through dark mixed forest of conifers and hardwoods. From a brushy clearing you can see a vineyard high on a hillside to the southeast.

Ascend by several switchbacks through the forest. By 2⅜ miles you gain a brushy ridgetop where the view opens up to the vineyard you saw from below, now at the same elevation as you. Climb gently below the ridgetop through forest where dark red Indian warriors bloom in spring.

Around 2⅝ miles a post marks a spur on the right. The short spur circles a gentle hill at 1959 feet elevation. It offers a view of Little Bald Mountain southwest, the mountain vineyard nearby and brushy Mt. Veeder (2677'), the southernmost peak in the Mayacmas Range, to the south-southeast, with 3849-foot Mt. Diablo rising beyond it. If it weren't all private property to the south and east, this would make an idyllic takeoff point for Bay

BRUSHY PEAKS LOOP:

DISTANCE: 7-mile loop.
TERRAIN: Along creek, up and down across alternating
    grassy and wooded hillsides, ascend brushy ridge to
    peak, then down ridges and canyons.
ELEVATION GAIN/LOSS: 1310 feet+/1310 feet-
BEST TIME: Spring for wildflowers. Any clear day for views.
WARNINGS: Carry water. Watch for poison oak, ticks and
    rattlesnakes. No horses on Creekside Trail—start from stables.
HOW TO GET THERE: Same as Trail #43.
FEES: Day use: $6/vehicle. Car camping: $15/night.
FURTHER INFO: Sugarloaf Ridge State Park (707) 833-5712.

Area Ridge Trail heading south toward the East Bay Hills.

If you don't have long enough to do the full 7-mile loop,
this pleasant, grassy spot makes a good turnaround point.
Where the spur rejoins the main trail you'll see many star
lilies, blue dicks and lupines in spring.

Continuing on Brushy Peaks Loop, the ridgetop trail heads
northeast as the vegetation turns to dense chaparral. Coast
live oaks grow as brush here, so different from the stately
trees down in the valley. You will also see chamise, buckbrush,
creeping ceanothus and manzanita.

Your trail offers continuous grand views as it roller coasters
up and down along the ridgetop. Lomatium, purple night-
shade and sticky monkeyflower join the jumble of brush and
wildflowers. Gain another hilltop at 2¾ miles, then dip and
rise again along the ridge crest.

You make the steepest ascent on this loop around 2⅞ miles.
At the top of this hill a big white X marks the spot. It is not
your spot though, so drop once again then ascend toward the
westernmost of several Brushy Peaks.

Your trail veers right at 3 miles to avoid the nearby summit and
ascend gradually toward the Brushy Peak on the right. Rejoin the
ridgetop at 3⅛ miles, in 200 feet meeting a fork on the right.

Take this right fork for a short, easy climb to top the highest
of the Brushy Peaks (inside the park) at 3¼ miles. From this
2243-foot aerie, your expansive view stretches in all directions. To the southeast, another slightly taller Brushy Peak

lies just beyond the park boundary. Then clockwise the vista encompasses the twin humps of Mt. Diablo on the far horizon, Mt. Veeder to the south, Mt. Tamalpais, Little Bald Mountain to the southwest with broad Sonoma Mountain rising beyond, Sugarloaf Ridge, Bennett Mountain at Annadel, Adobe Canyon, a ridge near the coast due west, the radio-towered top of Red Mountain, then Bald Mountain west-northwest.

As you return to the main trail, look north-northwest for a view of Mt. St. Helena, Snow Mountain to its right and, visible on the clearest days, the Yolla Bollys to the right of Snow Mountain.

After you turn right on the main track, a vista opens up into the Napa Valley, with Lake Hennessey nestling in the foothills beyond all the vineyards. Your trail makes numerous small dips and rises as you head north along the ridgetop. You might notice abundant scats left by the many coyotes, bobcats and other mammals that live in these hills.

Vegetation becomes more diverse on this north slope of the Brushy Peaks near the headwaters of Malm Fork. Look for both broad- and narrow-leaf mule ears, gooseberry, toyon, yerba santa and the fragrant bright green leaves of spicebush, which has large red wine-scented flowers in late spring.

Your trail continues its erratic way along the ridgetop. Descend steeply beyond 3¾ miles, only to ascend to another knob around 3⅞ miles. Dip and rise again to 4⅛ miles. As you descend, gray pines and interior live oak rise above the chaparral. Ascend two more knobs, passing beneath power lines at the first. At the second, where birchleaf mountain mahogany grows beneath gray pines, ignore the fork on the left—it's only a fire break.

Follow the ridgetop as it descends northwest to a signed junction with Gray Pine Trail at 4⅜ miles. If you have time and desire enough to ascend Bald Mountain today, turn right and climb slightly more than a mile to the summit. Our described loop goes left, descending on Gray Pine Trail. It is 2⅝ miles to the parking lot via Gray Pine, Meadow and Bald Mountain Trails (as described in reverse order in Trail #50), about ¼ mile longer via the Hillside and Creekside Trails.

52.

CRANE CREEK REGIONAL PARK
WILDFLOWER MEADOWS, OAK WOODLANDS AND VISTAS

Sonoma Mountain, which looms over the park, has volcanic origins. It formed as a low volcanic ridge about 7 million years ago, when Cotati Valley was a saltwater bay. Enormous fissures

*vented huge quantities of molten lava, and eruptions spread ash
and debris for miles. The mountain uplifted to its present height,
2295 feet, perhaps as recently as one million years ago. In relatively recent times, the Coast Miwok tribe reached its northern
extremity here, with the village of* Lumentakala *on the slopes
of Sonoma Mountain. Southern Pomo territory was just north.
The native people gathered acorns and basketry materials,
sedge roots and willow, along Crane Creek. The park is located
on land settled by Robert Crane in 1852. His descendents still
farm nearby today. Early settlers erected graceful stone walls
(perhaps built by Chinese laborers). You may see the remains
of one such wall in the northwest corner of the park. In 1975
the county purchased 128 acres for this pleasant park. Since
cattle graze the park in late spring to minimize fire danger, it
is important that you leave all gates exactly as you find them.
Wheelchair users can generally negotiate the first ½ mile of trail,
and perhaps Lupine Trail, possibly with assistance.*

From the parking area, head north from the trailhead by the
restrooms on a level, paved path through rolling grasslands
with scattered oaks. In 100 feet the trail turns to gravel. At ⅛
mile your trail swings left and forks. Narrow Poppy Trail (no
horses or bikes) continues straight behind a gate. Turn right,
crossing a bridge over a seasonal creek to follow Creek Trail.

Draw near Crane Creek at ¼ mile, where Buckeye Trail
forks right. It fords the creek, connecting with Fiddleneck
Trail and Sunset Trail on the park's north side. You can add
about 1¼ miles to your hike by ascending Sunset Trail to its
end at the highest vista point in the park, 466 feet above sea
level, and returning to here. Our described hike veers left to
follow Creek Trail northwest along the wooded creek. Spurs
on the right lead to picnic tables and creekside.

After you pass beneath two immense California bay trees,
Creek Trail skirts the edge of Wildflower Meadow on your
left, with hardwoods growing along the creek on your right. In
spring, keep an eye on the meadow for poppy, clover, thistle,
fiddleneck, brodiaea and other wildflowers.

Around ⅜ mile poison oak, blackberry and blue dicks
grow near the creek. You come to two rest benches beneath
a large California buckeye. The creek gurgles merrily below.
Wheelchair users may need to turn back here unless they have
assistance. Creek Trail continues across a seasonal creek,
meeting the junction with Lupine Trail on the left. It forks
left through the heart of Wildflower Meadow.

Continue on Creek Trail, soon drawing beside the murmuring creek. Then Creek Trail veers away from the creek,
crossing two seasonal streams.

CRANE CREEK REGIONAL PARK:

DISTANCE: 1½-mile loop, with options to add up to 1⅜ miles or more.

TIME: One or two hours.

TERRAIN: Gentle loop contours through grasslands, then descends along creek and climbs grassy ridge to overlooks.

ELEVATION GAIN/LOSS: 250 feet+/250 feet- for described loop. Climb to Sunset Trail overlook adds 160 feet+/160 feet-.

BEST TIME: Wildflowers in spring.

WARNINGS: Leave gates as you find them. Please keep bikes and horses on trails designated for their use. Watch for poison oak. Park open sunrise to sunset. No fires allowed.

HOW TO GET THERE: Exit Highway 101 at Rohnert Park Expressway. Go east 2.5 miles, then right on Petaluma Hill Road. In 1.2 miles go left on Roberts Road. Go 1.9 miles, the last .6 mile on Pressley Road, then turn left into park entrance and parking lot.

FEE: Day use $5/vehicle.

FURTHER INFO: Sonoma County Parks (707) 565-2041.

Come to a second junction with Lupine Trail around ⅝ mile. You can go left and return via Lupine Trail for the shortest, easiest hike. Our described hike stays right, following Creek Trail to its end in about 500 feet at its junction with Fiddleneck Trail. You can turn right on Fiddleneck Trail for another short, easy loop.

Our described hike crosses Fiddleneck Trail to follow Northern Loop Trail. At the top of a hill around ¾ mile, a dense patch of soap plant grows on your left. Descend to the northwestern corner of the park, passing a rest bench with a pastoral view. Follow the trail as it swings left to again meet Fiddleneck Trail at ⅞ mile.

Turn right and follow Fiddleneck Trail on a gentle climb south with a seasonal stream on the right. At one mile you pass a connector to nearby Lupine Trail on your left. Continue south on Fiddleneck Trail, passing Poppy Trail where it forks left in 150 feet.

Follow Fiddleneck Trail as it fords the seasonal creek and climbs moderately through grasslands. It climbs to a junction at 1¼ miles, with a nearby view bench. You can continue straight on Fiddleneck Trail, which soon loops back to the trailhead. I prefer to turn left on Hawk Ridge Trail (no horses or bikes). In 75 feet it comes to a rest bench at Bowden Bluff. From here you have a sweeping vista of the heart of the park and the surrounding hills of Sonoma Mountain.

Continue on Hawk Ridge Trail as it contours southeast near the ridgetop. It is bordered by lichen-encrusted rocks, blue-eyed grass and abundant soap plant. By 1⅜ miles, the parking lot is visible ahead, but follow the trail as it veers right to a junction. To conclude your hike, turn left and descend broad Fiddleneck Trail to the parking lot at 1½ miles.

If you are not quite ready to return, follow the short Overlook Loop Trail southwest, adding ⅛ mile to your hike. It descends slightly to a bench in 300 feet. From there you have a commanding view west over the Cotati/Santa Rosa flood plain and through Petaluma Wind Gap toward the Pacific. When you've had your fill of the view, it's about ⅛ mile to the trailhead.

OTHER SUGGESTION: FAIRFIELD OSBORN PRESERVE offers guided hikes on weekends to explore the beautiful canyons and ridges near the top of Sonoma Mountain. You must call (707) 795-5069 and get permission before going. To reach the preserve, where Pressley Road goes left, turn right on Lichau Road and go 3.5 miles to parking on right.

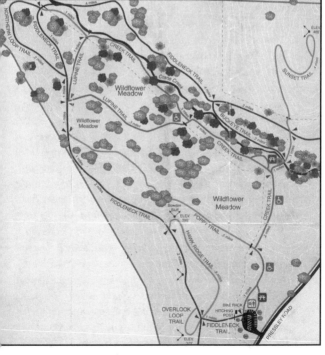

JACK LONDON
STATE HISTORIC PARK
INCLUDES NEXT TWO TRAILS

I liked those hills up there. They were beautiful . . . and I wanted beauty. So I extended the boundary up to the top of that ridge and all along it . . . I bought beauty, and I was content with beauty for a while.

Jack London was a brash and brilliant young Californian who never allowed himself the time to grow old. Born out of wedlock January 12, 1876 in San Francisco, Jack lifted himself from poverty to become one of the most popular and acclaimed writers of his generation, one of the first American authors to make a million dollars from his work. He succeeded with adventure stories, but wrote eloquently of the dilemma of the human condition. He lived for love and beauty, but died at age 40, exhausted and physically spent.

Jack's mother and step-father frequently moved the family from one bay area town to another, seeking a decent living. As an adolescent Jack worked various jobs, selling newspapers, setting pins in a bowling alley, keeping bees. At fifteen he became an oyster pirate on San Francisco Bay, robbing other people's oyster beds for excitement and easy profit. At seventeen Jack became a seaman on a sealing schooner, taking a seven-month cruise to Japan. These early experiences nourished his love of sailing.

Upon his return Jack worked several jobs of hard physical labor, "inhuman hours on barbarous jobs." Wanderlust soon sent him tramping cross-country. At Niagara Falls he was arrested for vagrancy and served a month in prison, then rode the rails back to Oakland.

The hardships and suffering Jack encountered on his tramping adventures pushed him toward his life-long commitment to socialism and encouraged him to seek an education. He attended Oakland High School for a year and enrolled in the University of California at Berkeley in 1896. But the impatient, restless young man soon dropped college.

When news of the Klondike gold rush reached California, Jack London put together a grubstake and headed for the Yukon. He found little gold during his year in the Northland, but the sojourn was one of the most important events in his life. "It was in the Klondike that I found myself," he said later. London returned to Oakland and began writing. He sold some stories to Overland Monthly and Atlantic Monthly. Within two years of his return from the Klondike, Houghton-

Mifflin published Jack's first book, The Son of the Wolf, to favorable reviews, launching his career.

Jack London married Bessie Maddern, and they produced two daughters. It was during this loveless marriage that Jack wrote The Call of the Wild, his great short novel that has been published in 70 languages. Jack and Bessie separated in 1903.

Jack first went to the Sonoma Valley to escape the notoriety caused by his simultaneous best seller and the break up of his marriage. He was immediately drawn to its marvelous natural landscape: peaceful wooded hills and year-round streams interspersed with orchards and vineyards. In Glen Ellen he met and courted the spirited Charmian Kittredge, whose family owned a lodge there. In 1905 Jack spent some of his royalties to buy 127 acres of a rundown farm on the wooded slopes of Sonoma Mountain, the start of his beloved Beauty Ranch.

> All I wanted was a quiet place in the country to write and loaf in and get out of Nature that something which we all need, only the most of us don't know it.

But Jack was too restless and eager for adventure to settle down and spend all his time there. He built a sailboat and set out with Charmian to sail around the world. They got as far as the South Pacific and Australia before Jack's health problems forced him to sell the boat and return to Glen Ellen.

From 1909 to 1914 he expanded his ranch. In 1911 they moved to a small house on the ranch and began work on Wolf House, the mansion where they planned to live out their days. Jack threw himself into scientific agriculture based upon the principles of his friend, Luther Burbank, farming and working the ranch. Jack and Charmian entertained friends here, including other literary giants of their times like novelist Frank Norris and poets George Sterling and Joaquin Miller.

Then in 1913, Wolf House burned, just before the Londons were to move in. They were painfully aware that someone, perhaps a friend, may have deliberately set the fire. The mystery remains unsolved. Jack never fully recovered from this disaster.

Jack wrote prolifically throughout the good and bad times, in fact right to the day he died. He almost never missed his early morning writing stint, consistently producing 1000 words a day. Between 1900 and 1916, he completed more than fifty books, hundreds of short stories and numerous articles on diverse subjects. Add to this his extensive touring, lecturing, socializing and voluminous correspondence, not to mention the operation of the ranch, it is easy to see why Jack tried to limit his "wasted" sleeping time to no more than four or five hours a night.

215

Suffering from an expanding variety of health problems, Jack ignored the advice of his doctors to relax his work habits, improve his diet, give up alcohol and get more exercise. If anything Jack worked even harder to realize his ambitions and pay off the mounting debts that his grand schemes produced. He generously continued to support friends and relatives.

Jack never grew complacent in his success. A few months before his death, he told Charmian, "I am standing on the edge of a world so new, so terrible, so wonderful, that I am almost afraid to look over into it." But look he did, writing prolifically and daringly up to the day he died, November 22, 1916, of an unintentional overdose of morphine, taken to ease his pain from gastrointestinal poisoning and a kidney condition.

The obituary in the San Francisco Bulletin *summarized the world's loss:*

> *No writer, unless it were Mark Twain, ever had a more romantic life than Jack London. The untimely death of this most popular of American fictionists has profoundly shocked a world that expected him to live and work for many years longer.*

Jack's old friend George Sterling correctly predicted that "[h]is greatness will surge triumphantly above race and time."

53.

JACK LONDON'S WOLF HOUSE RUINS
REMNANTS OF A DREAM NEARLY COME TRUE

From the lower parking area, head east on the paved path. In 350 feet you come to the House of Happy Walls, which serves as the park's visitor center (open 10–5). Be sure to drop in and explore the fine exhibits, so evocative of the Londons' time at Beauty Ranch.

Charmian London had the House of Happy Walls built in 1919–22, after Jack had died. She lived here (when not traveling) until her death in 1955 at age 84. Her will specified that the house be used as a memorial to Jack and a museum.

This house is similar to Wolf House in that it has walls of volcanic stone and a roof of Spanish tiles, but it is more intimate and formal. Much of the furniture was designed by the Londons and built for Wolf House. The library has

JACK LONDON'S WOLF HOUSE RUINS:

DISTANCE: 1½ miles round trip.

TIME: One hour.

TERRAIN: Easy descent through woodlands and grasslands
to ruins of Jack London's house, surrounded by redwoods.

ELEVATION GAIN/LOSS: 160 feet+/160 feet-.

BEST TIME: Spring for wildflowers. Nice anytime.

WARNINGS: Watch for poison oak and rattlesnakes. Park
open 9:30-5 daily, until 7 in summer.

HOW TO GET THERE: At M.30.7 on Highway 12 east
of Santa Rosa, turn south on Arnold Drive. In .9 mile,
in the town of Glen Ellen, as Arnold Drive veers left,
you go right on London Ranch Road. Go 1.25 miles to
entrance, then left to trailhead.

FEES: Day use: $6/vehicle.

FURTHER INFO: Jack London State Park (707) 938-5216.

furnishings from Jack London's study, which was in the cottage (see next trail).

From the visitor center, take the gravel path descending east. You pass a display of wagons and farm equipment from Beauty Ranch, although Jack's beloved passenger wagons are absent.

Your trail turns left, descending through forest of madrones, oaks, bays, buckeyes, toyon and young firs. Beyond ⅛ mile the path bends left again, passing massive live oaks. At ¼ mile your trail levels and skirts the edge of a meadow. In spring you will see Indian warriors, buttercups, hound's tongue, and poppies. Cross a tiny creek at the bottom of the meadow, climb briefly, then descend through forest where you may hear a murmuring creek. Pass a rest bench and a drinking fountain.

At ⅜ mile you cross another creek and meet a broad paved trail. Turn left on the paved path, which levels as the creek drops away on the left. The path swings right and climbs a hill, then descends.

At ½ mile you reach a junction, with another drinking fountain and bench. Go right, descending along the edge of a glade with fruit trees on your right, black and live oaks on the left. Sonoma Mountain rises to the southwest. At ⅝ mile your descent steepens, coming to Wolf House ruins, surrounded

217

by redwood forest above Asbury Creek.

Take the path that wraps left around the ruins. Climb the leather-leaf fern-draped stairs on the south wall to overlook the house. A floor plan there helps you visualize the Londons' dream. Notice the stag party room (for men only), the fireproof manuscript vault and Jack's sleeping tower. The rough-cut maroon volcanic rock of the interior and exterior walls presents a rugged look. Unpeeled redwood logs framed the front entrance and beautiful redwood paneling graced the inside walls. The double-thick concrete foundation and lower walls were intended to be fireproof. All the modern utilities and appliances then available were installed. The four-story house had 15,000 square feet, 26 rooms and nine fireplaces. The outdoor pool was to be stocked with bass.

With his Wolf House, poverty-born Jack London strove to realize a life-long dream. Construction began in 1911 on the house designed by well-known San Francisco architect Albert Farr with much input from the Londons. By August 1913 London had spent more than $80,000 and the project was nearly complete. On August 22 final cleanup began and plans were made to move the Londons' belongings into the mansion. In the middle of that night Jack received word that the house was burning. By the time the Londons arrived, the roof had collapsed and nothing could be saved. The Londons' grand dream and much of their fortune crumbled into ash. Today moss, lichen and ferns inhabit the space for which Jack and Charmian had such plans.

218

Continue clockwise around the ruins, returning to the graceful arches of the front entrance at ¾ mile. Perhaps you will see a red-tailed hawk circling overhead, its shrill, mournful cry piercing the silence. How easily our dreams can turn to ruin!

Retrace your steps uphill, returning to the junction at ⅞ mile. Take the side path on the right, climbing through oak woodlands to a knoll before one mile. Jack London knew this place and wrote about it in his novel *Burning Daylight*.

He came out abruptly upon the cypresses. They were enclosed in a small square of ancient fence; the pickets he could plainly see had been hewn and sharpened by hand. Inside were the mounds of two children's graves. Two wooden headboards, likewise hand-hewn, told the story: Little David, died [November 25, 1876]; and Little Lily, died [August 8, 1877]. "The poor little kids," Daylight muttered.

On the left a large block of red lava marks Jack London's grave. Only three years after the devastating fire, his ashes were buried in a copper urn sealed in concrete. Charmian was buried beside him many years later. Jack chose to have his remains rest beside the two young innocents in this tranquil spot.

Return to the paved trail and go right. When you reach the junction with the dirt path you descended, beyond 1⅛ miles, you can go right to return to the House of Happy Walls or continue on the paved path. Either way you come to the parking area at 1½ miles.

OTHER SUGGESTIONS: You can arrange guided HORSE-BACK TRAIL RIDES in the park by calling (707) 887-8700. JACK LONDON BOOKSTORE, which now only does telephone sales, has a wonderful collection of books by and about the sailor on horseback. Call (707) 996-2888.

54.

SONOMA MOUNTAIN

"MOST BEAUTIFUL PRIMITIVE LAND TO BE FOUND IN CALIFORNIA"

Jack London wrote eloquently of the wild upper reaches of his Beauty Ranch:

> *On the steep incline above the spring grew tiny maiden-hair ferns, while higher up were larger ferns and breaks. Great, moss-covered trunks of fallen trees lay here and there, slowly sinking back and merging into the level of the forest mould. Beyond it, in a slightly clearer space,*

SONOMA MOUNTAIN:

DISTANCE: (all round trip) 8⅛ miles to Mountain Spur, 10⅝ miles for Sonoma Ridge Trail, or 13¼ miles for full hike.

TIME: Four or five hours.

TERRAIN: Past vineyards and historical buildings to small lake, then climb through oak woodlands and grasslands to shoulder of Sonoma Mountain.

ELEVATION GAIN/LOSS: 1800 feet+/1800 feet−.

BEST TIME: Spring for wildflowers. Clear day for views.

WARNINGS: Watch for poison oak, ticks and rattlesnakes. Stay off adjacent private property. Dogs allowed on first ¼ mile. Park open 9:30–5 daily, until 7 in summer.

HOW TO GET THERE: On Highway 12 east of Santa Rosa (M.30.7), turn south onto Arnold Drive. In .9 mile, in Glen Ellen, as Arnold veers left, you go right on London Ranch Road. Go 1.25 miles to entrance, then right to trailhead.

FEES: Day use: $6/vehicle.

FURTHER INFO: Jack London State Park (707) 938-5216.

wild grape and honeysuckle hung in green riot from gnarled old oak trees. A gray Douglas squirrel crept out on a branch and watched him. From somewhere came the distant knocking of a woodpecker. This sound did not disturb the hush and awe of the place. Quiet woods' noises belonged there and made the solitude complete. The tiny bubbling ripple of the spring and the gray flash of tree-squirrel were as yardsticks with which to measure the silence and motionless repose. "Might be a million miles from anywhere."

From the upper parking area, where you'll find an updated map of park trails, your trail climbs southwest into a eucalyptus grove, one of several Jack London planted on his Beauty Ranch. In 250 feet you reach a pleasant picnic ground. Go straight, descending slightly to the road (from the equestrian trailhead) signed "Lake." To the left stand three stone buildings. The Sherry Barn dates from 1884, the pre-London winery days. Behind it stand London's Manure Pit and Stallion Barn.

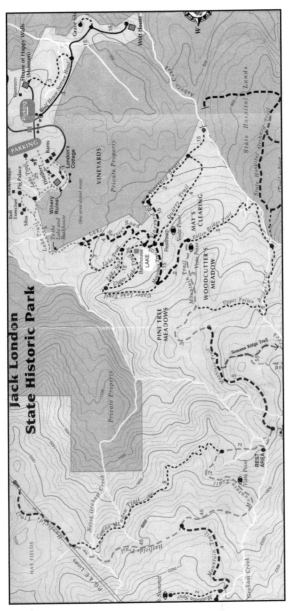

Go right on the dirt road, climbing past the stone Distillery Building on your left at ⅛ mile. A short spur on the left leads to the humble cottage where Jack London worked in his final years. Jack added the small room on the southwest side of the building after Wolf House burned in 1913. He wrote many of his later works, including *The Star Rover*, in this study overlooking the vineyards. On November 22, 1916, Jack London died in the glassed porch on the southeast side. The cottage has been restored recently and is open to the public on weekends from 12 to 4.

The main trail soon forks. Bear right and head along the mustard-dappled vineyard on your left. You can see stone retaining walls built to terrace the steeper fields, to prevent erosion and retain moisture. After meeting the horse trail, your road bends left,passing a spur on the right that leads to London's Pig Palace and silos. (No dogs beyond this point.)

Staying left, you climb gradually around the vineyard at ¼ mile. At ⅜ mile, you top a rise where a rare white eucalyptus stands on the right. Beyond it the view north encompasses Valley of the Moon and Hood Mountain, a volcanic outcrop of the Mayacmas Range (see Trail #48).

Your trail bends left at a corner of the vineyard and climbs, with wild forest (and a smattering of London's eucalyptus) on your right. As you approach a gate on the road, a trail branches right, entering the forest. Equestrians and mountain bikers must continue on the road. Hikers take the more intimate path that dips, then climbs through forest of redwood, Douglas fir, bay laurel, big leaf maple, madrone and eucalyptus. In the understory you may find toyon, coffeeberry, hazel, hairy honeysuckle, sword fern and assorted wildflowers. Around ⅝ mile your trail bends left, climbing through the forest, with trilliums and twisted stalk in the understory. The main trail climbs steadily, passing redwoods to three feet in diameter.

Around ¾ mile you climb past a split rail fence protecting redwoods on your left. Climb to a junction at a rest bench before ⅞ mile. Take the less traveled right fork.When your trail forks again, take the left fork.

This side trail provides a ⅜-mile side trip to the lake and back.It reaches the tules at the upper end of the five-acre lake in ⅛ mile, then follows the oak-shaded north shore to London's rustic redwood bathhouse and the beach and picnic area. Jack and Charmian London played here, often alone, sometimes with large groups of friends. A curving stone dam forms the east shore. If you come upon the lake quietly when no one is here, hundreds of birds might squawk and shrill, producing a joyous symphony of sounds.

Cyclists and equestrians will meet the lake at the dam and continue up the road from there. Our described hike returns to the junction north of the lake at 1⅜ miles. Go straight at the junction, climbing northwest toward Sonoma Mountain. You soon switchback left and climb gradually through forest above the lake. You can glimpse the lake through the trees.

Before 1⅝ miles you meet Mountain Trail (road) at a big bend where you go right, climbing steadily through mixed forest. Maidenhair and leather-leaf ferns grow on the bank on the right, as does poison oak.

At 1¾ miles you enter Mays Clearing, where a view unfolds

southeast along the flank of Sonoma Mountain and down Valley of the Moon to the north end of San Francisco Bay, with Mt. Diablo rising beyond. Fallen Bridge Trail forks left, descending ½ mile to old Sonoma State Hospital lands, now part of Jack London State Historic Park.

Mountain Trail veers right and climbs into the forest. At 1⅞ miles you climb steadily along the north slope of a ridge, where lady and maidenhair ferns grow beneath mixed forest. At 2 miles you meet the upper end of Fallen Bridge Trail at Woodcutter's Meadow. The spur goes left over a saddle, climbing to North Asbury Creek before descending steeply to the other end of its loop.

Your trail veers right, climbing through the forest. Around 2⅛ miles you skirt several glades, mapped as Pine Tree Meadows although only one pine grows here; large firs dominate the surrounding forest. The trail makes a big bend left as the sound of rushing water rises from Graham Creek. Return to the forest at 2¼ miles.

Mountain Trail ascends steadily, then descends briefly to cross two or three forks of South Graham Creek, where redwoods, elk clover and woodwardia ferns grow. Before the upper ford of South Graham Creek, the new Sonoma Ridge Trail forks left around 2¾ miles. You can turn left and take that out and back trail to add 2¾ miles to your hike. It is described at the end of this trail report.

Continue on Mountain Trail as it climbs steeply through rocky terrain in lush forest, meeting Upper Treadmill Road beyond 2¾ miles. Your ascent eases, continuing through redwood forest to cross Middle Graham Creek, lined with nutmeg and oceanspray, and reach London's Deer Camp at 2⅞ miles.

Marked as a rest area on the park map, Deer Camp offers a picnic table in a grove of redwoods along a spring-fed creek jammed with woodwardia ferns. The site looks north across a beautiful glade surrounded by oak forest. Jack London would bring his guests to camp and hunt here. An old stone wall rims the east edge of the clearing above the grove. Beyond it sits a knoll with a fine view east to Valley of the Moon and the Mayacmas Range.

Your trail climbs through the glade to a junction at 3 miles. On the right Cowan Meadow Trail climbs north. Your Mountain Trail goes left, climbing steeply through hardwood forest. At 3⅛ miles you round a big bend left, then make the steepest climb yet as your trail passes native bunch grasses beneath black oaks and bay laurels.

Your climb eases at 3¼ miles where an overlook on the left perches above a steeply rolling glade. Climb steeply again, around 3⅜ miles approaching the precipitous canyon of

Middle Graham Creek. The rugged climb continues through a beautiful meadow, then returns to oak forest.

At 3⅝ miles the trail levels and enters a rolling glade studded with mistletoe-draped black oaks. You meet Hayfields Trail, which branches right, meandering for nearly a mile to the park's north boundary. Go left, contouring through grasslands, then climbing to the largest glade yet at 3⅞ miles, stretching west to the summit of Sonoma Mountain.

Your road soon bends left, leaving the grasslands to return to oak forest. Beyond 4 miles, Mountain Trail bends right and draws alongside one of the headwaters of Middle Graham Creek. Climb along the creek, reaching the park boundary before 4⅛ miles.

The park map shows the trail ending here. In fact, a footpath climbs north along the boundary fence to reenter the immense glade. At 4¼ miles you climb a very steep, short hill to the park's summit, the crest of Sonoma Mountain's east ridge. At 2380 feet you are about 80 feet below the mountain top, visible with its forest of antennae and microwave relays ¼ mile west. Private property stands between you and the summit of the mountain, but the park's summit provides grand views and an aerie more peaceful than the rise to the west.

Jack London scaled Sonoma Mountain many times. He obviously loved it up here:

> There were no houses in the summit of Sonoma Mountain, and, all alone under the azure California sky, he reigned in on the . . . edge of the peak. He saw open pasture country, intersected with wooden canyons, descending . . . from his feet, crease on crease and roll on roll, from lower level to lower level, to the floor of [the] valley. Swinging his horse, he surveyed the west and north, from Santa Rosa to Mount St. Helena, and on to the east, across Sonoma Valley, to the chaparral-covered range that shut off the view of Napa Valley. . . . [H]e continued the circle of his survey to the southeast, where, across the waters of San Pablo Bay, he could see, sharp and distant, the twin peaks of Mount Diablo. To the south was Mount Tamalpais, and, yes, he was right, fifty miles away, where the draughty winds of the Pacific blew in the Golden Gate, the smoke of San Francisco made a low-lying haze against the sky. He was loath to depart, and it was not for an hour that he was able to tear himself away and take the descent of the mountain.

When you are able to tear away, return by the same route you ascended. If you stay on the main road all the way you will save about ¼ mile, making the total hike 8¼ miles. If you return late in the day, keep a sharp eye out for the deer, coyote, fox, racoon and other mammals that become active in the evening. Remember that the park closes at the hour posted at the entrance kiosk.

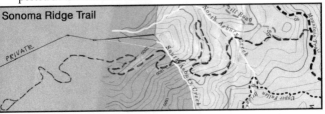

Sonoma Ridge Trail

If you still have two extra hours and enough energy, explore the new Sonoma Ridge Trail, which heads south from the 2¾-mile point, below Deer Camp and the Upper Treadmill junction, making a 5⅛-mile semi-loop. Sonoma Ridge Trail (open to hikers, equestrians and mountain bikers) climbs south gradually through mixed forest, soon turning east. Your trail ascends north briefly around ⅛ mile, then climbs northeast past maidenhair ferns and soap plant beneath a forest of mostly bays, with scattered buckeyes and Douglas firs.

Around ¼ mile you top a ridge and make a winding contour south, gaining filtered views of Sonoma Mountain and Valley of the Moon. At ⅜ mile your trail meets Lower Treadmill Road, which forks right to climb south. Stay on Sonoma Ridge Trail, climbing gradually southeast and south, then contouring across a side hill.

Beyond ½ mile our trail bends right to cross Asbury Creek near its headwaters, where a tiny waterfall makes an idyllic spot beneath redwoods. Elk clover grows at the ford. Your trail climbs gently through Douglas fir forest with scattered oaks and bays.

Climb gradually from ¾ mile, then moderately south. Around ⅞ mile you gain a vista across Valley of the Moon to the Mayacmas Range. Soon you switchback right to climb moderately north and northwest. By 1⅛ miles your trail ascends west, then makes a slow bend left, passing abundant wildflowers in spring.

By 1¼ miles your trail again climbs south, but soon switchbacks left on a gradual ascent east. As your trail levels at 1⅜ miles, Mt. St. Helena rises to the north beyond the Mayacmas Range.

Beyond 1½ miles, you make a steady, well graded climb south. Switchback right, then just beyond 1⅝ miles, switchback left below a fence. Climb moderately south and southeast to 1⅞ miles where your trail switchbacks right.

Sonoma Ridge Trail switchbacks left before 2 miles, climbing near the crest of the ridgetop now. Soon woodlands yield to steeply rolling grasslands just above the trail. Before 2⅛ miles you gain a view of the town of Sonoma's end of Valley of the Moon. Your trail leaves the woodlands for grasslands, then a slight descent returns you to forest before you reach a

225

broad grassland. Descend into the grasslands scattered with large oaks. A fence marks private property to the west.

Your trail bends left to contour north, then winds east and south above an immensely steep drop to Valley of the Moon. Descend slightly to cross the headwaters of a seasonal creek.

Just beyond 2⅜ miles you come to a junction marked "Sonoma Ridge Trail Loop Trail (BART). Turn right to make a scenic, view-studded loop. Climb briefly on an old double track paralleling the private property fence just west. From 2½ miles your trail descends. Soon you must veer left, with another fence marking private property to the south. An agreement was reached in 2006 to extend this trail south

The loop trail soon descends north to a CLOSED sign on the continuation of the the the double track. Veer left and ascend gradually northwest on single track, returning to the loop junction at 2¾ miles. Stay right and retrace your steps on Sonoma Ridge Trail, returning to Mountain Trail at 5⅛ miles. Turn right to descend Mountain Trail 2¾ miles to the trailhead.

55.

CANYON/RIDGE LOOP

SONOMA VALLEY REGIONAL PARK

In 1880 the San Francisco and North Pacific Railroad completed tracks from the shore of San Pablo Bay, through the bustling town of Sonoma and up Valley of the Moon to sleepy Glen Ellen. Their passenger train soon became a popular excursion for city-weary people fleeing to the country for a weekend or a week. The railroad chugged through what is now Sonoma Valley Regional Park before reaching the end of the line at the Glen Ellen Depot, less than a mile north. The line was extended to Santa Rosa before 1890, then discontinued in 1935 after business dwindled in the depression.

These rolling oak- and wildflower-studded hills served many years as the dairy farm for nearby Sonoma State Hospital. Sonoma County acquired the lush 162 acres in 1973 for a park. Today the trail system explores the canyons and ridges tucked among the folds of Valley of the Moon. The paved Canyon Trail is as gentle as the Ridge Trail is angular. You can stay on the former for an easy walk, also accessible to people with handicaps (with some assistance). Or you can climb to the top of the park for expansive views of Glen Ellen, Valley of the Moon and the Mayacmas and Sonoma Ranges. On a clear day the Ridge Trail provides ample reward for its short climb. Dog owners should

CANYON/RIDGE LOOP:

DISTANCE: 2⅝-mile loop.

TIME: One or two hours.

TERRAIN: Gentle descent on paved trail down wooded canyon, then along old railroad grade. Return by same trail for easiest walk, or climb footpath to ridge with views, then return to trailhead.

ELEVATION GAIN/LOSS: Loop: 320 feet+/320 feet-. Paved path: 160 feet+/160 feet-.

BEST TIME: Spring for wildflowers.

WARNINGS: Watch for poison oak and rattlesnakes. Stay off adjacent private property.

HOW TO GET THERE: On Highway 12 in Glen Ellen at M.31.1, turn west into Sonoma Valley Regional Park.

FEES: Day use: $5/vehicle.

FURTHER INFO: Sonoma Valley Regional Park (707) 539-8092 or 565-2041.

make a point of checking out the great new fenced dog park northeast of the parking area. Let your dog run free and social-ize, then put the dog back on leash and take it for a hike.

From the parking lot, paved Canyon Trail passes through a gate and heads toward two huge green water tanks. In 250 feet your paved path meets a junction with a gravel track on the left that climbs to the water tanks. Stay right on the paved path which soon starts a gentle descent, passing grass nut and poppies in spring. At ⅛ mile mimulus and tidy tips grow on the left in spring, with California poppies on the right. Also on the right is a picnic table beside blue oaks. A tiny seasonal creek starts here, burbling beside the picnic spot.

Trail and creek descend gently, following and crisscrossing each other. Your trail winds through Oregon and blue oak forest draped with the gray-green lichen called old man's beard. At ¼ mile the creek crosses to the left of your path. Lupine, bedstraw and Mariposa lilies grow on the right. Steep, grassy hills dotted with abundant oaks rise beside the trail, but you descend gently.

At ⅜ mile, as the creek returns to the right side of the trail, another picnic table sits beside the stream. Scattered

227

manzanitas, blue dicks, yarrow and other wildflowers grow here. Watch out for poison oak twining around oaks along the trail. You may also spot mule ears and miners lettuce beneath California black oaks.

At ½ mile a footpath on your left climbs a side canyon. Stay on the paved path, swerving left across the creek. Tiny white flowers called milkmaids grow abundantly here as early as January, with blue dicks and yellow fiddlenecks later in spring. As you continue your gentle descent, Sonoma Mountain rises to the west.

Pass another picnic table on the right at ⅝ mile. If you picnic here, stay away from the nearby oak wrapped in poison oak. In 75 feet, a massive Oregon oak three feet in diameter is on the right. Buckeye, bay laurel and coast live oak grow nearby.

Soon a tiny gully descends from the left. Beside it grow soap plants, a lily with many uses to Indians and early settlers. The local Wappo used glue from the bulb, green dye from the leaves for tattooing, and ate leaves and roasted bulbs. Settlers crushed the bulbs to make soap and shampoo. Soap plants grow profusely on this walk. Hikers rarely see soap plant's delicate white flowers which only open in the evening or on cloudy days. Growing nearby are iris, woodland star, buttercups and tall lupine.

Your trail climbs a slight rise as the creek wanders away on the right. At ¾ mile several picnic tables line the creek near an immense fallen oak as you approach the old railroad right-of-way. Your paved trail bends left, then right to join the level railroad bed. (You can turn right to follow the bed to the park boundary, a ⅜-mile side trip.) The main trail passes through a dense grove of madrones as houses appear on your right. As you turn south, Sonoma Creek parallels your path on the right. The road noise comes from busy Arnold Drive on the far side of the creek. Continue on the paved level path along the railroad grade. In spring, Chinese houses grow on the left, with narrow-leaved mule ears and blue dicks on the right.

At one mile a dirt trail runs between you and Sonoma Creek. Pass a large manzanita on the left. At 1⅛ miles the hill on your left is crowded with soap plants beneath live and Oregon oaks. Elegant brodiaea thrive here in spring. In 400 feet your paved path splits into three forks: a dirt footpath climbs the bank on your left, the graveled railroad bed in the center curves left, while your paved path swings right. The latter climbs a slight rise to two last picnic tables at 1¼ miles before coming to a gate and Arnold Drive. For the easiest walk, retrace your steps, returning to the parking lot at 2½ miles.

If you prefer a slightly more challenging hike, take the dirt footpath. It climbs north into oak forest. Many rocks lie beside the trail, some as large as Volkswagen Bugs. Climb steadily on rocky tread to 1⅝ miles, where soap plants and vetch grow beneath Oregon and live oaks, with blue-eyed grass beneath buckeyes. Scattered manzanita, bay laurel and toyon also grow along the trail. Stay right at an unmarked junction, the left fork descending steeply to the paved path.

You pass yarrow as your trail bends right and climbs steeply. At 1¾ miles you reach the ridge and pass a fence. You come to a T junction on the ridgetop. Turn left and descend northeast along the ridge. Milkmaid and sun cup brighten the way in winter, poppy, Indian warrior and paintbrush in spring. Your path bends left, descending along the ridgetop.

Continue a gradual descent near ridge and fence line. At 1⅞ miles you climb again, continuing along the fence. You soon reach a high top on the ridge. You look out over broken terrain

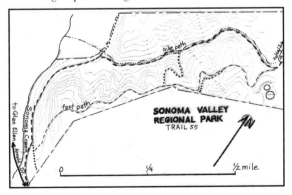

SONOMA VALLEY
REGIONAL PARK
TRAIL 55

to Glen Ellen   Arnold Dr.   Sonoma Creek

bike path

foot path

0   ¼   ½ mile

229

that supports the geological theory that Valley of the Moon is a series of basins rather than a true valley. Over time, Sonoma Creek has carved a channel to connect the separate basins.

Descend gradually along the ridge to 2 miles, where your trail levels. Then your trail dips to an unmarked junction, then climbs near the ridge crest, coming to a top where you immediately meet another T junction where you turn left. At 2⅛ miles another trail forks left, descending northwest. Your Ridge Trail goes northeast as views open up to Lake Suttonfield and Sonoma State Hospital. Continue along the contours of the ridge to a broad hilltop at 2¼ miles, where you descend north to a saddle by the fence line, then rise to another top. Turn left on the well-trod main path as it descends. Follow the obvious path to one last small ridgetop where you have a fine view over pastoral park lands and Valley of the Moon beyond. You can see Sugarloaf Ridge and Hood Mountain to the north.

Your path descends from here. Beyond 2⅜ miles you again meet a T junction. Turn left and descend to the left of the big water tanks, then veer left between large oaks and descend toward the parking lot. You join a gravel road that descends to the paved path. You reach the parking lot before 2⅝ miles.

56.

MAXWELL FARMS REGIONAL PARK
COUNTRY OASIS IN CITY OF SONOMA

Dedicated in 1988, Maxwell Farms Regional Park offers 85 acres of woods and fields bordering Sonoma Creek. Turn-of-the-century conservationist George Maxwell, an advocate for small farmers, had a farm here. Though the park is small, it provides peace and solitude not far from Sonoma Valley's busiest intersection.

From the west end of the parking lot, take the dirt path, signed "Verano Trail," that descends west around the athletic field. As your track angles left to parallel Verano Avenue, Sonoma Mountain towers in the background. Veer right at the first junction in 200 feet. Beyond the baseball diamond you meet another junction. The Upper Meadow Trail goes left, but our described hike continues west through riparian woodlands.

Descend into oak woodlands, then through a stand of English walnut trees. Himalaya blackberry and native snowberry and bay laurel grow along the trail. By ⅛ mile you cross a gully where periwinkle carpets the ground.

230

DISTANCE: 1-mile loop or 1¼-mile loop.
TIME: Less than one hour.
TERRAIN: Grasslands and woods along Sonoma Creek.
BEST TIME: Spring for wildflowers.
WARNINGS: Watch for poison oak. Stay off adjacent
    private property.
HOW TO GET THERE: Turn west off Highway 12 (at
    M.36, north end of Sonoma) onto Verano Avenue, then
    quickly left into park.
FEES: Day use: $5/vehicle.
FURTHER INFO: Sonoma County Parks (707) 565-2041.

You soon meet the broad Three Meadow Trail. Go left, following the top of the creek's cutbank south. In about 250 feet an unsigned trail on the left is confusing. Go right at the unsigned junction, heading generally southwest along the top edge of the cutbank, with Sonoma Creek visible below.

The path parallels the creek. You can see a meadow through the trees on your left. A immense bay tree on your right at ¼ mile stands 100 feet tall and eight feet in diameter.

Soon a fence on your right blocks a 20-foot plunge to the shallow creek. Your trail skirts the meadow merging with a broader trail from the left. Stay right on the lower path along the top of the creek bank. Wild anise, willows and young cottonwoods grow densely on the right.

At ⅜ mile you meet the junction of Three Meadow Trail and the creek access spur on the right, which descends 200 feet to deadend at the shore in a pretty spot. Continue straight to pass red flowering currant, quickly returning to shady bay laurel woodlands above the creek. Soon a spur on the right descends quickly to the creek. The main trail continues straight, then veers left to return to the fire break and meadow. A path goes straight to the parking lot, but you veer right on dirt Back Meadow Trail, heading southeast.

Your trail passes coast live oaks, then stays left of a fence. Turn left where you meet the southern park boundary beyond ½ mile. Head east through grasslands lined with oaks, paralleling

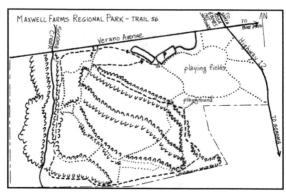

the boundary. Ignore several paths that fork left. Follow Back Meadow Trail across grasslands, meeting the south end of Bay Tree Trail. Continue on Back Meadow Trail through the dark, fragrant woods, a windrow of native trees left by farmer Maxwell to create a protected microclimate in the adjacent fields.

Your path finally veers left beneath a large coast live oak, breaks into grasslands and heads north toward a nearby shopping mall. Beyond ¾ mile the path bends left away from the mall and climbs to merge with a gravel service road. Follow the road north, then northwest.

At ⅞ mile your track meets another gravel road. The group picnic area lies on your left and the restrooms and playground on your right. You can turn right and follow the gravel for a quick return to the trailhead at one mile.

To extend your hike, bear left and cross the gravel to find the junction of Three Meadow Trail on the left and Upper Meadow Trail on the right. Turn right and follow Upper Meadow Trail northwest behind the big new community center building. Near the end of the building, the trail veers left to become a narrow footpath, following a gully on the left along the edge of the wild side of the park. Several paths branch left to cross the gully, but to conclude your walk stay right of the gully. By one mile laurels arch gracefully over the path ahead. Continue northwest along the windrow.

Before 1⅛ miles you have passed the ball field. Your path meets a junction on the left. Homestead Trail veers left to cross

OTHER SUGGESTIONS: A BIKE PATH connects Maxwell Farms Park with SONOMA STATE HISTORIC PARK, a must-see for first time visitors. Follow the bike path east to LACHRYMA MONTIS, General Vallejo's home for his last 40 years. The BIKE PATH continues to Fourth Street East, but the main attraction is SONOMA STATE HISTORIC PARK, a cluster of some of Northern California's oldest buildings that encircle large, shady SONOMA PLAZA. (It is 1¼ miles from MAXWELL FARMS to PLAZA.)

the gully and begin a second loop of the park. To return to the trailhead veer right before crossing the gully and head north on Upper Meadow Trail that soon meets Verano Trail. Turn right and go ⅛ mile to the trailhead and parking lot.

57.

SONOMA OVERLOOK
CLIMB FROM CITY TO PANORAMIC VISTAS

In the 1990s, developers wanted to build a resort hotel on this then-neglected, city-owned property overlooking the town of Sonoma from beside Mountain Cemetery. The fate of the land was put on a city ballot, and citizens strongly rejected any commercial development. Then, in community forums, residents expressed popular support for public access to the steep and hilly property. The Sonoma Ecology Center eventually teamed with city government to develop the great new Sonoma Overlook Trail here, built largely by volunteers.

The steep and rugged hill was originally a hunting ground for the Muchi branch of the Coast Miwok people. Later, when many native people lived on the grounds of nearby Sonoma Mission, they again used it for hunting. By the mid-nineteenth century, the land had become part of General Mariano Vallejo's estate. Vallejo soon gave the sloping portion of what was then called Battery Hill to the Pueblo de Sonoma for use as a community cemetery, a purpose it still serves today.

In the 1890s Solomon Schocken bought the rocky upper part of the hill, east of where Sonoma Overlook Trail now is, establishing a successful stone quarry. The stone was used in several Sonoma buildings, then in the rebuilding of San Francisco after the 1906 earthquake. Decreased demand for stone building materials led to the quarry's closure in the 1920s. Over the years the abandoned hillside came to be used as a garbage dump. But after the dump was closed in the 1950s, the city-owned property remained undeveloped and neglected for decades. Now it's become a pleasant and popular trail for hikers.

Follow the trail as it climbs from grasslands into woodlands of coast live oak and bay with sticky monkeyflower in a grassy understory. In 300 feet your trail fords a seasonal creek where nonnative vinca grows beneath oaks and California buckeye. Honeysuckle and poison oak vine through trees beside the trail.

Around ⅛ mile, climb along the chain link fence of Mountain Cemetery, passing soap plant and toyon. Your trail contours,

SONOMA OVERLOOK:

DISTANCE: 2½-mile loop.

TIME: One or two hours.

TERRAIN: Climbs through oak woodlands and grasslands to expansive views, then descends through a historic cemetery.

ELEVATION GAIN/LOSS: 410 feet+/410 feet-.

BEST TIME: Spring for wildflowers.

WARNINGS: Watch for poison oak, ticks and rattlesnakes. No dogs, smoking or bicycles allowed.

HOW TO GET THERE: From Highway 12 at west side of Sonoma Plaza, go north on First Street West .5 mile to trailhead beside entrance to Mountain Cemetery.

FURTHER INFO: Sonoma Ecology Center (707) 996-9744.

then dips across a larger seasonal creek at the bottom of a rolling grassland. Resume a gradual climb through the forest, where Chinese houses thrive in the grassy understory in spring.

At ¼ mile your trail switchbacks right and left, climbing through grasslands. Soon you climb in and out of woodlands, then switchback right to return to woodlands. By ⅜ mile your trail returns to grasslands, offering the first views south and southwest over Sonoma town and valley. You soon switchback left to ascend along the edge of meadow and woodland, passing wild geranium, coffee fern, then hedge nettle.

By ½ mile, you have climbed to the level of the big metal water tank across the canyon, with more vistas to its left. Continue an easy ascent along the ecotone (the border between two habitats). Around ⅝ mile your trail switchbacks right, briefly following an old rock wall. Return to woodlands, climbing past maidenhair ferns growing beneath a mossy rock. Soon you return to grasslands, where the yellow Mariposa lily relative called gold nuggets are abundant in spring, with some blue larkspur. Views are also abundant.

By ¾ mile the trail from the upper trailhead enters on the right. Our description will return that way. Return to woodlands briefly, then climb in and out of grasslands. Your trail soon switchbacks left, continuing its ascent in and out of the trail's two main habitats. In the grasslands around ⅞ mile, pink farewell-to-spring joins the gold nuggets.

Around one mile you pass through grasslands beneath a large rock outcrop. Abundant sticky monkeyflower, lupine, California fuchsia and California poppy grow here. Suddenly

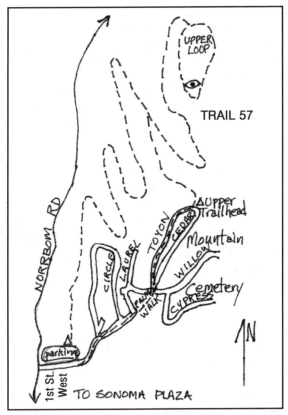

UPPER LOOP

TRAIL 57

NORRBOM RD

Upper Trailhead

CIRCLE

LAUREL

TOYON

CEDAR

Mountain

WILLOW

PALM WALK

CYPRESS

Cemetery

N

parking

1st St. West

TO SONOMA PLAZA

your trail climbs moderately, then fitfully by rocky tread. Beyond 1⅛ miles your trail climbs through shady woods. Soon the path bends right and climbs to the Upper Meadow Loop. Stay to the right, contouring to expanding vistas.

Before 1⅜ miles you reach a rock bench with a grand vista. You can see the south flank of Sonoma Mountain to the west, vineyards and Sonoma hills northwest, the town of Sonoma laid out like a map below, and on clear days, far to the south San Pablo Bay and the skyscrapers of downtown San Francisco. A California buckeye grows on the hill below the bench.

Beyond the bench, the trail climbs, passing a spur on the right to another view. The main trail ascends slightly, passing narrow-leaved mule ears, blue-eyed grass, brodiaea, morning glory, coyote brush, yarrow and a wine-dark farewell-to-spring. Your trail bends left to descend past three rock benches in a semicircle. These offer some shade at the right time of day.

Leave the upper loop by 1½ miles, descending the trail you came up. Before 2 miles you meet the side trail to the upper trailhead, now on your left. You can return the way you came, but our described hike turns left to descend toward Upper Trailhead. The trail drops in and out of meadows and oak woodlands

235

repeatedly. In the woodlands look for blue oak, black oak and valley oak along with more common coast live oak.

By 2⅛ miles the trail dips into cool woods along a seasonal creek to the upper trailhead. Climb past headstones in the cemetery to a narrow paved road. Turn right and follow the quiet road's shoulder, descending through shady Mountain Cemetery. Pass many pioneer graves, including well known names like Vallejo, Pedroncelli, Sebastiani, and less known ones like William Smith, the only veteran of the American Revolutionary War known to be buried in California (died 1846).

Soon a street sign confirms that you are descending Toyon. Then Toyon and Cedar end at Willow beyond 2¼ miles. Cross Willow and descend Palm Walk through the heart of the cemetery. By 2⅜ miles, Palm Walk ends at Laurel Lane. Descend to the cemetery entrance visible not far below and the trailhead parking area just beyond.

58.

BARTHOLOMEW PARK WINERY
HIDDEN JEWEL EXPLORES HILLS FULL OF HISTORY

These wooded hills, although still essentially wild, ring with the early history of the town of Sonoma. After California's last mission was established at Sonoma in 1823, Americans began arriving by 1827, more than twenty years before the Gold Rush. General Mariano Vallejo was sent by Mexico in the early 1830s to develop the town and establish military authority over the Catholic settlement. Vallejo laid out the 8-acre town square and the street grid surrounding it in 1835. His wife lent one of her family names to the lake on this hike, Benicia's Lake. A mission baptized Patwin chief, Solano, lent his name to a cave near hike's end. In 1856 Mariano Vallejo invited Baron Agostin Haraszthy, a Hungarian aristocrat then living in San Francisco, to move to Sonoma to develop the wine trade. Haraszthy found Sonoma Valley to be an ideal setting for wine grapes, soon proving that they could thrive here without irrigation. In 1857 the baron established his Buena Vista Winery, California's first winery. The impressive original building can still be seen beside the creek near hike's end. In 1861 California's governor sent Haraszthy to Europe to gather cuttings of wine grape varietals. He returned with 300 varieties that became the foundation of the state's vast wine trade. It is not known whether the Hungarian had a hand in naming Szeptaj Point, the overlook on this hike that's less than ½ mile from his winery. After your hike, you might want to stop at the winery tasting room to raise a glass in honor of the baron.

From the Bartholomew Park Winery parking lot, head northwest to cross the road and walk through the Wine Garden (signed "10–4 daily"). Take the left fork through the picnic area. In 200 feet you come to a white, thigh-high concrete marker, "TO TRAILS." It points west, downhill across the lawn of the picnic area. Pass the westernmost picnic table to find a mowed trail with a gate just ahead at ¼ mile. You'll find a trail map posted here.

As you pass through the gate, you leave the cultivated gardens and enter a wild garden beneath live oaks. Soon your trail, Grape Stomp Walk, dips across a seasonal creek and climbs steeply northwest briefly, then contours through oak woodlands with a dense tangle of vegetation: poison oak, coyote brush, bay laurel, madrone, chemise, toyon, manzanita, soap plant, and broad- and narrow-leaved mule ears.

From ⅜ mile your trail climbs gradually along the seasonal stream. You soon cross it again and climb steeply by steps, then dip to cross another fork of the tiny stream. Climb steeply again around ½ mile.

Beyond a switchback right, ascend through grasslands and chaparral where blue dicks and sticky monkeyflowers grow in spring. After the first of two summits, views open up to the south—over the town of Sonoma to the Carneros wine region and San Pablo Bay beyond. Near Grape Stomp Bench, golden fairy lanterns thrive with other wildflowers in spring. Continue on Climbers Delight Trail as it contours, gaining more vistas and passing paintbrush and bedstraw.

Descend gradually around ⅝ mile. The terrain is rocky here, with the same mix of chaparral and grasslands. Dip across another small seasonal creek, then climb steps. Soon your path bends sharply left to ascend along a ridgetop, quickly topping out about 40 feet higher than the bench. Descend moderately by more steps through oak woodlands around ¾ mile, passing Indian warriors and wild iris in spring. From the bottom of the steps your path descends fitfully.

By ⅞ mile you near Arroyo Seco Creek and follow it upstream. Your trail passes through a grove of redwoods and fords the creek, climbing to a trail sign and map at a paved road. Cross the road and ascend a wooden staircase to continue on Climbers Delight Trail. Beyond one mile it ascends generally east and northeast through a mixed forest of Douglas fir, redwood and black oak, with trees to three feet diameter.

By 1⅛ miles you reach a summit overlooking Benicia's

BARTHOLOMEW PARK WINERY:

DISTANCE: 2⅝-mile loop, plus ⅛-mile to Solano's Hideaway.

TIME: One or two hours.

TERRAIN: Climbs through oak woodlands, forest, chaparral and grasslands to vistas, then descends to creek and climbs to Benicia's Lake before descending through woodlands and grasslands to a creek, following it back to the winery.

ELEVATION GAIN/LOSS: 615 feet+/615 feet-.

BEST TIME: Spring for wildflowers.

WARNINGS: Watch for poison oak, ticks and rattlesnakes. No smoking or bicycles allowed. Open daily, weekdays 9:30 am-4:30 pm, weekends 10 am-4:30 pm. Winery open 10:30-4:30 daily.

HOW TO GET THERE: From Sonoma town Plaza on Highway 12, go east on Napa Street to 7th Street East and turn left. Follow 7th Street north for .4 mile, then turn right on Castle Road and follow it to its end and park in the Bartholomew Park Winery parking lot just south of winery.

FURTHER INFO: Bartholomew Park Winery (707) 935-9511, trail steward (707) 938-2244.

Lake. As you descend toward the creek and pond, California hazel and honeysuckle grow beside the shady trail. Descend steps to cross the East Fork of Arroyo Seco Creek, where redwoods and ferns thrive. Climb south, soon passing a dead-end spur on the right that ends at the lake's shore in a nice, shady picnic spot (signed "No swimming or fishing").

The main trail bends right and left as it climbs, partially by rough steps. Beyond the steps, Climbers Delight Trail ascends moderately southwest and south to a junction at 1⅜ miles.

At the junction, Angels Flight Trail on the right descends west, offering a shorter and easier way back to the trailhead in about ¾ mile. Our described route turns left to follow You-Walk Miwok Trail, climbing northeast on an old road. You soon leave the road for a narrow trail climbing south through forest. It soon reaches another summit, then contours before climbing. Beyond 1½ miles your shady forest path summits again. Contour, then climb to yet another summit at 1⅝ miles.

The forest yields to sparse oak woodlands here. Your trail

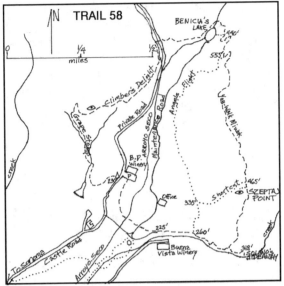

comes to a rest bench with a filtered view southwest. Descend slightly with a fire-scarred hill on your left. By 1¾ miles your descent steepens as you navigate more steps, with the woodlands receding for the best vista yet. Resume the steady descent through oak woodlands by numerous steps.

Before 1⅞ miles you reach a junction with Shortcut Trail, which descends west to meet Angels Flight Trail not far from its end. Our described hike continues on You-Walk Miwok Trail, descending south. In just 150 feet Szeptaj Point spur is on the right. Sonoma sage grows at the junction. The spur leads 150 feet to a bench beside a rock outcrop with a nice view west to the flanks of Sonoma Mountain being crowded by oaks. Szeptaj is Hungarian for beautiful view.

Continue down You-Walk Miwok Trail. By 2 miles your descent leads to a dry gully, leveling briefly before another steep descent to Miwok Trail's end at a junction above a rushing creek. A right turn leads back to the trailhead in only ¼ mile. But I suggest you turn left and hike up the creek briefly for a look at Solano's Hideaway, a shallow cave in a large rock outcrop. Solano, chief of the Suisun Patwin tribe, was a baptized member of mission culture and probably never really needed a hideaway, except perhaps for peace of mind. His "Hideaway" is a beautiful natural spot.

Returning to the nearby junction, descend west and southwest along the creek. You'll find a good place to get down to the creekside at 2⅛ miles. The banks are lined with elderberry, twisted stalk, sword ferns and variable-leaf snowberry beneath redwoods. The trail continues to a junction with Angels Flight Trail, then comes to a gate around 2¼ miles.

239

Beyond the gate, your trail follows a fence and the creek past the historic old stone cellar building of Buena Vista Winery on the other side of the creek. The vegetation turns lush but nonnative, with English ivy and vinca minor beneath eucalyptus trees. Continue west, passing a drinking fountain and sometimes-open restrooms. When your path joins a paved road, step to the right to follow the gravel path beside it It leads to Bartholomew Park Winery and the parking lot by 2⅝ miles.

59.

SHOLLENBERGER PARK
AVIAN OASIS HIDING IN PETALUMA

Petaluma's Shollenberger Park has become a busy place. Created in 1995 when city crews added a walking surface to the levees that had contained the dredge spoils from the nearby river since the 1970s, today the park hums with activity even on weekdays. Joggers, dog walkers, cyclists, parents pushing baby strollers, wheelchair riders and many birders circle the loop trail in search of exercise, fresh air and bird sightings.

This is a landscape that has been in transition for the past 200 years. Long before there was a city here, the Coast Miwok people saw a wild, meandering slough, a tidal extension of San Pablo Bay that harbored abundant game and fish. In 1776 a party of Spanish sailors were the first Europeans to navigate Petaluma Slough, unsuccessfully searching for an inland passage to Bodega Bay. In 1836 General Mariano Vallejo built a fort upstream on Adobe Creek, which flows through the park. His Petaluma Adobe is still there today. After many more Europeans settlers arrived, by 1860 the slough was being dredged and straightened, at first by Chinese laborers using only shovels and buckets. Farmers drained much of the adjacent wetlands as Petaluma became an important agricultural center. By the early twentieth century, Petaluma Slough was the third busiest inland waterway in California. In just one year, 14,000 passengers were ferried along the river, as well as nearly 8000 cattle and horses, 33,000 poultry, and nearly 3.5 million dozen eggs. Other barges hauled grain, wine, trees and much more.

In the 1950s the city tried to get the Army Corps of Engineers to take over the dredging that kept the slough passable, but the Corps only dredged navigable rivers. So in 1959 the local congressman drafted a bill declaring that Petaluma Slough was hereafter to be Petaluma River. After the bill was passed and signed into law, the Army Corps took over dredging. They

DISTANCE: 2¼-mile loop, plus one mile side trail through Alman Marsh.

TIME: One or two hours.

TERRAIN: Nearly level paved and gravel trail circles marshlands beside the Petaluma River, with side trail that explores adjacent Alman Marsh.

BEST TIME: Winter for best birding, although white pelicans visit in summer.

WARNINGS: Stay on trails. Stay off adjacent property. Park open 6 am to 10 pm.

HOW TO GET THERE: Exit Highway 101 in South Petaluma onto Highway 116/Lakeville Highway. Go east about a mile. Turn right on South McDowell Blvd. for .3 mile. Turn right on Cedar Lane, marked by a "city park" sign.

FURTHER INFO: Petaluma Parks Dept. (707) 778-4380.

dredge the "river" about every four years, and since the 1970s they've dumped the 250,000 cubic yards of mud at the spot that today is Shollenberger Park. Water and shore birds discovered this cache, which contained many tiny organisms and plants, a virtual smorgasbord for the avians. Today more than 150 species of birds have been sighted at Shollenberger Park.

This wet and nearly level little park now has the potential to become much larger. In 2004 the city purchased the adjacent Gray's Ranch, a 251-acre parcel where oat hay had been grown. The city plans to develop more wetlands on the site in a project modeled after the Arcata Marsh, a notable and wonderful birding venue up in Humboldt County that's featured in our Hiker's hip pocket Guide to the Humboldt Coast. The Gray's Ranch property would hold four new ponds planted with vegetation that would remove contaminants left in the treated sewage, thereby allowing the water to be recycled or released into the river. While the timetable for this ecological development has not yet been spelled out, the eventual park would have more than 400 acres, becoming one of the largest publicly accessible wetlands in the bay area, and a mecca for birders from all over.

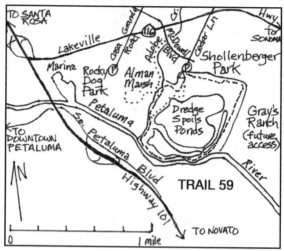

TRAIL 59

From the parking lot, pass the restrooms and drinking fountain to head south on the paved trail as it climbs slightly to an interpretive sign and map in 200 feet. Nearby rest benches and picnic tables overlook the park's ponds and surroundings. It's a peaceful, verdant setting surrounded by city.

Take the trail on the right. Except around times of high water in winter or spring, you have a choice of the paved trail on the right or the broad dirt track beside the shore. Head southwest with the manmade slough on your right and the dredge spoils pond on your left.

Beyond ⅛ mile both trails bend right, heading northwest along the shore. On your right, the slough ends as it empties into tiny Adobe Creek, which now flows between your trail and Alman Marsh. Coyote brush and ceanothus grow on your right. Around ¼ mile both trails bend left and head southwest. The dirt trail rises to the levee and turns grassy as it parallels the paved path.

By ⅜ mile Alman Marsh Trail forks right, crossing a sturdy bridge to explore the marsh. Continue on the paved or grassy trail past more rest benches. Beyond ½ mile the grassy path ends, merging with the paved path, which has gravel shoulders here. The next stretch of trail is the only portion of trail not directly along the shore of the central wetlands, although Adobe Creek on your right flows toward its confluence with the Petaluma River.

Around ⅝ mile an unnamed pond appears on your left. Suddenly you come to the Petaluma River. The confluence of Adobe Creek with the river lies on your right, with Alman Slough beyond. Across the muddy brown river or slough, dilapidated building and derelict boats rise from the mud flats, remnants of the the river's colorful industrial past. Look for a small stand of eucalyptus trees that sometimes houses a colony of nesting egrets and herons.

Follow the paved trail as it turns left to follow the riverbank. Soon a short grassy loop trail on the left offers a route closer to the central ponds. The paved path turns to gravel by ¾ mile, continuing along the river. Around ⅞ mile trail and river bend to the left. The small pond on your left links with the larger dredge spoils pond when the water is high enough.

The trail bends left to head east around 1⅛ miles, with open water on both left and right. To the southeast you can see the broad tidal lands the Petaluma River follows to San Pablo Bay.

By 1¼ miles your gravel trail swings away from the Petaluma River and aims for the lands of Gray's Ranch, a 251-acre parcel that the city recently purchased to add to the wetlands and public access here. Hay is still grown on part of the ranch. On your left abundant poison hemlock grows between you and the open water of the ponds.

By 1⅜ miles your path parallels the open waters of the dredge spoils ponds, with the marsh and hayfields of Gray's Ranch on the right. Continue northeast toward Sonoma.

At 1¾ miles you reach the northeast corner of the dredge spoils pond. Your trail turns left to head northwest on its final leg. Cattails and native willows grow in and along the manmade slough on your right, where red-winged blackbirds sometimes sing their raucous songs. Office buildings rise beyond the slough. Beyond 1⅞ miles your trail jogs left and right, continuing between the slough and pond. You return to the trailhead by 2¼ miles. Want to go round again?

60.

SONOMA'S OTHER SHORE
LOWER TUBBS ISLAND WILDLIFE REFUGE

This trail differs from any other in the book. A level, easy hike passes through farmlands, with views offering an unusual perspective on San Francisco Bay and its surrounding landmarks. After 2¾ miles you reach the marshes of 332-acre Lower Tubbs Island Wildlife Refuge, where over 200 species of resident and migrating birds may be found. The bird population and diversity are highest in autumn and winter, but some birds are here year round. Try to time your visit with a low tide, when birds will be busiest (and most visible) feeding on the mud flats along the bay and in the marshes. If you have a compass, bring it to help pinpoint the landmarks. The entire hike is less than 20 feet above sea level.

Behind the brown gate, a dirt road heads south atop a levee surrounded by level farmlands on the left, and recently restored Upper Tolay Lagoon on the right. Tolay Creek is beyond the lagoon. Soon a sign indicates that this area is closed to hunting.

At ⅛ mile your broad trail bends right to head west on the levee beside the lagoon. Wild turnips, fennel, mustard, coyote brush and grasses grow at roadside. Red-winged blackbirds dart across the fields. Quail and pheasants are more reclusive, but you may flush them from cover. As your trail bends left before ⅜ mile, you enter the posted "Steel Shot Zone" (hunting OK). A picnic table and information board are on the left. Head south and southeast on the double track, which runs left of the top of the levee.

At ½ mile the stump of a lone eucalyptus stands on the left. It once offered the only shade on the entire hike. If you brought a compass, climb atop the levee and aim due south. If visibility is good the Bank of America and Transamerica Pyramid skyscrapers rise above Point Richmond. You might see part of the Richmond Bridge to their right.

Continue southeast. Around ⅞ mile your road bends left, then back to the right. The confluence of two sloughs is on your left, with Lower Tolay Lagoon on your right. Beyond one mile you pass a farm road that forks left, as your road bends right to head toward Mt. Tamalpais. You curve right again before 1¼ miles. Around 1⅝ miles your road makes a gradual bend left. When you tire of walking on the hard-packed road, walk the levee on the right. I flushed a pheasant here that had been hiding in the grass. The slight elevation gain of the levee enhances the views on this flatland.

By 2 miles your road bends left to head south, following a power line. Soon your road swings left again, passing a metal pumphouse. From atop the levee here, an east tower of the Richmond Bridge is due south. The tip of the Pyramid is 3 finger-widths (at arm's length) to the left. Two fingers to the right of the east bridge tower, a more easily visible west tower of the bridge rises above the bay. Three fingers to the right of that, a tower of the Golden Gate Bridge rises above Tiburon. Each mile divulges a few more landmarks, which seem to float on the bay and horizon. As the road winds, the landmarks shift their positions relative to each other.

Your trail turns toward Mt. Diablo on the levee road, passing coyote brush. Soon a lagoon on your right. Around 2¼ miles road and levee jog left. Before 2⅜ miles, a boardwalk to the right of the levee provides some birding access. At 2½ miles your road swings right and heads due south. First Angel Island is left of a tower of the Richmond Bridge, then wanders to the right. At one point Sutro Towers are left

DISTANCE: 5½ to 8⅛ miles round trip.

TIME: Three hours to all day.

TERRAIN: Level road along sloughs to bay shore.

BEST TIME: Low tide in fall or winter for best birding. Spring for wildflowers.

WARNINGS: Use caution in hunting season: mid-October to mid-January, especially opening weekend. Watch for ticks. No dogs, fishing or jogging allowed.

HOW TO GET THERE: Trailhead is on Highway 37, .7 mile east of intersection of Highways 37 and 121. From intersection go east .7 mile on Highway 37 across railroad tracks and Tolay Creek. Parking area is on right, beside brown gate (do not block gate). No access from Highway 37 west. Use extreme caution to turn around at Highway 121 intersection, or at turnaround .8 mile east of trailhead after hike.

FROM NORTH: Exit Highway 101 south of Petaluma onto Highway 116 East (M.3.95). Go 12 miles to Highway 121, then south on 121 for 6.5 miles to Highway 37.

FROM SOUTH: Exit Highway 101 south of Novato onto Highway 37 (at M.18.7, Marin County). Go 7.5 miles to intersection with Highway 121.

FURTHER INFO: San Pablo Bay National Wildlife Refuge (510) 562-3000.

of Angel Island, then they are on the right. The changing perspectives create a dreamy effect.

At 2¾ miles, climb a slight rise and come to a picnic table, rest bench and interpretive sign. The trail forks here. Take the right fork 250 feet to another sign, which informs you that you are entering Lower Tubbs Island Wildlife Refuge, no dogs, fishing, hunting or shooting allowed beyond this point. From the second sign, take the left fork, heading southeast ¼ mile to the open bay. (Another trail forks right, the end of your loop trail.)

Former farmland on the left has been restored to the tidal salt marsh it was 100 years ago. More marsh is on the right. Pickleweed, saltbush and other salt-tolerant plants cover the marsh.

Beyond 3 miles your road splits as you meet the bay shore. During a plus tide it is all water to the south and east, but at zero or minus tide mud flats line the shore. In fall and winter migrating birds feed here. You may see dowitchers, killdeers, sandpipers, sanderlings, curlews and many more.

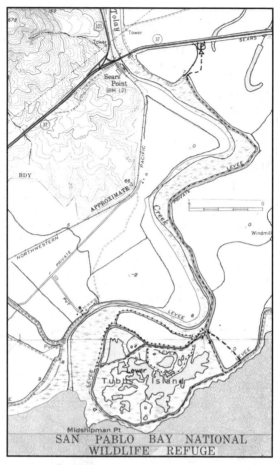

SAN PABLO BAY NATIONAL
WILDLIFE REFUGE

Your route turns right, with salt marsh on the right and
bay tidelands on the left. The bright blue roof of Marin Civic
Center snuggles at the base of Mt. Tamalpais. Pt. Richmond
is due south, surrounded by other Bay Area landmarks. The
Berkeley Hills are south-southeast. Mt. Diablo rises to the
southeast, with Carquinez Straits now visible to its left.

At 3⅜ miles cross a gate where slough and marsh on the
right empty into the bay if the tide is ebbing, the opposite if
it is rising. Your road soon bends toward Mt. Tamalpais. Road
and levee wind right and left around 3⅝ miles.

Pass the ruins of an old dock on the left. Until the advent
of railroads in the 1870s, ferries transported most people
from the bay area to the Sonoma bay shore. Passengers and
freight were transported by stage to Sonoma.

Continue along the levee road. At 3⅞ miles you cross
another gate where slough and marsh empty into the bay. In
250 feet you reach the southern extreme of this hike. The
Sonoma-Marin county line is one mile south, the Richmond

city limits, five miles. San Francisco's skyscrapers still rise above Pt. Richmond. Angel Island can be seen beyond the Richmond Bridge. Your road bends right. Midshipman Point is the green marshy promontory due west.

Beyond 4 miles the ruins of another ferry dock settle into the bay shore. Weathered redwood and iron rest on rip-rap at the edge of the mud flats. Today the ruins teem with mussels, barnacles, and lively purple shore crabs. Imagine this site a bustling ferry landing, bringing settlers and commerce to booming Sonoma via this lonesome bay shore. You have a view west to the mouth of the Petaluma River, still navigable to the town of Petaluma, where other ferry landings were in the 1800s.

Continue on the levee road. Near the mouth of Tolay Creek it turns northwest. At 4¼ miles you cross another slough gate. Your road bends right, heading north-northeast.

At 4½ miles you turn right, taking Mid Marsh Trail across a slough, winding northeast toward the interpretive sign. Great and snowy egrets live here. Wind through salt marsh and ponds rich in bird life, with dense pickleweed lining the path. At 4⅝ miles a pond is on your left, bird tracks wander across the mud flat on your right. At 4¾ miles red and green algae-covered marshes are on your left.

At 4⅞ miles your road forks. The path on the right makes a loop to explore Mid Marsh Pond in the heart of Lower Tubbs Island. Your described hike continues straight. At 5 miles pass a big pond on the right surrounded by dense salt marsh. While it may look as if nothing lives in the marsh, in fact salt marshes are among the most nutrient-rich, productive habitats in the world. They harbor many birds, small mammals, shellfish and the larval stages of many fish and invertebrates that live elsewhere as adults. Your path gets brushy, then slightly swampy, but quickly climbs to higher ground. At 5⅛ miles your road bends left to head straight for the interpretive sign.

Before 5¼ miles you merge with the outer loop path and your tread improves. At 5⅜ miles you complete the loop, returning to the sign and main road. Head north, retracing your steps 2¾ miles to the trailhead at 8⅛ miles.

WHAT KIND OF TRAIL
ARE YOU LOOKING FOR?

continued from page 10

TRAILS FOR BACKPACKING
28. Half-a-Canoe Loop
29. South Shore to Old Sawmill Camp
31. Austin Creek

BEACH WALKS
1. Headlands to Beach Loop
5. Other Sea Ranch Trails
8. Fisk Mill Cove to Stump Beach Overlook
9. Stump Beach/Plantation/North Trail Loop
11. Salt Point to Stump Beach
14. Fort Ross North Headlands
16. Fort Ross Creek
17. Sonoma's Lost Coast
18. North of Jenner
20. Blind Beach to Shell Beach
22. Shell Beach to Wrights Beach
23. Bodega Dunes Loop
24. Bodega Head North to Dunes
26. Pinnacle Gulch to Shorttail Gulch

COMMON & SCIENTIFIC NAMES
OF PLANTS ALONG THE TRAILS

*Fine grass covered the slope-spangled with flowers, with here
and there patches of color, orange and purple and golden.*

—Jack London, *All Gold Canyon*

*acacia, *Acacia spp.*
alum root, *Heuchera micrantha*
*alyssum, *Lobularia maritima*
angelica, *Angelica tomentosa*
azalea, *Rhododendron occidentale*
baby blue eyes, *Nemophila menziesii*
bay laurel (Calif. bay, pepperwood),
  Umbellularia californica
beach morning glory, *Calystegia
  soldanella*
beach pea, *Lathyrus japonicus var.
  glaber*
beach primrose, *Oenothera cheiran-
  thifolia*
beach strawberry, *Fragaria chiloensis*
bear grass, *Xerophyllum tenax*
bedstraw, *Galium spp.*
bee plant, *Scrophularia californica*

big leaf maple, *Acer macrophyllum*
bird's-eye gilia, *Gilia tricolor*
bird's foot fern, *Pellaea mucronata*
Bishop pine, *Pinus muricata*
bitterroot, *Lewisia rediviva*
black oak (Calif.), *Quercus kelloggii*
black sage, *Salvia mellifera*
bleeding heart (western), *Dicentra
  formosa*
blueblossom (Calif. lilac), *Ceanothus
  thyrsiflorus*
blue dick, *Dichelostemma capitatum*
blue elderberry, *Sambucus mexi-
  cana*
blue-eyed grass, *Sisyrinchium bellum*
blue-eyed Mary, *Collinsia sparsiflora*
blue flax (western), *Linum perenne*

*blue gum eucalyptus, *Eucalyptus globulus*

blue larkspur, *Delphinium decorum*

blue oak, *Quercus douglasii*

bracken fern, *Pteridium aquilinum var. pubescens*

broadleaf ceanothus, *Ceanothus griseus*

buckbrush, *Ceanothus cuneatus*

butter and eggs, *Triphysaria erianthus*

buttercup, *Ranunculus californicus*

California aster, *Lessingia filaginifolia var. californica*

California blackberry, *Rubus vitifolius*

California boxelder, *Acer negundo*

California buckeye, Aesculus californica

California fuchsia, *Epilobium canum*

California gooseberry, *Ribes californica*

California nutmeg, *Torreya californica*

California poppy, *Eschscholtzia californica*

California rose, *Rosa californica*

California sycamore, *Platanus racemosa*

*calla lily, *Zantedeschia aethiopica*

calypso orchid (redwood orchid), *Calypso bulbosa*

camas lily, *Camassia quamash*

canyon live oak, *Quercus chrysolepis*

cattail, *Typha spp.*

chamise, *Adenostoma fasciculatum*

chaparral pea, *Pickeringia montana*

checker lily, *Fritillaria lanceolata*

checker mallow, *Sidalcea malvaeflora*

Chinese houses, *Collinsia heterophylla*

chinquapin, *Castanopsis chrysophylla*

clintonia, *Clintonia andrewsiana*

coast buckwheat, *Eriogonum latifolium*

coast lily, *Lilium maritimum*

coast live oak, *Quercus agrifolia*

coast silktassel, *Garrya elliptica*

coastal manroot (wild cucumber), *Marah oreganus*

coastal onion, *Allium dichlamydeum*

coffee fern, *Pellaea andromedaefolia*

coffeeberry, *Rhamnus californica*

columbine, *Aquilegia formosa*

common blue cup, *Githopsis specularioides*

corn lily, *Veratrum fimbriatum*

cottonwood, *Populus spp.*

cow parsnip, *Heracleum lanatum*

coyote brush, *Baccharis pilularis*

coyote mint, *Monardella villosa*

cream cup, *Platystemon californicus*

cream fawn lily, *Erythronium californicum*

creeping ceanothus, *Ceanothus prostratus*

*creeping myrtle, *Vinca minor*

*crimson clover, *Trifolium incarnatum*

cypress, *Cupressus spp.*

dandelion, *Taraxacum officinale*

deer fern, *Blechnum spicant*

dogwood, *Cornus nuttali*

Douglas fir, *Pseudotsuga menziesii*

Douglas iris, *Iris douglasiana*

Dutchman's pipe, *Aristolochia californica*

dwarf brodiaea, *Brodiaea terrestris*

elegant brodiaea, *Brodiaea elegans*

elk clover, *Aralia californica*

*European beach grass, *Ammophilia arenaria*

evergreen huckleberry, *Vaccinium ovatum*

evergreen violet (redwood violet), *Viola sempervirens*

fairy bells, *Disporum smithii*

false baby stars, *Linanthus androsacea*

false lily of the valley, *Maianthemum dilatum*

fat Solomon's seal, *Smilacina racemosa*

*fennel, *Foeniculum vulgare*

fiddleneck, *Amsinckia intermedia*

five-finger fern, *Adiantum pedatum var. aleuticum*

flannel bush, *Fremontia californica*

forget-me-not, *Hackelia floribunda*

Fort Bragg manzanita, *Arctostaphylos mendocinoensis*

*foxglove, *Digitalis purpurea*

giant horsetail, *Equisetum telmateia*

godetia (farewell to spring), *Clarkia spp.*

gold back fern, *Pityrogramma triangularis*

golden brodiaea, *Triteleia ixioides ssp. ixioides*

golden fairy lantern (Diogenes lantern), *Calochortus amabilis*

goldfields, *Lasthenia chrysostoma*

grand fir, *Abies grandis*

grass nut (Ithuriel's spear), *Triteleia laxa*

gray pine, *Pinus sabiniana*

gum plant, *Grindelia stricta*

249

hairy cat's ear, *Hypochaeris radicata*

hairy honeysuckle, *Lonicera hispidula*

hairy manzanita, *Arctostaphylos columbiana*

Hartweg's sidalcea, *Sidalcea hartwegii*

hazel (California), *Corylus cornuta californica*

hedge nettle, *Stachys bullata*

hen and chicks, *Dudleya farinosa*

*Himalayan blackberry, *Rubus procerus*

Hinds walnut, *Juglans hindsii*

horsetail, *Equisetum spp.*

hound's tongue, *Cynoglossum grande*

huckleberry, *Vaccinium spp.*

*ice plant, *Mesembryanthemum spp.*

Indian pink, *Silene californica*

Indian potato, *Wapeto pterideridia*

Indian warrior, *Pedicularis densiflora*

inside-out flower, *Vancouveria spp.*

interior live oak, *Quercus wislizenii*

iris, *Iris spp.*

knobcone pine, *Pinus attenuata*

Labrador tea, *Ledum glandulosum var. columbianum*

ladies' tresses, *Spiranthus romanzoffiana*

lady fern, *Athyrium filix-femina var. sitchenense*

leather fern (leather-leaf fern), *Polypodium scouleri*

licorice fern, *Polypodium glycyrrhiza*

live-forever, *Dudleya spp.*

Lobb's buttercup, *Ranunculus lobbii*

lomatium, *Lomatium spp.*

lovely clarkia, *Clarkia concinna*

lupine, *Lupinus latifolius, L. littoralis, L. nanus, L. polyphyllus, L. bicolor, L. subvexus, L. varicolor, L. rivularis*

madrone, *Arbutus menziesii*

maidenhair fern, *Adiantum jordanii*

manzanita, *Arctostaphylos spp.*

Mariposa lily, *Calochortus luteus*

Mendocino cypress, *Cupressus govenia ssp. pygmaea*

Mendocino gentian, *Gentiana setigera*

milkmaids, *Dentaria californica*

miners lettuce, *Montia sibirica*

monkeyflower, *Mimulus guttatus*

mountain mahogany, *Cercocarpus betuloides*

mugwort, *Artemisia douglasiana*

mule ears, *Wyethia spp.*

*narcissus, *Amaryllidaceae spp.*

narrow-leaved mule ears, *Wyethia angustifolia*

oceanspray, *Holodiscus discolor*

Oregon ash, *Fraxinus latifolia*

Oregon grape, *Berberis spp.*

Oregon white oak, *Quercus garryana*

owl's clover, *Orthocarpus attenuatus*

paintbrush, *Castilleja latifolia, C. affinis, C. foliosa, C. hololeuca, C. wightii, C. mendosensis*

*pampas grass, *Cortaderia selloana*

pearly everlasting, *Anaphalis margaritacea*

pennyroyal, *Mentha pulegium*

penstemon, *Penstemon spp.*

*periwinkle, *Vinca minor*

phacelia, *Phacelia spp.*

phlox, *Phlox spp.*

pickleweed, *Salicornia subterminalis*

plantain, *Plantago spp.*

*poison hemlock, *Conium maculatum*

poison oak, *Toxicodendron diversiloba*

popcorn flower, *Plagiobothrys nothofulvus*

poppy, *Eschscholtzia californica*

purple larkspur, *Delphinium spp.*

purple milkweed, *Asclepias cordifolia*

Queen Anne's lace, *Daucus carota*

raspberry, *Rubus leucodermis*

*rattlesnake grass, *Briza maxima*

rattlesnake plantain, *Goodyear oblongiflora*

red alder, *Alnus rubra*

red elderberry, *Sambucus callicarpa*

red flowering currant, *Ribes sanguineum*

*red hot poker, *Kniphofia uvaria*

red huckleberry, *Vaccinium parvifolium*

red larkspur, *Delphinium nudicaule*

redwood, *Sequoia sempervirens*

redwood lily, *Lilium rubescens*

redwood sorrel, *Oxalis oregana*

rein orchid, *Platanthera leucostachys*

rhododendron, *Rhododendron macrophyllum*

rush, *Juncus spp.*

salal, *Gaultheria shallon*

salmonberry, *Rubus spectabilis*

saltbush, *Atriplex spp.*

sand verbena, pink, *Abronia umbellata*

sand verbena, yellow, *Abronia latifolia*

Sargent cypress, *Cupressus sargentii*

scarlet fritillary, *Fritillaria recurva*

*scarlet pimpernel, *Anagallis arvensis*

*Scotch broom, *Cytisus scoparius*

scouring rush, *Equisetum hyemale*

sea rocket, *Cakile maritima*

seaside daisy, *Erigeron glaucus*

sea thrift, *Armeria maritima var. californica*

sedge, *Carex spp.*

self-heal, *Prunella vulgaris*

shield fern, *Polystichum californicum*

shooting star, *Dodecatheon spp.*

shore pine, *Pinus contorta ssp. contorta*

Siberian miners lettuce, *Montia siberica*

silverleaf lotus, *Lotus argophyllus*

silverweed, *Potentilla egedei var. grandis*

skunk cabbage, *Lysichitum americanum*

slim Solomon's seal, *Smilacina stellata*

slink pod (fetid adders tongue), *Scoliopus bigelovii*

smooth cat's ear, *Hypochaeris glabra*

snowberry, *Symphoricarpos rotundifolius*

soap plant, *Chlorogalum pomeridianum*

Sonoma sage, *Salvia sonomensis*

*spearmint, *Mentha spicata*

spicebush (western), *Calycanthus occidentalis*

star lily, *Zygadenus fremontii*

star tulip, *Calochortus elegans*

starflower, *Trientalis latifolia*

sticky monkeyflower, *Diplacus aurantiacus*

stinging nettle, *Urtica dioica*

stream violet, *Viola glabella*

sun cup, *Oenothera ovata*

sweet clover, *Melilotus spp.*

sword fern, *Polystichum munitum*

tanoak, *Lithocarpus densiflorus*

tarweed, *Madia capitata*

thimbleberry, *Rubus parviflorus*

*thistle, *Cirsium spp.*

tidy-tips, *Layia platyglossa*

toyon, *Heteromeles arbutifolia*

trail plant, *Adenocaulon bicolor*

trillium, *Trillium chloropetalum, T. ovatum*

tule, *Scirpus acutus*

twinberry, *Lonicera involucrata*

twisted stalk, *Streptopus amplexifolius*

two-eyed violet, *Viola ocellata*

valley lupine, *Lupinus subvexus*

valley oak, *Quercus lobata*

variable-leaf snowberry, *Symphoricarpos albus var. laevigatus*

*vetch, *Vicia spp.*

vine maple, *Acer circinatum*

wallflower, *Erysimum menziesii*

wally basket, *Triteleia laxa*

water fern, *Azolla filiculoides*

watercress, *Nasturtium officinale*

wax myrtle (bayberry), *Myrica californica*

*weeping willow, *Salix babylonica*

western bistort, *Polygonum bistortoides*

western coltsfoot, *Petasites palmatus*

western dog violet, *Viola adunca*

western hemlock, *Tsuga heterophylla*

white alder, *Alnus rhombifolia*

white brodiaea, *Triteleia hyacinthina*

*white eucalyptus, *Eucalyptus albens*

white fritillary, *Fritillaria liliacea*

whitethorn, *Ceanothus incanus*

wild geranium, *Geranium spp.*

wild ginger, *Asarum caudatum*

wild grape, *Vitis californica*

*wild mustard, *Brassica campestris*

wild rose, *Rosa spp.*

willow, *Salix spp.*

windflower, *Anemone deltoidea*

wood fern, *Dryopteris arguta*

wood rose, *Rosa gymnocarpa*

wood strawberry, *Fragaria californica*

woodland buttercup, *Ranunculus uncinatus*

woodland madia, *Madia madioides*

woodland star, *Lithophragma heterophylla*

woodwardia fern, *Woodwardia fimbriata*

wooly mullein, *Verbascum thapsus*

yarrow, *Achillea millefolium*

yellow mat, *Sanicula arctopoides*

yellow water iris, *Iris pseudacorus*

yerba buena, *Satureja douglasii*

yerba de selva, *Whipplea modesta*

yerba santa, *Eriodictyon californicum*

*Introduced (feral) species

251

FURTHER READING

Adams, Rick and Louise McCorkle, *The California Highway 1 Book*, Ballantine Books, New York, 1985. (o.p.)

Alt, David D. and Donald W. Hyndman, *Roadside Geology of Northern and Central California*, Mountain Press Publishing Co., Missoula, Montana, 2000.

Becking, Rudolph, *Pocket Flora of the Redwood Forest*, Island Press, Covelo, Ca., 1982. (o.p.)

Burton, Jack, *Sonoma Picnic*, Bored Feet Press, Mendocino, CA, 2000.

California Coastal Commission, *California Coastal Access Guide*, sixth edition, University of California Press, Berkeley, 2003.

California Coastal Commission, *California Coastal Resource Guide*, University of California Press, Berkeley, 1987.

Edwards, Don, *Making the Most of Sonoma County*, Alameda, Ca., 1988. (o.p.)

Hanse, Harvey J., *Wild Oats in Eden, Sonoma County in the Nineteenth Century*, self-published, Santa Rosa, Ca., 1962. (o.p.)

Hinch, Stephen W., *Guide to the State Parks of the Sonoma Coast and Russian River Region*, Annadel Press, Santa Rosa, CA, 1998.

Howard, Arthur D., *Geologic History of Middle California*, University of California Press, Berkeley, 1979. (o.p.)

Jenny, Hans, *The Pygmy Forest Ecological Staircase*, Nature Conservancy, 1973. (o.p.)

Keator, Glenn, *Pacific Coast Berry Finder*, Nature Study Guild, Rochester, NY, 1978.

Keator, Glenn and Ruth Heady, *Pacific Coast Fern Finder*, Nature Study Guild, Rochester, NY, 1981.

Kroeber, A.L., *Handbook of the Indians of California*, Dover Publications, New York, 1976.

Lyons, Kathleen and Mary Beth Cuneo-Lazaneo, *Plants of the Coast Redwood Region*, Shoreline Press, Soquel, CA., 2003.

Munz, Philip A., *Introduction to California Spring Wildflowers of the Foothills, Valleys, and Coast*, revised edition, University of California Press, Berkeley, 2004.

Munz, Philip A., *Introduction to Shore Wildflowers of California, Oregon and Washington*, revised edition, University of California Press, Berkeley, 2003.

Niehaus, Theodore F. and Charles L. Ripper, *Field Guide to Pacific States Wildflowers*, (Peterson Field Guide Series), Houghton Mifflin, Boston, 1976.

Randall, Warren R., Robert F. Keniston, Dale N. Bever and Edward C. Jensen, *Manual of Oregon Trees and Shrubs*, Oregon State University Bookstores, Corvallis, OR., 1988.

Russo, Ron and Pam Olhausen, *Pacific Intertidal Life*, Nature Study Guild, Rochester, NY, 1981.

Sholars, Robert, *The Pygmy Forest and Associated Plant Communities of Coastal Mendocino County, California*, self-published, Mendocino, CA., 1982. (o.p.)

Watts, Phoebe, *Redwood Region Flower Finder*, second edition, Nature Study Guild, Rochester, NY, 1979.

Watts, Tom, *Pacific Coast Tree Finder*, second edition, Nature Study Guild, Rochester, NY, 2004.

Wilson, Simone, *Sonoma County: The River of Time: An Illustrated History*, Windsor Publications, Chatsworth, CA, 1990.

Young, Dorothy King, *Redwood Empire Wildflowers*, Third Edition, Naturegraph Publishers, Happy Camp, Ca., 1976.

INDEX

253

ABOUT BORED FEET

We began Bored Feet in 1986 to publish *The Hiker's hip pocket Guide to the Mendocino Coast*. We've grown our company by providing the most accurate guidebooks for California, including the award-winning two-volume series, *Hiking the California Coastal Trail*. Thank you for supporting quality independent publishing with your purchase, helping us to bring you more information about gorgeous and fascinating California. We love to hear your feedback about his or any of our other products.

Updates for several of our books are available at our website, **www. boredfeet.com**, where you can easily order any and all of our great books and maps. You can also get updates or a catalog by sending us your name and address on a stamped envelope, specifying your areas of interest.

We offer quick (standard shipping) and lightning fast (rush) order service for the more than 150 books and 100 maps we carry about California and the West. **To order items, go to www.boredfeet.com, or send name, address, check or money order, or call one of the phone numbers listed below.**

Hiker's hip pocket Guide to the Mendocino Coast, 3rd ed., Lorentzen	$15.00
Hiker's hip pocket Guide to the Humboldt Coast, 2nd ed., Lorentzen	15.00
Hiker's hip pocket Guide to Sonoma County, 3rd ed., Lorentzen	16.00
Hiker's hip pocket Guide to the Mendocino Highlands, 2nd ed., Lorentzen	17.00
Great Day Hikes in & around Napa Valley, 2nd ed., Stanton	15.00
Mendocino Coast Glove Box Guide: Lodging, Eateries, Sights, History, 3rd edition, Lorentzen	17.50
Sonoma Picnic: A California Wine Country Travel Companion, Burton	15.00
Napa Valley Picnic: A California Wine Country Travel Companion, Burton & Stanton	15.00
Day Trips with a Splash: Swimming Holes of California, Pancho Doll	18.95
Hiking the CA Coastal Trail, Vol. 1: Oregon to Monterey, 2nd ed., Lorentzen & Nichols	19.50
Hiking the CA Coastal Trail, Vol. 1: Monterey to Mexico, Lorentzen & Nichols	19.00
Coastal Trail Gift Set: Volumes 1 & 2, Lorentzen & Nichols	37.00
Trails & Tales of Yosemite & Central Sierra, Giacomazzi	17.50
Exploring Eastern Sierra Canyons: Sonora Pass to Pine Creek, Giacomazzi	15.50
Geologic Trips: San Francisco & the Bay Area, Konigsmark	13.95
Geologic Trips: Sierra Nevada, Konigsmark	17.50
Visual Guide to Coastal County Plants from Santa Cruz to Mendocino, Pikkarainen	16.95

Please add $3 shipping for orders under $30, $5 over $30 ($5 /7 for rush)
For shipping to a California address, please add 7.25% sales tax.
Prices subject to change without notice.

BORED FEET PRESS
www.boredfeet.com
P.O. BOX 1832
MENDOCINO, CA 95460
888-336-6199 toll-free, 707-964-6629